CLEANING UP
THE MESS

CLEANING UP THE MESS

—

AFTER THE MPs' EXPENSES SCANDAL

IAN KENNEDY

Biteback Publishing

First published in Great Britain in 2019 by
Biteback Publishing Ltd
Westminster Tower
3 Albert Embankment
London SE1 7SP
Copyright © Ian Kennedy 2019

ISBN 978-1-78590-494-3

10 9 8 7 6 5 4 3 2 1

A CIP catalogue record for this book is available from the British Library.

Set in Adobe Garamond Pro

Printed and bound in Great Britain by
CPI Group (UK) Ltd, Croydon CR0 4YY

CONTENTS

Introduction   vii

Chapter 1   The Expenses Scandal   1
Chapter 2   Take-Off and Turbulence   9
Chapter 3   Thinking Things Through and Setting Things Up   17
Chapter 4   The Scheme of Expenses   23
Chapter 5   A Changed World   31
Chapter 6   Getting Started   51
Chapter 7   The Speaker's Committee on the IPSA (SCIPSA)   73
Chapter 8   Communication, Contact, Compliance   83
Chapter 9   Open and Closed   95
Chapter 10   Meeting MPs   103
Chapter 11   Independence   129
Chapter 12   SCIPSA Again   137
Chapter 13   Ordeal by Committee   147
Chapter 14   Freedom of Information   167
Chapter 15   Money – Funding for MPs' Staff   177
Chapter 16   Money – Remuneration of MPs   183
Chapter 17   Carrying On   231
Chapter 18   General Election of 2015   235
Chapter 19   Phase II   245

Epilogue   251
Appendices   259
Acknowledgements   347
Index   349

INTRODUCTION

When I stood down in May 2016 as the chair of the Independent Parliamentary Standards Authority (IPSA) after nearly seven years, I described my job as 'broken down into component parts, it has been part constitutional reform, part mud-wrestling, part pioneer frontiersman, and part voyager through Dante's Inferno'.[1]

Subsequently, I decided to write an account of this experience. What follows is that account. It does not claim to be a detailed history. Rather, it is my personal story.

I describe the challenges of seeking to establish from scratch a system for regulating a group of people who were not used to the idea of regulation and, on the whole, resented it. It mattered little that the system was one familiar to anyone who enjoyed the benefit of other people's money and understood that expenditure had to be accounted for. It mattered even less that the idea of creating a regulatory system independent of Parliament was their idea – one that had been voted for by Parliament itself.

To varying degrees, IPSA's approach was unpopular with MPs, though enthusiastically embraced by those who elected them. The

---

1   *IPSA's First Parliament*, IPSA (2016).

third constituency, the media, never quite worked out how to respond. They had called for regulation, but if we regulated MPs too effectively their stories of scandals would dry up. And the stories were immensely popular among a disaffected public convinced of the venality of all MPs. For the most part, therefore, the media opted to have their cake and eat it: IPSA was an inefficient quango wasting taxpayers' money, and MPs were still on the take. Neither of these positions was justified on the facts. But, as you learn very quickly in public life, the facts are always negotiable.

As you read on you may become concerned at what appears to be a level of cynicism and occasional despair in how I describe things. Well, that's how I often felt. I was surrounded by brilliant people – including colleagues on the board, senior executives and staff. But, ultimately, I was the person who copped the almost ceaseless flak. That said, it never got me down. Rather, it made me determined to press on, to serve the public, look after those who worked so hard and with such dedication for IPSA and to serve MPs. There were, after all, many MPs who deserved our best and were a delight to work with. And, perhaps most important, by the time I stepped down we had succeeded in doing what we were established to do – we had sorted out MPs' expenses and their pay.

CHAPTER 1

THE EXPENSES SCANDAL

The scandal that engulfed MPs and Parliament in 2008–09 needs no retelling.

It was a saga which, as it unfolded, left the nation appalled and fascinated in equal measure. The things that MPs (albeit only *some* MPs) got up to beggared belief. The ways they found to tap into taxpayers' money suggested that, for some, any moral compass that they might have once possessed had long ago gone on the blink. The slow drip of stories in the *Daily Telegraph* that were then repeated throughout the media painted a picture of MPs living up to the caricature: snouts firmly in the trough. Duck houses, moats, flipped second homes all entered the nation's lexicon of outrage. The Speaker of the House of Commons was moved to remark in a speech to the Hansard Society:

I cannot think of a single year in the recent history of Parliament when more damage has been done to it than this year, with the possible exception of when Nazi bombs fell on the chamber in 1941.

The difference is that the physical wreckage then was done by

dictators whereas responsibility for the reputational carnage inflicted this year lies with the House.[2]

MPs reeling under the onslaught of invective that their abuses gave
rise to went into 'something must be done' mode – and did something. They introduced, debated and enacted a piece of legislation, all
in a matter of weeks, that challenged over 300 years of constitutional
practice. The legislation contemplated a new body, independent of
Parliament, which would be responsible for distributing taxpayers'
money to MPs and would be able to look into possible abuses of the
new system of 'allowances', which was to be put in place.

In its original form, the act took this new body into territory fierce-
ly guarded by MPs over the centuries: the freedom to say what they
wished in Parliament. By article 9 of the Bill of Rights 1688, Parliament was its own master.[3] No one could place limits on it performing
its role, including the right of MPs to speak freely within Parliament
without challenge in the courts or elsewhere. But could controlling
their money lead to controlling how they performed their role? Wasn't
this what article 9 was about?

Well, that all went out of the window. MPs tripped over themselves
in agreeing that from henceforth the determination of the amount
of money made available to them from the public purse to do their
job as MPs would be made by a body independent of Parliament. So
much for the constitution. So much for the British love of tradition.
Welcome to damage limitation. Welcome to IPSA (the Independent
Parliamentary Standards Authority).

---

2   Reported in the *Daily Telegraph*, 1 December 2009.
3   'The freedom of speech and debates or proceedings in Parliament ought not to be impeached
    or questioned in any court or place out of Parliament.'

WHAT'S THIS ALL ABOUT?

In 2010, there were 650 MPs. They represented constituencies in all corners of the United Kingdom. With Parliament based in Westminster, it is an easy commute to Parliament for those MPs representing constituencies in London. For MPs representing people in the Shetland Islands, Northern Ireland or in rural areas in the south-west or north of England, by contrast, many hours of travel are needed to get there. Most MPs necessarily work in two places: Westminster and their constituency. They need a place to live in both locations. They also need staff to manage their offices in their constituencies and in Westminster. They (or the vast majority of them) need an office in the constituency at which to see members of the public and hold 'surgeries'. And they need to equip the office. These are legitimate requirements: what an MP needs to do the job.

The scandal of 2008–09 had demonstrated that if the system by which taxpayers' money was distributed to MPs was not properly regulated, MPs could and (some, at least) would exploit it to their own advantage – and to the detriment of the taxpayer. This was the crux of the scandal: that the system was exploited by many. Over the decades, a system for distributing taxpayers' money to MPs had emerged which was designed by MPs for MPs; it was opaque, had increasingly limited accountability, had ever-expanding benefits and operated against the background of a growing culture of exceptionalism and entitlement.

IPSA

IPSA was the response. It was created to establish a new order in which the taxpayer got a good deal, the MP got what was needed, and good governance prevented abuse.

Parliament passed the legislation creating IPSA in 2009. It was called the Parliamentary Standards Act. As originally conceived, IPSA was given wide powers in what was an orgy of self-flagellation. IPSA was given authority not only in relation to MPs' financial expenditure but also over the behaviour of MPs (the standards to be observed).

This meant getting rid of the House of Commons' Committee on Standards and Privileges, created by the House and consisting of MPs. As one might imagine, this provoked considerable pushback once the parliamentary dust had settled and MPs began to wake up to what they had done. The idea of independent, external accountability regarding financial matters was challenging enough. Giving IPSA the power to regulate the propriety of MPs' conduct was widely regarded by MPs as a step too far. That it would take IPSA into the territory marked out by article 9 seemed to have escaped attention.

Arguments to amend the act were put to the then Lord Chancellor, Jack Straw, who was responsible for the legislation. Given that IPSA would not open for business until after the election of 2010 and was still working on its regulatory approach, there was an opportunity for reflection. There was time, if needed, to amend the act. The arguments which were advanced related most specifically to what is called parliamentary privilege. This reflects directly the principle in article 9: things said in the House are privileged in that they cannot serve as the basis for any challenge in the courts or elsewhere. Some of the matters coming to the Committee on Standards and Privileges, which, if the proposed legislation went through, IPSA would replace, related to things said in the House. While MPs could investigate them, it would not be possible for IPSA, as an external body, to look into such matters, because constitutionally they were free from challenge from the outside. Of course, there was a big slice of special pleading here. After all, if a complaint of misconduct were made, it could be open to the House or the MP to waive the claim of privilege. Indeed, failure to do so by an MP might not go down well. But the argument from first principles was valid.

In my meetings with Mr Straw concerning the act, I also favoured amending it. But my reasons were different. They were as much pragmatic as principled. I saw the points about privilege but thought that they could be overcome, given good will and time. But both of those commodities were in short supply. The atmosphere was febrile. To say that we were in 'tricky' territory is seriously to understate what was involved and what was at stake. In their desire to signal a break with the past, I feared that there was a real danger that the break would cripple IPSA from the start. If IPSA started to tinker around with parliamentary privilege, MPs would be entering a completely unfamiliar world in which they would have to mind their Ps and Qs in what they said in Parliament, when they previously never had to, and even when doing so was not in the public interest. Without thinking it through, and in their urgency to act, Parliament risked doing serious harm to established constitutional practice. And IPSA would be in the middle, beset by regular enfilading fire: a sitting duck before we had even started work.

In the background, there was also a growing sense of anxiety among MPs about what IPSA would do; the sense that they had been unwitting midwives at the birth of what – from their perspective – could turn out to be a monster. In that atmosphere, the last thing I wanted was daily running battles concerning the boundaries of parliamentary privilege and whether a particular issue fell on my side or the other side. And, in meetings with the MPs and officials involved, the sense of my tanks and their lawns was pretty strong. As I put it to Mr Straw, it would be all that we could do to get a system of expenses up and running, given the logistical challenges and growing antipathy. Being drawn into other matters would probably be the final straw (pun intended).

Within a few months, Mr Straw deferred to the weight of opinion.

A bill was going through Parliament (the Constitutional Reform and Governance Bill – the CRAG Act when it became law) and a rethink about IPSA and its role was ordered. New provisions were tacked onto the bill. The provisions kept IPSA well away from matters of parliamentary privilege and the MPs' code of conduct. IPSA's role was made more limited. It was to establish a scheme for regulating and administering the distribution of taxpayers' money to MPs so that they could carry out their parliamentary functions. IPSA was also required to ensure that MPs complied with the requirements of the scheme and to investigate allegations of non-compliance. Concerns involving the privileges of the House were safely reassigned to the House's Committee on Standards. A new creature, an independent commissioner, was created to deal with cases of alleged breaches of the House's code of conduct as they related to financial irregularities committed by MPs, such as failing to register interests. The new commissioner would report to the House's Committee on Standards. IPSA would not be involved and those concerned about article 9 could sleep easier. Phew!

As will be clear, the creation of IPSA was not the most carefully planned and thought-through exercise. MPs and Parliament had been desperate to get everything done before the summer recess, thereby being able to suggest, at least to themselves, that the problem of the expenses scandal had been put behind them. As Sir Alan Duncan MP observed:

> We should all face up to the fact that the Bill is essentially a panic measure. The Government have been forced to make it up as they go along. Even before the ink is dry it is not perceived, in the eyes of many, as a permanent solution. One of the great remaining problems is that the various elements that make up a Member's remuneration are assessed in an utterly fragmented way. The authority will consider only expenses and allowances. There is a pressing need for some

structure or system that can examine pay, pensions, allowances and expenses as one, so that the House does not have to suffer being chewed in different places at different times, as we have been in the past few weeks.

Sir Alan was right. The government and Parliament did make it up as they went along. And he was also right that dealing with expenses in a vacuum, without addressing the larger question of MPs' remuneration in the round, was not a good idea. Indeed, if we were not able to deal with pay, we ran the risk of being unable, clearly and indisputably, to achieve one of our most important tasks: to signal to the taxpayer and to MPs that the past confusing and confused mixing of 'allowances' and pay was over. Henceforth, pay and expenses were always to be kept separate. I made the point repeatedly, but carefully, lest IPSA be thought to be engaged in that greatest of all sins of quangos – mission creep. I referred repeatedly to the view expressed nearly forty years previously by the Top Salaries Review Body:

> As a general rule we believe that, in the future, a clear separation should be observed between salary, on the one hand, and provision for expenses on the other…

To his credit, Jack Straw conceded the point. The CRAG of 2010, apart from dealing with the concerns about privilege, gave IPSA the additional power to set a scheme for MPs' pay and pensions, as well as for expenses. That addition, while it was the right thing to do, was never going to make life easy for IPSA. So it proved. I'll get to that part of the story in due course.

CHAPTER 2

TAKE-OFF AND TURBULENCE

What follows is my account of the first seven years of IPSA. It is not a comprehensive historical account. Nor does it represent the views of IPSA. Rather, it is a form of autobiography, wherein the life being described is my life as IPSA's chairman. It describes my experiences. It is subjective. Others may see the world differently, but, alongside a handful of others, I was the closest to the action.

I was appointed as the chair of IPSA in November 2009. Within two days, I realised that this was going to be a different job from anything I'd previously done. I'd had my fair share of difficult jobs, often operating in the rough and tumble of Whitehall and Westminster with regular attention from the media and commentators. Over the previous ten years I had chaired a public inquiry into the deaths of babies and children after paediatric cardiac surgery at Bristol Royal Infirmary and then established and chaired the Healthcare Commission, the first organisation to regulate the NHS. I thought I was used to the press. I thought that my reputation was secure – someone who was his own man and told things as he saw them without fear or favour. That's probably why I was handed IPSA.

Well, within two days I felt the full force of the political press, an animal I was relatively unused to. In previous lives, I had found that

9

reasoned argument and honesty ensured, more or less, that the story came out with some semblance of the truth. Things were about to change.

At this point, in late November 2009, IPSA barely existed. There was a chairman, an acting chief executive, some eager young civil servants seconded from the Ministry of Justice, and some advisers. One adviser came up with the notion that I should meet the lobby journalists, a clique which move as a pack and are given privileged access, on terms that no one would be quoted, not even through that much-loved device of 'a source'– in other words, they were given the inside story on a non-attributable basis.

I knew the media specialising in healthcare, science, and higher education. I didn't know the lobby. They filed into a tiny room in the temporary offices that IPSA shared with the Boundary Commission. There were about nine or ten of them on that Wednesday morning. My adviser, a long-term veteran of Whitehall media, welcomed them and explained that I was giving them an opportunity to put a name to a face and to ask some general questions. Nothing was to be on the record. One of them, Tim Shipman, then of the *Daily Mail*, pressed the point. Could something be attributed to a 'source'? No, this was to be a completely off-the-record conversation.

Several in the group did not look happy but appeared to acknowledge that these were the accepted rules of engagement.

Now, before I go any further, we need to back up for a moment.

IPSA had only recently been established by Parliament. The four other members of the board in addition to me as the chairman had not been appointed. Meanwhile, in another part of the Whitehall jungle, the Committee on Standards in Public Life, under the chairmanship of Sir Christopher Kelly, had been invited by (then) Prime Minister Gordon Brown to offer its views in response to the scandal over MPs' expenses that had so shaken Westminster and Whitehall. The committee chose to seize the moment and fill the vacuum of comment and recommendation on what should be done. Sir Christopher had decided that he was the person who should speak for an outraged nation. So, he called a press conference and spoke. His committee had considered the matter and drawn up a report. It included a lengthy list of things that should be done. And, yes, he said in response to questions, they not only should be done, they *must* be done, and done straight away.[4]

Back to my meeting with the lobby journalists. Those most closely associated with the expenses story had liked what Kelly had said. It was suitably draconian. It seemed to be in sympathy with their anti-politician, anti-politics agenda. So, the first question put to me was, quite simply, not a question but, rather, a proposition: 'You are here to implement Kelly, aren't you?' This, after all, had been what the media had been calling for – to 'implement Kelly'. Many MPs, including political leaders, had echoed this call, recognising that there was no mileage in anything other than in breast-beating declarations of guilt and remorse. The charge was led by Rosa Prince of the *Daily Telegraph*, who was seeking to hold on to the notion that the expenses scandal was the *Telegraph*'s and her story, and by the *Daily Mail*'s Tim Shipman, who saw himself as head boy.

My response was, I thought, measured. I remarked that legislation had been enacted, IPSA was being created, and IPSA's job would be to look at what might be needed so as to carry out its statutory mandate, not least to help to restore confidence in Parliament and parliamentarians. This response was met by the journalists with an incredulous and vaguely frustrated repetition of the proposition, 'Yes, but you are here

---

4 Anything other than a cursory reading would have revealed that much of what Sir Christopher was recommending would in fact have required primary legislation.

to implement Kelly.' When I explained, in my perhaps professorial style, that IPSA was there to make up its own mind as an independent body (that was what the I in IPSA stood for), it was clear that I had lost the room. I wasn't on message. I was referring to another and quite unacceptable script. And who was I, anyway, to think that I might have a mind of my own, that I might for a moment imagine such a thing as independence existed? The meeting ground to a halt with an angry lobby not getting its way.

By the Friday and over the course of that weekend, the convention that lobby briefings were confidential, non-reportable and non-attributable was in tatters. I was attacked for my views. Front pages and banner headlines in the *Daily Telegraph*[5] and the *Daily Mail*[6] were dedicated to the fact that I knew Alastair Campbell, who until recently had been the press spokesman for Mr Blair. Indeed, I was so close to him that I had been his 'phone-a-friend' when he appeared on TV in *Celebrity Who Wants to Be a Millionaire?* Pages of Alastair's published diary were splashed across the papers describing how we holidayed together in the summer. The point was obvious: I was a patsy, in thrall to the political elite. My appointment had been fixed so that IPSA would not stand up to MPs.

Not true, but who cares? In fact, as regards the TV show, I had been asked by Alastair to help him raise money for Leukaemia Research, a worthy cause, except in the eyes of those who see the world according to their values. As regards summer holidays, our children went to the same school, and Alastair's partner drew our attention to

---

5 *Daily Telegraph*, 6 November 2009.
6 The creative Tim Shipman, under a headline reading, 'MPs' expenses report WON'T be torn up: Sir Ian Kennedy caves in over reform', talked of 'frantic phone calls between the two', 11 November 2009. In fact, no such telephone calls took place. Members of IPSA's staff merely agreed with Kelly's staff that we would keep Kelly's report in mind as we did our work. In the event, much of what we came up with was similar to elements of Kelly's report.

a place she knew of in a village near where they spent their summer holidays. And, in any event, I had declared this friendship, and other connections to politicians whom I knew socially, to the chair of the interviewing panel when I was interviewed for the appointment as chairman. But why let facts get in the way of a smear?

These same newspapers also turned their fire on my family life. Journalists worked the houses on my street asking neighbours for whatever might be hurtful or damaging. Drawing a blank (my neighbours were decent folk), they pitched camp outside my house, such that on one occasion when I was due to take my younger son to watch Chelsea play his beloved Manchester United, I had to climb over the back wall to avoid the photographers massed at the gate. My older son was harassed by a journalist as he came home and followed as far as the front door. When he (politely) closed the door, the journalist shouted through the letter box and left a note with her phone number on it urging him to call her. Having found that my wife and I had recently separated, the story in the *Mail* became that I was so bereft that I was not up for the job.[7] The journalist, one Simon Walters, resorted to the old device of citing a 'friend' so as to peddle his humbug. (Journalists don't reveal their sources, which is particularly convenient when the source is made up.) The 'friend' was reported as referring to me as 'the poor chap'. Even in the very unlikely event that a friend would talk about me to a journalist in such circumstances, my friends don't speak like that. And, so as not to leave any stone unturned, a journalist was sent to 'doorstep' my mother-in-law and sister-in-law, who happen to live 100 miles north of Los Angeles (over 5,000 miles away). And my wife and her friends and colleagues were harassed.

What was my sin? I was someone who had dedicated his life to

---

7   8 November 2009.

public service. There were no skeletons. Why, then, this attack? Why this attempt to suggest that I was unsuitable as chairman on political or personal grounds?

Simple. I, who was to them a nobody, had the temerity to indicate that I was my own man and would decide for myself and with my board, once appointed, what IPSA would do. The collective had decided that I was to be undermined. I was to be shown what would happen if I didn't go where elements of the media wanted me to go. Welcome to the birth of IPSA!

Word got back, as it always does in Westminster, that I was being harassed by the media. I had taken one of my sons to the local pub for dinner. We ordered our food and my mobile phone rang. I stepped outside into a chilly November night. First, Harriet Harman, then Leader of the House, and then the Speaker, John Bercow, called me. Both were keen to show solidarity with me. Also, of course, having seen me appointed they didn't want to start all over again if I got cold feet and quit. It was good of them to call. I indicated that I had no illusions about the press, but that there was an important job to be done and that I would do it. I was on the phone and in the cold for over two hours. My son had waited patiently but had the good sense to eat his food while it was still warm. My own dinner was long since cold when I finally got back inside.

TWO POSTSCRIPTS

First, two days after meeting the lobby journalists, I received a handwritten letter from Patrick Wintour, *The Guardian*'s lobby correspondent, apologising for the behaviour of his colleagues and saying that in all his time in the lobby he had never known such a flagrant disregard for the conventions. He went on to apologise that he had himself used the story, once it had appeared elsewhere, under pressure from his editor. It was good of him to write and I appreciated it.

The second postscript concerns the appointment of members of IPSA's board. As the very newly nominated chairman, I was to join the panel that had recommended my appointment so as to take part in the process of selecting my future colleagues. The *Telegraph* had by then published its front-page story about my knowing Alastair Campbell. As I joined the group, the obligatory ex-judge on the panel, Sir Christopher Rose, immediately went into his best cross-examination mode and pompously demanded to know why I hadn't mentioned my involvement with *Who Wants to Be a Millionaire?* I was struck by the aggression of his questioning. Whatever it said about the individual, it also demonstrated the power of the media to distort reality and massage prejudices. I was somewhat reluctant to reply. I had declared my links with Alastair and others in politics whom I knew socially when I was interviewed. Moreover, my involvement in the particular TV programme could not have the slightest relevance to my fitness to chair IPSA.[8] So, I simply said that I was not going to let the *Telegraph* pick my friends. But Sir Christopher was not appeased. He persuaded the chair of the panel that though I might be involved in the interviewing, I should be barred (for some reason – perhaps my keeping bad company) from involvement in the decisions to be made, once the interviews were over, as to who should serve as my colleagues on the board. No reason was given, perhaps because prejudice is hard to substantiate in reasoned terms. It was a shabby display by him. But it was an important lesson about the world that I was entering: that it would be lonely and the knives could come from anywhere.

---

8   As it happens, I gave the wrong answer and wrecked Alastair's fundraising!

CHAPTER 3

THINKING THINGS THROUGH
AND SETTING THINGS UP

When I have taken on tasks, my approach has always been to sit down and try to work out what it is I am being asked to do and how I might go about doing it. Intrinsic in this approach is a disinclination to look backwards, to what has been done in the past. Of course, when you are asked to set something up from scratch, there is no past. This does not stop those who are nervous about leaping into the unknown from looking around for some kind of model which, even if it doesn't particularly match, at least means that there's something on the paper. The sheet isn't blank. This approach is what I encountered when I sat down with the team of bright young civil servants who had spent the past several months between the passage of the legislation and my appointment mapping out what IPSA might look like. Being good civil servants, they wanted me to have something to work with when I came on board, both to help further thought and to ensure that any further thought would be within already determined (by them) lines. Free thinking is always a bit scary to those who work in Whitehall. Being good civil servants, they searched about for a model which could serve as a starting point, something to have on paper. The model they chose was the existing system of MPs' allowances. What was to be changed was that the system was to be administered by IPSA as an independent body. But the content of the system – what MPs were to receive and the basis on which they were to receive it – was to remain more or less as it was.

This was not what I wanted. I indicated at the outset that we must map out a different way forward. I made it clear that there were a number of matters which, taken together, should set the shape of IPSA.

First, we should ignore what had gone before, not only because it was thoroughly discredited,[9] but also because our job was to proceed on first principles so as to build a new system.

Secondly, although the statute talked of 'allowances', which was the language of the old system, it was absolutely crucial to use a different language, the language of 'expenses and budgets'. This wasn't just some linguistic fetish. It was intended to signal a fundamental shift in culture. The language of 'allowances' is the language of money which is there to be spent. Sitting alongside the culture of entitlement which had developed among MPs, the language of 'allowances' translated into the notion that the money made available was the MPs' money to spend, rather than the taxpayers' money to be used to serve the taxpayers' interests. It was the language of 'allowances' and the culture of entitlement that it fostered that had given rise to the excesses which figured so prominently in the expenses scandal.

My insistence on this change of language also reflected a further cultural shift. We had a statutory duty to have regard to 'efficiency [and] cost-effectiveness'. This meant (in ordinary language) that we had to remember that we were there for the taxpayer as well as the MP. This had not always been apparent in the past.

---

9   Notwithstanding the hard work and dedication of the staff of the fees office in the House of
     Commons which administered the old system, many of whom came to work at IPSA.

Thirdly, over the years, the previous system of MPs' 'allowances' had become increasingly extensive and malleable in its operation. As political leaders set their faces against the pay rises for MPs that were regularly recommended by the Senior Salaries Review Body (SSRB), there developed a range of devices to channel money to MPs in lieu of an increase of salary. If IPSA was to replicate or reflect the previous system of multiple allowances, we would risk disappearing into the same mess that we were created to clear up.

So, I asked a simple question, again from first principles: what are the general areas of activity that MPs might need financial support for?[10] It was clear that they are: travel; the employment of staff; renting an office in the constituency, together with associated equipment and operating costs; money for somewhere to stay in London, if the constituency was outside London; and money for somewhere to stay in the constituency if they did not live there. These would be the activities for which MPs needed funds and that we needed to support.

THE SCHEME

We then had to design the architecture of the new system for meeting MPs' needs. The statute creating IPSA required us to establish a 'scheme' and, before introducing it, to submit it to consultation. The statute also set out a list of those to be consulted: the Speaker, certain office-holders and MPs. I took the decision that consultation should not be restricted to the Westminster bubble. It was the taxpayer whose money had been used and abused in the past. It was the taxpayers' money that IPSA would be distributing. So, it seemed appropriate that any consultation on the 'scheme' should include consulting the public. This is what we did right at the outset, and have done ever since.

---

10   Other than pay and pensions, that is.

The scheme initially concerned what we called 'expenses'. We did not use the term 'allowances' though that was the word used in the statute. Over time, some MPs complained that the public, and, in particular, their electorate, did not understand that 'expenses' actually referred to the costs of renting and running an office and hiring staff. We saw the force of this complaint and a couple of years later changed the name to the 'MPs' Scheme of Business Costs and Expenses'.[11]

Apart from travel costs, where there was no fixed budget as costs varied greatly (travelling from the Shetlands costing rather more than coming into London from the Home Counties), the basis of the scheme was that it consisted of rules setting out what was allocated to each MP by way of a budget under various headings and describing how to make a claim for reimbursement. The approach was crucial. An MP could only be reimbursed against a claim for such expenditure as was allowed under the scheme. I will come back to various aspects of the scheme as it developed over time, but here I'm concerned with describing it in general terms.

Although crucial, an approach based on claims for reimbursement suffered from an inherent initial weakness that we recognised but could not immediately rectify. If MPs were to be reimbursed only after the event, they would have to find the money themselves in the first place. Running costs could be paid for out of pay, but there were also start-up costs, particularly for newly elected members (and after the scandal, the general election of 2010 produced 227 new members). Many MPs did not have the necessary money to meet the outlay involved in setting up an office and paying a deposit on a place to live, if their constituency was outside London, nor for the rent of a constituency office. The answer, in the long term, was an IPSA credit

---

11   Now called the 'Scheme of MPs' Business Costs and Expenses'.

card. But a proper system of credit cards would take time, and we had not been able to set one up in the time available. So, once we were made aware of the problem, we scrambled to set up a system whereby MPs could take out a loan of up to £4,000, to be repaid at the end of the parliament. We advised MPs accordingly.

This should have solved the problem. It didn't, unfortunately, for many MPs, because of a different problem which dogged IPSA from the start: many MPs didn't read what we told them! The cynic might say that this is a form of selective blindness. Others might say that the modern MP is besieged by emails and other forms of communication and that we should have found better ways of communicating. Both are true. IPSA struggled with how best to get things across to MPs; very often specifically in terms of advising them how they could avoid unnecessary and damaging publicity if rules were broken. As time went on, however, loans were taken up and another bump in the road was negotiated.

CHAPTER 4

THE SCHEME OF EXPENSES

The scheme which was to be presented for consultation had to be constructed from scratch around the various areas of financial need. We also had to decide how we were going to deal with those practices that, under the old system, had given rise to the greatest abuse. We dealt with many simply by moving from a system of allowances to a system of budgets with payments following claims, supported by receipts: a new world for MPs, which I captured in one speech with the expression 'No ticket, no laundry'!

The process of putting the scheme together was the first big test for the board. The four other members had been appointed by the beginning of 2010. We also had a distinguished acting chief executive in Andrew McDonald, a senior civil servant and veteran of policy-making, and a director of policy, John Sills, another senior civil servant. They were both on secondment from the Ministry of Justice. They were supported by an energetic group of young policy officials including 'fast-streamers'.[12] Given that there had not been time yet to recruit our own staff, there was also a group of consultants, brought in to

---

12   Civil servants who entered the civil service through a path intended to accelerate their progress.

help us set up.[13] They included specialists in IT, human resources and communications. Of particular – and lasting – importance were the IT specialists. Their early decisions as to what we needed, what we could afford (we had a small interim budget), and, crucially, what could be set up by the early spring (we had to be ready in time for the coming election) were to have a profound effect on IPSA's operational capacity and the way in which IPSA was viewed by MPs. And typically, once the decisions were made, we were locked into service contracts which extended for several years. There is no doubt that if we had had the luxury of time, the IT system – the key to almost everything in operational terms – would have been significantly better. But we didn't have that time. We had to do the best we could.

During February and March of 2010, with the threat of an early, surprise election always in the background, the board embarked on a marathon series of meetings and seminars, six in all, each lasting several hours. The executive would bring forward papers for consideration. The board would slowly and carefully move from general principle to detailed action.

Consideration of MPs' travel costs can serve as an illustration. The starting point was that the costs of travel from an MP's constituency to London should be met if the constituency was outside London. As a matter of principle we decided that MPs should be held to their claim that they wished, as far as possible, to live as their constituents lived. So, we distinguished between travel costs and the cost of everyday commuting. We decided that IPSA should not meet the cost of commuting within London because this is a cost that all people travelling from home to work have to meet.

But that decision raised the need for a further decision: what

---

13   The process of recruitment was made slower by the need for everyone to obtain security clearance.

should be the outer limit for travel in London which would be treated as a commute? We considered various options. Initially, we decided that IPSA would not meet the cost of travel if the journey took less than an hour, based on railway timetables. This proved, however, to be impractical. Some constituencies could be reached by a fast train journey in an hour so did not qualify for support even though they were significantly distant from London and if an MP had to catch a slower train it took a long time. A story circulated that one MP was sleeping in his room in the Commons to avoid the cost of travelling to and from his constituency. We were sent photographs of camp beds in Westminster offices. Another option was to use the outer zone of the London Underground transport system as the limit. But this proved to have drawbacks also. So, in the end, in April 2011, we settled on drawing a line around London with a radius of twenty miles. Those within the line would not be reimbursed for the cost of travel, those outside would. Naturally, there is always an inevitable arbitrariness in drawing lines, notwithstanding the apparent justification. Some MPs fell just the wrong side of the line and complained that they were put to considerable expense as a consequence. But, for the most part, the twenty-mile rule worked well.

But then there were other details to settle. As a reaction to the excesses of the expenses scandal, the call went up to curtail MPs' recourse to first-class travel on trains. The reaction of MPs, on hearing of this possibility, was swift and strong. First-class travel, they argued, allowed them to read papers in a quieter atmosphere which was more conducive to maintaining any necessary confidentiality (a better class of snoopers and eavesdroppers, perhaps!). Also, they said, MPs were at the mercy of the parliamentary timetable. It was impossible to predict when debates might end. Last-minute travel was common and first-class tickets were often the only ones available. Well, while it was clearly not for IPSA to tell MPs how to organise their business, there was at least an argument that if the House's business was organised differently last-minute arrangements could be avoided, save in exceptional circumstances, allowing time to plan journeys and secure tickets, and save taxpayers' money in the process.[14]

After considerable discussion we settled for a rule which, rather than insisting on a certain class of travel, made price the criterion. The maximum that could be claimed was the price of a standard open ticket. If a first-class ticket cost less than this limit, it would be paid in full. If it cost more, IPSA would only pay for the standard amount. This gave MPs some scope to claim for first-class travel if they planned their journey in advance, and some have used this flexibility. The rule remains in place to this day, despite intermittent interest from the media in first-class travel.

In time, despite the opposition of the House's travel office, we were able to come to an arrangement with an online booking agency. This offered a dedicated service for MPs which they could log onto and make the most economic booking, which was ordinarily a standard-class ticket but might, rarely, even be in first class.

The insistence on using standard-class travel, unless first class was the most cost-effective means of travel, then took us into the details of airline travel. MPs flying to Scotland told us that there was a particular fare which, though first class, was cheaper than regular standard class. We duly made the relevant adjustment. Over time such details were ironed out and things settled down.

But there were still other areas to address. The first was what to do about taxis. The general atmosphere of austerity in the context of

---

14 Within hours of my floating the idea that at least part of the problem lay in how the House organised business, I received a curt message from the then Leader of the House, Sir George Young, advising me to keep out of the House's affairs.

spending taxpayers' money persuaded us to limit claims for taxis to certain specified circumstances: when the House sat late and otherwise when the MP had a good reason to need to take a taxi – where, for example, there was no reasonable option of using public transport. There was much concern expressed about MPs, particularly female MPs, if they were to be expected to travel home after a late sitting only to arrive at some dark station in the early hours. Clearly, there was a difference between expecting MPs to use public transport during the day and late at night. Moreover, it was a common practice for employers in the public as well as the private sector to pay for taxis after a certain hour. How late the House chooses to sit is a matter for the House, but we accepted that an MP might properly claim for the use of a taxi after 11 p.m.

The extent of the challenge to the prevailing culture that even our decision about taxis represented can be illustrated by the conversation I had with an MP while we were still making up our minds. He stressed the inconvenience that he would be put to on returning from his constituency if he could not use a taxi from the mainline train station in London to his flat in central London. I suggested that he try the Underground. He said that this wasn't possible: he could not take his two dogs on the Tube. I reflected for a moment and then enquired whether he wanted it to be a matter of public knowledge that he expected the taxpayer to pay for his dogs to travel by taxi. He didn't.

The second issue related to families. Should the rules cover the cost of partners and children travelling to London to visit the MP? Conscious of the desirability of ensuring that MPs had as much of a family life as was possible, but conscious also of the fact that the taxpayer would not ordinarily in other contexts pay for partners to travel to be together, we decided on a variation of the previous system. We proposed that MPs should be able to claim for a set number of journeys (thirty) per year by their families, but they could not claim for partners travelling alone (unless it was so as to care for dependents). In the event, the compromise worked but, like all compromises, it was either too little or too much depending on whom you listened to.[15] Scottish MPs, in particular, were not happy.

Then there was a third issue. We had to address a further means of travel. Some MPs who were not commuting within London travelled to Westminster by car. We began by requiring MPs to claim for each journey made. Since this usually involved simply their going from and to their constituency, MPs saw our rule as unnecessarily bureaucratic and burdensome. There was some justification in this complaint. But we were beginning from scratch and needed to establish a system which maximised accountability and probity above everything else. Over time, we were able to develop our systems so that claims for travel by car could be dealt with routinely.

As was the case in relation to travel costs, there were very many detailed decisions in all the other areas covered by the scheme. The board had to work through each of them with the help of the executive before we could settle on the consultation document that the statute required.

Since we were creating a scheme from scratch, it was clear that we were not going to get everything right first time. The value of the process of consultation was that some decisions could be modified or changed in the light of arguments advanced by MPs, commentators and members of the public. Of course, there were issues of principle which, though they met with opposition, we were not minded to change. But obviously, there were other areas where we were open to persuasion; for example when it became clear that the

---

15   The rules were simplified in 2017 allowing, among other things, claims for partners travelling alone, see Chapter 19.

one-hour-journey rule relating to travel by train had produced unintended consequences.

The board's approach to establishing the scheme was informed by two fundamental principles. The first was that it would have to consist of detailed rules and, initially at least, quite a lot of them. This was not only to ensure that MPs were left in as little doubt as possible as to what was permitted, but also so that the taxpayer could be reassured about what their money could be spent on. Yes, the rules could be relaxed over time as lessons were learned, but the initial imperative, reflecting the context of the recent scandal, was to err towards proscription and to leave the notion of MPs having more discretion to catch up later.

The second principle was to seek to capture and reflect the zeitgeist; that MPs needed to be reined in and could not be trusted to exercise self-regulation, without going too far so as to impinge on MPs' ability to do their job. There is no doubt that we didn't always get the balance right. Indeed, once the scheme was put into operation there were occasions when it became clear pretty soon that some decisions were wrongheaded such that we amended the scheme as promptly as we could.

One example is really a comment on the whole approach adopted by IPSA when devising the original scheme. It related to accommodation and what arrangements to make for MPs with children. We were very conscious that being an MP put significant pressure on those with families or planning to start a family. There was a view that IPSA should, in fact, seek to draft the rules of the scheme in such a way as to make them family friendly. We took the view that this was beyond our statutory remit, but nonetheless in principle we were sympathetic to the point. At the same time, we assumed that children of school age would live at home with a parent and go to school where that parent lived. Thus, we introduced a rule that an MP's budget for accommodation in London would be increased by that amount which data from the Royal Institute of Chartered Surveyors (RICS) showed that it would cost to rent a flat with a second bedroom (or more if there was more than one child). This rule, however, would only apply to children until they reached the age of five.[16] After that, children would be expected to live and go to school wherever their home was rather than in London.[17]

It soon became clear that this policy was far too family *unfriendly*. The permutations of family life and how MPs managed living in two different places were just too complicated to be addressed by some simple and, it has to be said, fairly draconian rule. This was brought home to me by a chance meeting with Alan Johnson MP as I was on my way from IPSA's offices to Westminster. I knew Alan from his time as Secretary of State for Health when I was chair of the Healthcare Commission and found him easy to get on with and down to earth. He was not one of the head-bangers railing against IPSA.[18] He had a young family and explained the adverse effect that our rule on accommodation for families was having. When I reported the conversation to my chief executive, he told me that there was a growing sense among MPs who were affected, and among our staff, that the rule should be changed. Clearly, we had got it wrong. We acted after consultation in 2011. We amended the rules so that the accommodation budget would extend to any child until the age of sixteen, children aged sixteen to eighteen if in full-time education and until twenty-one if in full-time education and the child of a sole carer. The same criteria applied to eligibility for claims for travel. Even these changes did not please everyone and there were regular calls for the rules to be made more generous.

---

16   Except for children of a sole carer up to the age twenty-one if in full-time education.
17   London MPs do not get an accommodation budget.
18   Though he did call the director of policy a 'Stalinist' when he was explaining the rules about accommodation and families.

CHAPTER 5

A CHANGED WORLD

SECOND HOMES

Perhaps the biggest single abuse of the old system of allowances involved the notion of 'second homes'. Taxpayers and newspaper readers were introduced to a new term – 'flipping'. MPs 'flipped' the designation of homes as first and second so as to improve them, and their value, at the taxpayers' expense. What this involved perhaps provided the clearest evidence of the culture of entitlement and the wilful blindness of many MPs as to how they used taxpayers' money. It went as follows. Under the system in existence before the scandal broke, an MP could have two 'homes'. One had to be designated the first home. The other was the second home. The assumption was that the first home was the MP's actual home and the second home was where MPs stayed, in London or the constituency, given the need to have somewhere to hang their hat. An allowance was available under the old system to provide for the payment of rent or mortgage costs and the upkeep of the second home. So far, so good. But it was not long before some MPs spotted the opening and went for it. All MPs had to do was to indicate to the authorities in the House that there had been a change in their arrangements and that what had been the second home would thereafter be the first home. So now the MP had a new second home on which to spend taxpayers' money, thereby also enhancing its value. Whichever house might be sold, the MP got the best of all 'I win–you lose' deals. The MP kept one, suitably improved, and could sell the other at an enhanced value because of the taxpayer-funded improvements. Plus, 'flipping' also created the opportunity to minimise liability for capital gains tax since first homes are exempt.

This had to end. Our solution was clean and simple. We abolished the institution of the second home. We accepted that most MPs (except those living in London and representing London constituencies) had to live and work in two places: in London and in their constituency. It followed that many non-London MPs would need a place to stay in London while working in Westminster, while some who lived in London but represented constituencies outside London would need a place in or near their constituency. But they did not need a second home. Rather, they needed a place to stay. The solution was to give MPs a budget which would allow them to rent a flat or stay in a hotel (up to a maximum rate). If they had families routinely living with them, the budget was set to allow them to rent additional rooms.

How did we fix the budget? Many MPs who needed accommodation in London had fallen into the habit of choosing accommodation close to Westminster. This is an expensive area in which to rent. If MPs were to be held to their oft-proclaimed intention of living lives similar to those of their electorate, the net of possible places to rent had to be cast wider. Indeed, in a subsequent consultation when we asked whether MPs should be funded so as to live within walking distance of Parliament, a position maintained by many MPs, there was a sense of surprised outrage from the public that MPs should even think this. The 'disconnect' is well illustrated by the pained expression of surprise (not far off shock) of an MP who told me that she had had to stay in a hotel in Euston on a visit to London so as to keep within budget.

Euston is just a few stops on the Underground from Westminster or a 25-minute bus ride, but this was clearly asking too much.

We chose to analyse the data on the cost of renting accommodation made available by the Royal Institute of Chartered Surveyors. As regards London, we chose as the budget for accommodation a sum of money which would allow MPs to rent a one-bedroom flat within a reasonable travelling distance from Whitehall.[19] Of course, they could rent at a higher cost should they wish to continue to live close to Parliament but they would have to pay the difference themselves. Equally, what was available was a budget. MPs did not have to spend it all if they chose to rent at a lower cost or share the cost with others. This was one of the crucial effects of moving away from a system of 'allowances'. For those renting accommodation outside London, we used RICS' data to set budgets for various regions, depending on the prevailing cost.

MORTGAGE INTEREST

There was another feature of the second homes scandal that we had to deal with. A good many MPs had taken out mortgages to buy a second home in London. Under the previous system, the payment of the interest on the mortgage could be claimed as an allowance: that is, it was paid for by the taxpayer. This was a particularly pernicious practice. Property in London was and is one of the safest and most lucrative forms of investment, with values rising ineluctably. MPs were thus able to finance a very profitable asset at the taxpayer's expense. When the property was sold, the profit went, of course (after paying off the mortgage), not to the taxpayer, but to the MP. This had to be stopped.

---

19   Eventually, the London accommodation budget was explicitly linked to rents in Westminster and Lambeth.

We announced, as part of the initial consultation on the scheme of expenses, that, after 'a reasonable period of time', we would no longer pay claims for the interest on mortgages (the mortgage interest subsidy).

This change was probably the one most welcomed by the public in the consultation. It was not popular with MPs. They made the point that, often, the cost to the taxpayer represented by the payment of the mortgage interest was significantly less than the budget made available by IPSA under the scheme for renting a flat. While this was true, when we consulted the public on whether we should introduce the change even if it might be more costly in the short term, the practice was so resented that the answer was a resounding yes.

It was also put to me by the then Leader of the Opposition, David Cameron, when I went to see him to brief him on aspects of the scheme, that owners of property would simply rent out the property to cover the cost of the mortgage once IPSA ceased to pay the mortgage interest. They would then draw on the budget available from IPSA for renting a flat. This would allow them to benefit twice over from our attempt to secure the interests of the taxpayer. My response was that it was not our business to tell MPs what to do with their assets, though it might look like profiteering to some. All we could do is tell the public about MPs' decisions and arrangements and leave it to the electorate to judge accordingly. This commitment to make such arrangements known to the public became, over time, the most important regulatory tool available to IPSA. MPs became increasingly aware that whatever they did with taxpayers' money would be made public.

In our report arising from the consultation on the payment of mortgage interest we announced that the 'reasonable period of time' would be a period of roughly two years, and would end on 31 August

2012. This would allow for a grace period so that those MPs who were claiming would have time to reorganise their affairs. To continue to claim during this period, MPs had to register that they would be claiming.

The board also decided that those MPs who continued to benefit from this subsidy during the grace period should repay any capital gain made on the property subsidised by the taxpayer. So, if IPSA was paying 100 per cent of the interest charged on the property, MPs would have to return 100 per cent of the capital gain made between the time they started claiming and when they stopped. The latter would be either when they sold the property, if that was before August 2012, or the deadline for the ending of the subsidy, 31 August 2012.

If MPs had not sold the property they would not actually have realised any capital gain. However, it would have been accumulated for the future. So, to address this, the board decided that in order to claim for the mortgage interest subsidy, MPs would have to pay back a sum equal to the notional capital gain. This was a condition of our meeting their claims – by claiming, they thereby agreed to do so. To make this approach work, MPs had to get two valuations of their property. The first was before they registered to claim, so that we knew the value of their property at the start of the period during which they made claims. The second was the value of the property on 31 August 2012, if they claimed until the end of the grace period. If they sold the property before then, we were prepared to rely on the sale price.

From these two values we could calculate any capital gain owed to the taxpayer. To avoid the prospect of their remaining liable to capital gains tax in the future – notwithstanding having repaid the capital gain to IPSA already – we discounted the amount owed to us by 28 per cent to reflect the capital gains tax.

Seventy-one MPs chose to register to continue to claim mortgage interest subsidy. Twenty-nine made a capital gain.[20] This relatively low number can be explained by the fact that the economy was in a prolonged recession as a result of the financial crash in 2008 and the austerity measures which followed it.

While the policy that we adopted was clear, the actual process of recouping money from MPs was not without its difficulties. Over time, with varying degrees of reluctance, MPs ultimately paid what the valuations of their properties indicated was the amount of money due to the Treasury. They did so notwithstanding that IPSA was put under significant pressure by the government beforehand to soften the impact of our decision. The board considered this and the executive provided some examples of potential hardship. The difficulty affecting some MPs was that their property had, in fact, lost value as a result of the recession such that they could not viably sell their asset in order to repay the capital gain between 2010 and 2012. Consequently, they had to find the money from their own resources. To respond to the pressure, however, would have meant waiting for the unlikely event of a change in the economy or causing a significant policy decision to unravel. So the board held to its position.

There were a number of recalcitrant MPs. There were difficult conversations and even threats of legal action which never materialised. Eventually, all but one MP returned the gains to the taxpayer. The exception was Stewart Jackson, then MP for Peterborough.[21]

THE JACKSON CASE

As a result of the two valuations of his property, in 2010 and then 2012, Mr Jackson was required to return £54,000. This was after we had taken 28 per cent off the capital gain. It was the second highest

20 Later reduced to twenty-eight.
21 He lost the seat in the general election of 2017.

sum owed, the highest being £70,000. The valuations were carried out by RICS-approved valuers, as the scheme's rules required. The valuations were commissioned by Mr Jackson himself, not by IPSA. As in all cases, we took the valuations provided to us at face value.

Mr Jackson refused to pay the money owed. There were various exchanges with legal representatives towards the end of 2012 and into 2013 which did not lead to a resolution, save that IPSA would adhere to the rules of the scheme; the same rules that had allowed him to receive mortgage interest subsidy from 2010 until August 2012.

Eventually, after Mr Jackson's lawyers had requested a number of extensions of the time by which payment was due, IPSA issued proceedings in the High Court in June 2013.

At the same time, both IPSA's legal advisers and the director of policy felt that we should try to find a solution which avoided taking Mr Jackson to court, winning (which was deemed highly likely) and saddling him with our costs as well as the £54,000 repayment. We were concerned that this was a significant amount of money for Mr Jackson. IPSA wasn't in the business of creating genuine hardship for MPs, no matter how they behaved towards us. Indeed, if we were to have to enforce payment and Mr Jackson were bankrupted, he would have had to stand down as an MP. In addition, the court is concerned to see efforts to resolve cases out of court wherever possible. Our proposal was that IPSA and Mr Jackson should jointly approach RICS and ask them to identify an independent valuer who could review the 2010 and 2012 valuations. There was a good deal of scepticism internally about the prospect of a successful resolution, but I agreed to back the director of policy's judgement.

The approach was eventually agreed with Mr Jackson, and we instructed RICS in September 2013. They took some time to identify a valuer, and we finally received the revised valuations in February 2014.

These showed no capital gain between 2010 and 2012, which was no surprise given the state of the economy. The case was permanently stayed by the High Court on 20 February 2014.

We agreed with Mr Jackson that the agreement would remain confidential, but he breached the agreement by making a statement on 1 March 2014. We issued a public statement in response, which said:

> For two years, Stewart Jackson claimed taxpayer support to pay his mortgage – this was a legacy of the old expenses regime, which IPSA brought to an end. The terms of this interim agreement were clear – if there was a capital gain, the taxpayer would share the benefits.
>
> When we stopped MPs claiming for their mortgages, Mr Jackson commissioned and provided two valuations from RICS-registered valuers, as we requested, which showed that the property had risen in value and the taxpayer was due £54,000.
>
> Only at this point did Mr Jackson take the view the valuations he provided were fundamentally flawed.
>
> He produced no acceptable evidence to support this and refused to pay the taxpayer back, in contravention of the rules.
>
> And so in looking after the taxpayers' interest we were left with no option but to seek legal advice.
>
> In the interests of preventing an unnecessarily lengthy and expensive legal process, we proposed to get a final, independently appointed surveyor to value the property at Mr Jackson's expense.
>
> Following this initiative, the valuer judged that there had been no rise in the property value between 2010 and 2012. We are happy to accept the surveyor's assessment.
>
> If Mr Jackson had submitted accurate valuations in the first instance, or produced suitable evidence in the months of discussion

about this, we would not have had to escalate this issue or seek legal support to try and conclude the matter.

Having ended the practice of MPs claiming mortgage repayments from the taxpayer – this situation can never arise again.

And that was the end of the matter: a year and a half after the subsidy ended.[22]

MPs EMPLOYING RELATIVES

Another feature of the old system which gave rise to considerable concern was the practice whereby MPs employed relatives, usually spouses, as members of their staff, paid for from the public purse. There had been a scandal involving Derek Conway MP, who claimed money for the services of his son who, on closer examination, happened at the relevant time to be attending university nearly 300 miles away. Further allegations were made subsequently regarding the MP's claim for the payment of a salary to his other son. The abuse of the system was clear.[23]

For the most part, however, the general view was that family members worked long hours on behalf of MPs and were applauded and appreciated as a helpful link between the MP, away in London, and constituents. But though this may have generally been true, and there were no other cases of demonstrable abuse, the sense lingered that MPs were swelling the family coffers at the taxpayers' expense through this practice.

So, there was the perception and there was the evidence. We had

---

22   As a postscript, Mr Jackson complained to the information commissioner that I and the chief executive had spoken to the Whips' Office about our concerns – a standard route for transmitting concerns informally. The information commissioner dismissed the complaint.

23   On 2 February 2009, Mr Conway apologised to the House for breaking the House's rules. He did not stand in the subsequent election in 2010.

made it clear from the beginning that, while we were in the business of making judgements, any judgement we made should take account of, and be underpinned by, the relevant evidence. In the perception corner was the large majority of the population who, by then, through the good offices of the media, were thoroughly persuaded of the venality of MPs. And there was Sir Christopher Kelly's Committee on Standards in Public Life, which condemned the practice in forthright terms.

In the evidence corner, apart from one case, there was no hard evidence of abuse. And there was significant endorsement of the practice during our consultation (which, in the case of evidence from MPs, was, of course, to a degree self-serving). On the other hand, there was no evidence of compliance with the ordinary employment practices that you would expect in publicly funded appointments, such as: that the job be advertised, that the relevant skills and experience be set out, and that the job be open to all. We consulted on the basis that we were minded to abolish the practice. Once the consultation was over – with considerable public antipathy to the practice being expressed, but with most MPs supporting it – we had to decide.

The board was divided. There was the absence of evidence of abuse and considerable evidence that taxpayers in some constituencies got a bargain. But there was also the feeling that, as a practice, it was out of sync with the modern world of employment with its insistence on openness in hiring and good governance when public funds are involved. In the event, the decision was taken to continue the practice with safeguards. The safeguards included the creation of a broader group than just family members, which we called 'connected parties'. An MP could henceforth only employ one connected party. And the salary of connected parties would be published in bands of £5,000. This allowed for greater assurance that, for example, their pay was not out of kilter with that of others with similar responsibilities. While the salaries of other members of staff were not made public, we published a range of job descriptions by reference to which members of staff recruited after the scheme came into effect could be appointed, together with the respective pay ranges. We also decided to keep the employment of connected parties under review and revisit the practice when the scheme as a whole was next examined.

MPs' STAFF

The largest amount of funding made available to MPs was for their staff. We inherited a system whereby each MP was judged to need the equivalent of 3.5 full-time staff. This was a figure arrived at in 2007 after research carried out for the Senior Salaries Review Body by a major firm of consultants (PwC) into what MPs needed by way of staff. The reality, of course, was that needs, both real and perceived, varied considerably. Some MPs felt that they needed more than the allotted 3.5 staff (some, many more) and some did not, in fact, draw the whole of the funds available. To some extent, the difference lay in how safe the parliamentary seat was; the MP, and the staff, in a marginal seat being more active locally in a variety of ways. Moreover, since MPs resisted the notion that there might be a job description for being an MP ('each MP performs her/his role differently' was the standard mantra), there was no obvious norm as regards their requirement of staff that could be applied across the board. So, initially, we continued to operate the existing system of 3.5 members of staff per MP until we could do our own analysis.[24]

Meanwhile, in working out how to manage the funding of staff, two factors weighed heavily. The first was the fact that MPs were the

---

24   See Chapter 15.

employers of the staff. IPSA might be paying the salaries, but the MP was the employer. In effect, MPs were running a small business. But many, indeed most, MPs had no experience of doing so. The general perception was that many were very poor employers, unaware of the basic principles of employment law and practice.

The second factor was that the system whereby the taxpayer handed over tens of thousands of pounds to MPs for staff seemed to be rooted in the nineteenth century. Proceeding from the premise that MPs should be able to employ whomever they wanted and that this would ordinarily mean someone of similar political views, very many of the staff, while being politically aware, had little or no skills in running or managing an office, and no experience of dealing with a regulator, thereby adding to IPSA's difficulties in dealing with MPs' offices. Moreover, ordinarily there was no advertisement of jobs, very little (if any) job description, and few of the formalities which ordinarily attend the employment of staff.

To begin to instil some discipline into the system, IPSA made a number of changes. We introduced a system of budgets to replace allowances, model contracts to be used for all staff employed after 2010 and pay bands. We also abolished bonus payments, which had frequently been used in the past to distribute any part of the annual allowance which had not been used by the end of the financial year.

This was a start, but I thought it remarkable (and still do) that such a cottage industry approach should be adopted towards staffing the offices of the nation's legislators. I floated the idea of a kind of civil service, organised perhaps on a regional basis to train people to service the offices of MPs in an ordered and efficient manner. If MPs wanted a member of staff who would be charged with more overtly political responsibilities (although, remember that the staff are paid by the taxpayer exclusively to support parliamentary functions rather than political activities), I suggested that they could hire just one from their allocated complement.

MPs brushed aside any suggestion of change, and continue to do so. They want to be able to trust their staff, they say. Well, civil servants working in government spend their working lives being entrusted with the secrets of their political masters. The system works and is the envy of the world. In truth, the reason was partly because they wanted to hire people whom they knew and had worked with in a previous life, and partly because they wanted suitably zealous staff who would reflect their political views in dealings with constituents. Efficiency and accountability were secondary to political loyalty. It is not clear to me that this is what the taxpayers' support of MPs' offices is meant to achieve. But merely to suggest otherwise was to run into a storm of protest. Who was IPSA to tell MPs whom to employ? The answer, of course, is that IPSA is the guardian of the public interest and the public purse. But the argument fell on very deaf ears.

NO TIME TO TEST THINGS

All of the elements of the scheme had to be put together at breakneck speed. Although it was assumed that the general election would be in the May of 2010 (giving me just five months to set up and pull the whole thing together), it could have been called at any time before then, if the Prime Minister judged it appropriate (fixed-term parliaments – of five years – were established by the coalition government after the election of 2010). Given that we had only effectively been in existence a few months, it was a constant fear that we would not be ready to take on our regulatory and administrative tasks, including paying out money to incoming MPs. I was asked by one of the innumerable groups of MPs whom I appeared before as we were preparing for the launch of IPSA's scheme whether we would be ready by May. I said that I thought that we would be – just about. I was then asked what we would do if a snap election was called before May. I replied that we would be buggered (perhaps somewhat earthy, but true!).

In establishing IPSA at breakneck speed, we had to put in place all of the necessary infrastructure to operate a system which is basically concerned, as regards IPSA's administrative responsibilities, with paying out money: in the form of salaries for MPs and their staff and in meeting claims for repayment under the several budgets. We needed appropriate information technology. There existed on the market a number of products to manage the sort of things we were dealing with, such as Expense@Work. If we were going to be ready in time to meet the demands to be made on us, we figured that we had no option but to buy a number of these products, each of which existed and operated separately from the others.

If ever there was an illustration of 'act in haste, repent at leisure', this was it. The systems, although perfectly adequate in their own right, could not readily be integrated. In layman's language, they could not easily be made to talk to each other. The upshot was a system which was, at best, clunky. Add to this the fact that, in its initial form – and for good reason – the scheme of rules was relatively complex, and you have a state of affairs which was less than ideal, to put it mildly. Those MPs who regarded IPSA as a mistake, an over-reaction to the scandals, were not slow to seize on the technological weaknesses of our systems as a reason for daily condemnation. They were not interested in the reasons behind the choices made. They accepted none of the responsibility for demanding that IPSA be a fully functioning organisation offering a Rolls-Royce service, despite an impossible set of deadlines, an uncertain starting date, and with no opportunity to pilot anything. They just knew that the end result was less than ideal. And, in one sense, they were right. To this day, IPSA, and those it exists to serve, are victims of unavoidable decisions taken in 2010.[25]

Change was on the way as I stepped down in May 2016. But it has been a battle. And, to add to the problems, because the various systems do not readily talk to each other, IPSA has had to use what are called 'work-arounds', whereby human beings insert themselves into the systems to ensure that one system can deal with another. The moment humans are introduced, the risk of human error arises. And, given that much of the information that IPSA handles is confidential (private addresses, telephone numbers, details of bank accounts), the consequences of any error could be considerable. This meant that a system of checking was put in place to seek to guard against error. It has worked with very, very few exceptions. But it slows things down and adds to costs.

THE MANTRA: FAIR, WORKABLE AND TRANSPARENT

Prior to the election of 2010, after which IPSA would be operational, I had set out some of my thinking in a speech.[26] It was well attended by senior MPs, policy wonks and academics. The MPs were there to take the measure of me. Many of the latter two groups were there largely to explain how I would fail. They knew only the old system and were, indeed, part of it. A radical new approach meant that they would have to learn new tricks. In the speech, I coined a mantra which has stayed with IPSA ever since: that IPSA would work in a manner which was 'fair, workable and transparent'. Of particular importance was the stress laid on openness or transparency.[27] We would, I made clear, work in the open. The details of dealings with MPs would be there for

---

25   It should be recorded, however, that the staff at Expense@Work did a good job of seeking to customise their product for us and were very responsive to requests for changes.

26   At the Institute of Civil Engineers on 23 March 2010 – see *Daily Telegraph*, 24 March 2010.

27   We were under a statutory duty to be 'transparent'.

all to see. The aim was that the taxpayer would be able to see where the money paid over to MPs was going. Of all the decisions made in the early days, this was one of the most important. If MPs live and die by reference to their standing in the public's eye, the thinking was that they would not wish to be seen to be taking the expenses regime for a ride. Indeed, the incentive would be to adhere, and be seen to adhere, scrupulously to the rules. Making MPs' dealings with IPSA public was the single most important mechanism for achieving compliance with the new system.

LIMITS

During the discussions of amendments to the initial Parliamentary Standards Act 2009, two matters stood out. They can both be seen as gaps in the architectural structure that was being put together. In this most political of subject matters, they were both matters which were particularly sensitive politically. One gap was filled through the device of amendments to the Constitutional Reform and Governance Act 2010. The other was not, and we live with the consequences.

As regards the first, the expenses scandal had arisen in part because MPs felt that they were underpaid. I was constantly buttonholed by MPs complaining of how they dealt with leading members of the community in their constituencies such as doctors in the NHS, head teachers, or senior executives in the local authority, who were paid significantly more than they were. The suggestion was that their authority or legitimacy was in some way undermined by the fact that they were paid less. It was a very British concern with status, with income seen as the relevant proxy. And since MPs tended to be concerned about status, they were also concerned about money.

Before the creation of IPSA, MPs' salaries were subject to periodic review by a body called the Senior Salaries Review Board. The board had recommended on a number of occasions that MPs be paid more. Successive governments on receipt of their advice had for many years routinely rejected it. 'Now is not the time' was the recurring refrain. MPs fell into line, conscious of the political fallout if they were seen to be giving themselves a pay rise. To soften their disappointment, the various Whips' Offices were said to tour the tea rooms advising MPs privately to 'use their allowances'. Indeed additional 'allowances' were created over time, such as £10,000 for each MP as a 'communications allowance'. This approach took up some of the slack. And, because the mechanisms of control were weak to say the least, the system of allowances grew and was increasingly abused by a number of MPs. Moreover, seeing the increases in the salaries of others with whom they dealt in their constituencies every day, allowances came increasingly to be seen as an entitlement. This was not money to be spent as needed. This was 'my money', as one MP put it to me.

Against this background, my view was that to give IPSA the responsibility for getting 'allowances' back into shape while leaving the issue of pay unaddressed was to approach the problem of remunerating MPs from the wrong end. As I laid out in my first speech, the 'big exam question' was: 'How much money should MPs receive from the public purse to enable them to do their job?' The answer to this question must include salary and pensions and other associated benefits such as the quaintly titled 'resettlement allowance',[28] as well as costs and expenses. IPSA must, therefore, I argued, be given responsibility for these other matters.

As it happens, there was little or no opposition to this proposal. It was accepted as a matter of politics that IPSA should determine MPs' pay and pensions. Previously, they had been free to accept or

---

28   See Chapter 16.

reject the SSRB's recommendations. Giving the responsibility for pay and pensions to IPSA meant that MPs would no longer have any say. In the temper of the times this was seen as both inevitable and right. As we will see, when IPSA actually got round to the issues, sweet reason and pragmatism took a back seat to the trench warfare of politics.

The other gap in the legislative architecture was any mention of the House of Lords. This is the second of the two Houses of Parliament. There are clear distinctions between the roles and responsibilities of the two groups of members. Members of the House of Lords are not elected (save among themselves in the case of replacing hereditary peers), do not have constituencies and so, unlike MPs, do not need a constituency office nor staff to run it, though they could argue that they need staff to assist them in carrying out their duties. Historically, they were not paid a salary, though they could claim various allowances including an attendance allowance. But, accepting these differences, the case could be made for introducing the same level of scrutiny and accountability in terms of the use of taxpayers' money as regards the second chamber of the legislature, the House of Lords, that had been decided on for the Commons.

Indeed, I was asked to call on a senior member of the Lords who wanted to sound me out as to whether what we were proposing for the Commons could also be made to apply to the Lords. It was made clear to me that the meeting had no formal standing and that the person sounding me out, though very senior, had no formal authority to do so, indeed would attract significant criticism and opposition if it were known that we were talking. I made it clear that I thought that, as a matter of principle, restricting what were very significant changes to the relationship between the taxpayer and legislators just to one House did not make sense. But I added that it would require an amendment to the legislation to extend IPSA's role to include the Lords and that this was not likely.[29]

In fact, nothing was done about extending IPSA's role to the Lords. But the story was not without its twists. My understanding is that, in the wake of the scandal of 2008–09, the House of Lords, seeing the writing on the wall as regards external independent regulation for the Commons, saw the need to act promptly to preserve their position before they were caught up in what they saw as the general panic. An elder statesman was given the task of drawing up a system for the Lords which would ensure that IPSA was not allowed near the place, but which, to a relatively friendly and partially sighted observer could be said to have addressed the issues to the extent that they might be relevant to their noble Lordships. The recommendations which emerged did not give the right answer. The right answer was something along the lines of the famous words of the Prince in Lampedusa's *The Leopard*: that everything must change so that everything stays the same. What was being recommended was, in fact, real change.

The only possible response of their Lordships, in the form of Lord Strathclyde, was to commission a second review. This one, crafted by Lord Wakeham, came up with the right answer. I was called to see the author. He explained to me how important the developments were as regards the Commons and wished me well. He went on to explain that for various obvious reasons the system being planned for the Commons was not needed as regards the Lords. They had agreed their own way forward. This involved every member who attended the

---

29   During the second reading of the initial Parliamentary Standards Bill, Jack Straw observed: 'It is envisaged that in due course the arrangements relating to the Independent Parliamentary Standards Authority should indeed apply to the other place [the House of Lords]; that is why we sought to create an authority that covers both Houses. I hope that that matter will be dealt with in subsequent legislation. At the moment, however, the specific parts of the Bill cover only this House.'

Lords being entitled to an attendance allowance of £300 per day, plus various allowances for such activities as participation in parliamentary delegations and for travel between home and Westminster and when on parliamentary business. I would no doubt, he ventured, admire the simplicity of the approach and the ease of its administration. I withdrew, reflecting on the fact that it might be simple, but, from the point of view of the taxpayer, it was somewhat lacking in rigour and accountability.[30]

The House of Lords has not been without its scandals relating to expenses over the past several years. But I suspect that the system of allowances will prove as difficult a nut to crack as the bigger question of which it is only a small part – reform of the House of Lords.

---

30   The current system, as of May 2018, is somewhat more rigorous, see www.parliament.uk/documents/lords-finance-office/members-guide-may-2018.pdf

CHAPTER 6

GETTING STARTED

A PRESS CONFERENCE

In the helter-skelter countdown to the forthcoming general election of 2010, not only did we have to work out what the new scheme would look like, but consult on it, as required by the statute. Notwithstanding my previous unhappy exposure to the lobby, we decided to hold a press conference to launch the consultation and respond to questions. The lobby listened to my short presentation rather in the way diners might listen to a waiter describing the menu, only half attending since they knew what they wanted and were keen to get their teeth into it. The questions were aggressive. The journalists wanted MPs to be hammered. There was no room for careful consideration of how one might design a system which would reflect the twin needs of taxpayer and MP.

Of particular interest was the issue of MPs employing members of their families. Even to consult on this was seen as a betrayal, proof – if proof were needed – that I was soft on MPs, or out of touch with the mood of the nation. It was put to me that if over 65 per cent of the population, as suggested by one poll, thought that the practice should stop, how could I think otherwise? I confess that it seemed to surprise these particular representatives of the press when I replied that I, and I suspected they, did not necessarily believe in right by numbers (save when the numbers confirmed their prejudice). Majoritarianism, I urged, had its place, but also its dangers in making public policy.[31] I went on that we preferred to rely on evidence and reasoned argument. I could see a seminar coming on! We were right at the heart of arguments about democracy: when is it right for those with authority to follow and when to lead public opinion, and from where do organisations like IPSA derive their legitimacy when the leaders were not elected, not accountable save in matters of finance and not recallable? But it was not the time or the place for such reflections, central as they may be to the questions being asked. The press conference fizzled out. The leader of the pack huddled with his colleagues to agree what the story was. We went back to the office to get on with things.

There was work to do. What the media made of it would be a task for the long term, a task of persuading people that IPSA was doing what was asked of it, referring to what we did rather than anything we or others might say. Of course, we had members of staff who dealt with the media, but only a couple (reduced soon afterwards to one). We tried to reach out and explain. But the animosity of some MPs, their command of the ears of friendly journalists, and the reluctance on the part of the media to let go of a story which played well with a distrusting and cynical public, meant that we just had to dig in. As I said in one of my early speeches, we were there for the long haul. We were not going away.

One concrete demonstration of this was my continuing a policy I had adopted in other high-profile positions. Every day, and sometimes several times a day, an agency that we had engaged would send to the email accounts of all senior staff the reports about IPSA which had

---

31   I hesitate to mention the referendum in 2016 on remaining in or leaving the EU.

appeared in the media, from *The Times* to Radio Norfolk. I simply deleted them. I was not concerned with the ephemera of the moment. If there was anything important that I needed to know, I would be alerted (usually well in advance). If there was something requiring my attention, I would respond. Otherwise, I had a job to do. In doing it, the agenda was better set by those around me and the evidence that we were gathering than by this or that journalist or media outlet.

EARLY ENGAGEMENT

IPSA opened for business on 7 May 2010. There was a range of procedures to complete. MPs had been advised of this in a package of material which IPSA had arranged to be given to them by the returning officer on their election. Among other things, there was a copy of the scheme of rules and instructions as to how to get whatever was needed. One of our most pressing tasks was to take down relevant details (such as bank accounts) and provide information. Subsequently, we also had to make sure that MPs received the tokens for their computers which they needed to gain access to IPSA's systems. Staff were duly sent off to the House of Commons.

To new MPs this was just another chore, part of the rite of passage from ordinary citizen to MP. For many of those returning, however, there was a sense that something had changed. Some organisation that they had no familiarity with, indeed could barely remember voting for, was telling them what they had to do to get their hands on what they saw as their money. Some MPs clearly resented the change. They had just been elected/re-elected. They were here to do the nation's business, not to be bothered by some jobsworth telling them what to do. Several of them made this point in what might in the context be described as un-parliamentary language. To be more plain, staff were, on occasions, bullied, shouted at and even sworn at.

This was reported back. The chief executive, Andrew McDonald, a very experienced ex-civil servant, used his contacts in the House to complain, but in the early days, with Whips' Offices still being put together, it was hard to get the message through. For my part, I immediately advised that those members of staff working in the House during this process should each take a pad of paper and a pen and place them prominently on their desk. I told them that if there continued to be any form of abuse or bullying they should immediately reach for the pen and begin to record what was being said and make it clear, if asked, that they were making a record which would be reported to the board (and thus be amenable to a request under the Freedom of Information Act and so made public). This approach began to have the desired effect, at least in terms of face-to-face dealings.

The MailOnline of 23 May 2010 reported what was going on under the headline 'Bullying MPs warned to stop "abusing" expenses staff or risk legal action':

Bullying MPs could be prosecuted for threatening and intimidating staff who are overseeing a crackdown on their Commons expenses …
The warnings went up after MPs' protests over the tough new expenses shake-up went too far, forcing the new Independent Parliamentary Standards Authority (IPSA) to demand a stop to the bullying.
The *Mail on Sunday* understands:

- MPs yelled and gesticulated at junior staff trying to explain the new regime in special one-to-one sessions in Westminster's Portcullis House.
- Some civil servants – often drafted in temporarily from other Whitehall departments – have been left close to tears after being subjected to the full wrath of MPs.

- A meeting with IPSA policy director John Sills and Labour MPs was so stormy that one MP said: 'If there'd been a rope handy, we'd have used it.'

A subsequent meeting was cancelled.

Last night, an IPSA source said: 'The behaviour of some MPs has been disgraceful. We don't have to take this and they need to know that we can take legal action if necessary.'

MPs who bully expenses staff are potentially liable to prosecution for breach of the peace or even affray, which could land them with a hefty fine or a jail sentence.

However, MPs hit back by accusing the IPSA of 'total incompetence', and claiming that the new slimmed-down expenses regulations are 'totally unworkable'.

They are particularly livid that they now have to pay out the money first for office and accommodation costs, and then claim it back.

To add to their anger, the IPSA – an independent body that replaces the discredited Commons fees office and costs £5.8 million a year to run – plans to pay performance-related bonuses to its own staff.[32]

Last night, an IPSA spokesman said: 'We have held one-on-one induction sessions with over 550 MPs and the vast majority have been productive.

'But there have been instances where MPs have been very forceful in expressing their views about the new approach to how they can claim expenses.'

---

32   This was not so.

Following a request made under the Freedom of Information Act, on 20 August IPSA published an anonymised response setting out in detail various 'incidents' when members of staff had been abused.[33]

The following gives a flavour of the 'incidents':

INCIDENT ONE

Member in lift – Asked how he was getting on with IPSA – the reply was 'awful'. I offered help – he declined and said, 'You're all fucking idiots'.

INCIDENT TWO

Meeting with [deleted] MP

Date: Monday 26 July 2010

[Deleted] greeted me very pleasantly. He had staff members in attendance at all times, which created an intimidating atmosphere at the points at which [deleted]'s behaviour was inappropriate.

After an initial discussion, I outlined the basic principles of the scheme. These were met with ridicule and derision by [deleted] and his staff.

I then endeavoured to take [deleted] through the basic processes of the system. At several times during the session, he exclaimed, 'This system is a fucking abortion!' which I found deeply inappropriate and offensive. His staff laughed and agreed with this and other comments which [deleted] made.

Other comments included, 'It [the system/scheme] will make the only people who want to be MPs rich people and losers; that lawyer (Sir Ian Kennedy) is a stupid [offensive swear word that I am no longer able to recall], he has no idea what we do'; and 'I don't have a constituency office, but I might get one now to spend the budget

---

33   The request and IPSA's response are set out in Appendix III.

because I am that pissed off'. At one point an external visitor entered the office. [Deleted] said to him, 'I'm doing my fucking IPSA expenses. It's fucking shit!'

INCIDENT THREE

[Deleted] MP

Date: Monday 10 May

Came to say that he would not be doing an induction session, throwing his personal details form across the desk at the facilitator [deleted]. When told that he would have to, became angry and patronising and would not accept the message. In addition to being angry and raising his voice, his body language and physical behaviour was unacceptable – he struck the laptop on the facilitator's desk and loomed over the facilitator in an intimidating manner. Incident witnessed by: [deleted].

INCIDENT SIX

[Deleted] MP

Complete unwillingness to engage with volunteer [deleted], system, or induction session – rude, abrupt, disparaging ('I don't do administration') used the word 'fuck' and other violent language (e.g. 'I'm going to murder someone today'). Very angry until she realised she could give it all to her proxy; refused to sign declaration as her stated intention was to share her log-in details with her member of staff. Witnessed by [deleted] and [deleted] volunteer.

The BBC TV programme *Newsnight* promptly dedicated a slot on the following Friday evening, 28 May, in which actors read the transcripts of the various 'incidents'. It was both funny and chilling in equal measure.

The bullying and worse, while they lasted, were both very real and very shocking. There may only have been a few MPs who behaved in this way, but the behaviour had a lasting effect not only on some of IPSA's staff but on the struggle to create a proper working relationship between IPSA and MPs and their staff.

OF TELEPHONES AND EMAILS

The very strong sense of anger felt by some MPs in those early days did not go away. Indeed, it took years for it to dissipate (and it only needed the smallest sense of a slight for it to be rekindled, albeit in a somewhat less florid form). The anger was most commonly expressed in the form of telephone calls and emails.

As regards telephone calls, we had a pool of staff whose job it was to handle questions from MPs and their staff about the scheme and, more commonly as time went on, about IPSA's systems. Given the limits imposed by our funding and the myriad calls on the staff's time, we usually had a complement of about five staff who dealt with telephone calls. They were specially trained not only in how to respond but also in the details of the scheme and our operation since questions raised by MPs or their staff could be on anything.

About six months after beginning operations, we analysed the use made of the telephone service and found that the very large majority of calls were made in the afternoon and early evening. To improve our overall efficiency, we decided to operate the telephone service from 2 p.m. onwards. This allowed us to redeploy staff to other tasks in the morning. When this change was made known to MPs it attracted significant criticism. Each MP was an island. Their needs had to be met. The overall efficiency of IPSA and the value for money of the telephone service were of no real concern. They or a member of their staff had a question and wanted an answer. Eventually, an all-day telephone service was reinstated, but only when we had the necessary resources.

We were handling over 250 calls a day. On occasions we were close to being overwhelmed. Staff were routinely reassigned from other tasks to help, provided that they had been trained. But even then we did not always have enough staff to meet the demand, a demand which, until the IT systems are reformed, will never abate, though it became less severe as we slowly simplified the scheme. The director of operations in the early days had previously managed a call centre so brought considerable expertise. But the burden was heavy. Callers on occasions had to wait, not an inordinate amount of time, but undoubtedly too long. And, to an MP, any length of time was too long. The irony was that MPs might complain about having to hold on for twenty or thirty seconds, while at the same time, once connected, would demonstrate little or no awareness of the fact that the longer they spent detailing this or that point, the longer others had to wait. An email could have done the job, but an early lesson was that MPs like to talk to someone. A further irony was that many MPs would routinely condemn IPSA as being a bloated bureaucracy while at the same time urging that more staff be hired to deal with their telephone calls.

One consequence of all this was that, too often in those early days, staff were shouted at and abused. We recorded all telephone calls. Staff were encouraged to ride with the punches but if it got too bad they were advised to let the chief executive know. He in turn either spoke or wrote to the particular MP asking that due respect be shown to members of our staff. This sometimes worked.

Emails posed similar problems. The fact that they were received an instant after being sent was increasingly accompanied by the assumption that the response would be equally instantaneous. Well, we did not have enough staff to operate in this way, plus some of the emails raised questions that called for research and careful thought. But this did not stop the staff from receiving angry and sometimes offensive messages calling for a response. Members of staff were frequently criticised as incompetent and as failing to appreciate the needs and standing of the correspondent. A favourite was the MP whose email, after detailing his complaint, read in capital letters: 'DON'T YOU KNOW THAT I HAVE THE MOST IMPORTANT JOB IN THE WESTERN WORLD', which might be considered a tad overblown for an MP for a medium-sized constituency in the east of England. Some staff members took to pinning up the more egregious messages by their desks. They also pinned up the occasional thank-you email which they received.

The problem was that the very need for emails was itself resented by many MPs. It was not understood, though explained a number of times. Many MPs raised on the previous regime for managing taxpayers' money were used to seeking what they called 'pre-approval' for some expenditure or other. They would telephone the old 'fees office' operated by the House of Commons' authorities, and seek verbal approval for such-and-such expenditure. The stories were of last-minute phone calls, against the background, for example, of a train to catch, or that some item was urgently needed. A common feature of these stories was that staff ran the risk of being browbeaten if they demurred. So, they often conceded. Thereafter, whatever might have been the case as a matter of fact, if challenged as regards this or that expenditure, MPs were able to say that they had been given the green light by the fees office. And, of course, in the absence of evidence either way, there was no real way to introduce discipline into a system which, lest it be forgotten, was dispensing public money.

One of the very early decisions that I took was that every claim must be supported by evidence – the 'No ticket, no laundry' mantra. The aim was to put an end to the pre-approval of expenditure. If staff were asked about a particular matter, they were instructed to refer

MPs to the scheme, its rules and guidance. If MPs wanted to pursue any particular matter further, they were advised to send an email to which we would respond. In that way, there would be a 'paper trail' and there would be no room for subsequent claims about what had been said by whom. This was of great importance if IPSA was going to be a regulator that the public could put their trust in.

The approach was resented by many MPs. It appeared to be bureaucratic and it meant that instant answers were not available. It also meant that the Freedom of Information Act cast its shadow in that any email could be subject to a request for disclosure under the act. This made MPs nervous. The prospect of their local media reporting requests for office supplies in headlines referring scathingly to MPs' claiming for paper clips was unwelcome, even if the claim was entirely proper and justified. We understood the point, but it was clear to us that at the outset of IPSA's life there must be a clean break from a past which had operated on a basis which offered little or no assurance to taxpayers as to how their money was spent.

More importantly, but less obviously, the approach was essential as part of a larger vision of how IPSA would develop over time. IPSA did not want to continue to be prescriptive beyond the point where it was absolutely necessary. The aim was gradually to vest more and more discretion in MPs as regards their expenditure. Our not giving pre-approval and, instead, referring MPs to the rules was part of this approach. It was designed to encourage MPs to decide for themselves. And, to help, we offered guidance alongside the rules. Gradually, the approach took hold, although some MPs continued to hanker for a yes or no answer, rather than being advised to consult the rules and guidance.[34]

---

34   We had, for example, requests for advice as to whether the purchase and display of a fridge magnet with the details of the MP's constituency surgery on it was allowed by the rules. We were also asked whether the purchase of a Christmas tree for the office was allowed. I awaited the call to ask, 'What about ornaments for the tree?'!

The reason for their desire for an answer is obvious. MPs wanted some form of insurance if expenditure was later challenged, for example, in the media. They want reassurance that the rules of the scheme allow them to proceed in a particular way. This is different from those MPs who bridled against the very existence of rules. This latter camp is made up of MPs who remember the old days and lament their passing. They routinely would attack IPSA for a range of failings, but it was IPSA's very existence that got up their noses. They wanted to be given 'their' money to spend as they saw fit. I am not concerned with them here. I am concerned with those seeking confirmation that some expense is within the rules. They want 'rulings', as it were, on the rules. They do so out of concern that otherwise they may transgress and then be held up to obloquy.

This concern grows out of the fact that we announced from the outset that, in keeping with our statutory duty to work transparently, we would routinely publish all the claims for expenses made by each MP.[35] This served as a significant incentive to observe the rules. But it also created this desire in MPs to get a definitive answer as to whether X or Y was allowed under the rules. At the very least this provided cover – 'Well, IPSA said it was OK'. By and large, we would not give such answers. Our position was that the rules are there. They cannot, nor should they try to address every possible eventuality. Rather, we leave the MP with discretion, but a discretion to be exercised in the knowledge that if the choice was made to make a claim, the claim would be published. Our aim was to wean MPs off seeking approval, away from the very bureaucracy that they railed against in other contexts. Our vision was to encourage over time the transition to a

---

35   We consulted on publication in the middle of 2010 and proposed publishing monthly. After further consideration, the board settled on every two months. Crucially, in terms of subsequent events, we decided not to publish actual receipts but rather a summary of them, thereby avoiding the labour-intensive task of deleting personal data.

values-based system whereby the MPs had to serve as their own censors. Experience suggests that it will be a slow process.

Many MPs greatly dislike having to make their own judgements. I have no doubt, however, that it is the right approach. But I accept that the effect, at least in the short term, was that some MPs did not claim for certain expenditure, not because it fell outside the rules but because to claim might have caused them some kind of reputational damage at the hands, particularly, of the local media in their constituency. In my view the answer was not to abandon the system of rules and publication but to wait until the feeding frenzy of poring over the claims of MPs as they appeared every two months waned.

PUBLISHING CLAIMS

And, initially, it really was a feeding frenzy. Once we felt confident that the data was sound and that we were tooled up to do so, we launched our policy on publication in the November of our first year (2010) and released the first tranche of MPs' claims in the December. The media, particularly certain newspapers which had first published the stories that grew into the scandal of 2008–09, had created the image of the MP as venal, greedy and crooked. Some MPs, not so very many, had been. Most were not. The new system made it very hard to be so, even if they wanted to be. This might be good news for our democracy, but it was bad news for these newspapers because it meant that a story which had made careers and moved a lot of papers was dying if not dead. So, every effort had to be exerted to keep it alive. MPs were pilloried for claiming for paper clips or a jar of coffee, though it was never clear why, given that these were legitimate office costs. I'm sure the journalists writing the stories didn't have to buy the tools of their trade, but the cry was often heard, 'This is public money.' It's beyond me to understand why those who are paid from the public purse should be judged by a canon of behaviour which those in the private sector would scoff at if they even recognised it.

Given the initial increase in the temperature around MPs and expenses, I was repeatedly lobbied by MPs to publish claims less frequently, or not at all, because of the corrosive effect of the media's attention. I took, and still take, the view that it was important to hold our nerve. Regular publication would, I argued, become routine, barely noticed except by the obsessives. It would gradually dawn on the media that there was no longer a story about MPs' expenses and they would move on. Of course, to talk in the longer term did not allay the concerns of MPs who live permanently in the present. Nor did it help that a number of MPs who had abused the previous discredited regime eventually found themselves before the courts. The media, either through laziness or a wanton disregard for the truth, pounced on these cases as evidence of the continued venality of MPs. 'They still don't get it', was the cry. It was unwarranted. MPs *had* got it. But it fitted a different agenda to claim otherwise. It is true also that the occasional MP succeeded in scoring an own goal by putting in a claim for a birthday card for a constituent or a wreath for Remembrance Day. But they were exceptions that proved the rule.

NO SURRENDER

I say that MPs did 'get it'. But in these early days that I am describing, it was clear that some MPs did not get it and did not want to get it, so deeply opposed were they to IPSA. Why was this? There were the oft-repeated complaints that we were slow and bureaucratic, that our IT was clunky, and so on. To some extent, the complaints were justified. But no account was taken of the circumstances under which we had to set the organisation up. Nor, most significantly, did I ever receive an offer from MPs generally or any particular MP, to work with us in a practical, focused and constructive manner to find ways to improve what we did. Some MPs in private were kind and thoughtful and expressed discomfort at the behaviour of colleagues. Others accepted us as one accepts that February is an unpleasant month and that one just has to get through it. But, and this is a crucial insight into the behaviour of MPs, once they were in a group, tribal behaviour or 'group think' took over. MPs seek to attract attention (and thereby move on from base camp up the slippery slope of advancement towards a place in the executive or the chairmanship of a select committee). Speaking on behalf of their fellows in the face of IPSA's threat to the life that they felt was their due was a sure-fire way of winning admiring supporters.

We were just treated to litanies of shortcomings. We would call meetings to seek views or explain what we were planning or doing, which soon descended into what we came to call 'war stories'. MPs would take it in turns to describe occasions on which they, or more usually someone else, had fallen victim to IPSA's incompetence. Of course, by referring to someone else's experience, the opportunity to embellish was tempting, as was the claim that the person reporting the outrage was 'not familiar with all the details, but...' This would usually be the first time that we had heard of the particular problem, if it existed at all. Those MPs who genuinely wanted things to be sorted out would ordinarily have simply contacted us and we would have found a way forward. But the naysayers preferred the route familiar to readers of *Alice's Adventures in Wonderland*: 'Sentence first – verdict afterwards'. We were reduced to that most pathetic of responses, saying lamely that we would look into the matter.

In my view, the complaints raised were really only a symptom of a deeper antipathy, an antipathy by no means felt by all MPs, but felt very strongly by some. In the early months, I put the number at around 50–75, the other 575 or so tolerating us with various degrees of reservation. But, although relatively few, they made a noise far out of proportion to their number. What drove them? I say drove in the past tense because it is accepted now that IPSA is here to stay and that MPs have an interest in making it work.[36]

I think the answer is that IPSA was seen by these few MPs as an affront. It was an affront to suggest that they needed to be regulated as regards their financial affairs. It was an affront in that they had been elected in 2010 and were largely innocent of the excesses of their fellows in previous parliaments. It was an affront that they were regarded as in some way still guilty (as they saw it) and made to pay (as they saw it) by losing their freedom and suffering the indignity of regulation. And it was an affront that the regulation was in the hands of an external and independent body. They saw the response in the form of legislation creating IPSA as a constitutional aberration. Quite simply, they saw the legislation as a mistake and one which, on reflection, Parliament would recognise as such, and correct.

Of course, MPs' constituents wanted more regulation rather than less. The standing of MPs could not have been lower. But for these MPs, the public simply did not understand. They had been brainwashed by the media. In an analogy I used on occasions, the MPs were like the soldiers of the Japanese army found in the jungles of the Philippines in the 1950s for whom the Second World War was not over.

The notion, which I advanced on numerous occasions, that IPSA was good news for MPs and that it was in their interests to support us was simply not accepted by these MPs. We were, I argued, the bulwark against accusations of corruption. We could demonstrate month after month that MPs were complying with the scheme and

---

36 Though animosity towards me personally survived my stepping down as chairman, as you will see in the Epilogue.

managing taxpayers' money with proper care. But this would have been too much to stomach. IPSA was a 'bad thing'.

IPSA's first two years were spent handling this existential threat. Rationally, it was clear that no government would want to go back to the old regime. But politics is not always about reason! Thus, much of my time was spent working behind the scenes building understanding and support. I had learned over the years I had spent as a regulator that you should not aim to be liked, though neither should you aim to be disliked. What you should aim for is to be understood as having a job to do and then to do that job well. We were not always able to do the latter in the early days, but that was largely a consequence of circumstances relating to how we had been set up.

THE OFFICE OF GOVERNMENT COMMERCE

This chapter recounts how we got started. It is important to separate out the process of setting up IPSA as a functioning organisation from how it functioned thereafter. As regards setting up, I have already explained the helter-skelter nature of building an organisation from scratch. The legislation was being revised on the hoof. There was no template. There was a skeleton staff (around a dozen) seconded from the Ministry of Justice. And there were a few consultants trying to cobble together a number of information technology systems, given that there was no time to create one which was custom-made. The complexity of the IT challenge was, of course, exacerbated by the fact that the legislative mandate was evolving and changing, thereby calling for concomitant adjustments in our approach. Put shortly, it was difficult to tell the IT people what we wanted the technology to do when we didn't know ourselves.

In the public sector, the use of public funds to establish an organisation is usually subject to independent review to determine whether the process of setting it up was a success in terms of timeliness, efficient use of resources, operational readiness and the like. The review was carried out by the independent Office of Government Commerce (OGC).[37] In due course, the OGC examined IPSA's performance. Its review observed that:

> in October 2009, the task looked well-nigh impossible … Eight months later, the impossible has been delivered … this has been a success story, and deserves to be recognised as such.

The National Audit Office (NAO) echoed this view. They concluded that IPSA:

> began providing services to MPs on time in May 2010; this was a major achievement by the Authority.[38]

These judgements from independent bodies were heartening, particularly when seen against the backdrop of relatively incessant criticism from a core of MPs. To take just one example of the 'challenges' that IPSA faced, we had to pay the salaries of MPs. This meant that at the end of May 2010, we needed to have the bank or other details for each MP so that we could pay their salary into their accounts.[39] Repeated requests were made of MPs to let us have the necessary information. Yet, there were still over 200 MPs who had not done so by the date that we set as the deadline for letting us know so as to be sure to

---

37   Absorbed into the Cabinet Office's Efficiency and Reform Group in 2011. Subsequently an Infrastructure and Projects Authority was created in the Treasury which seems to have the same role as the old OGC.

38   And, I would add, a significant feather in the cap of the acting chief executive, Andrew McDonald and his small band of fellow executives.

39   Except for Sinn Féin MPs, who were/are not paid (though they may claim expenses) because they refuse to take the oath of allegiance to Her Majesty the Queen.

receive their pay. And there were still some forty odd who hadn't done so on the last day of May when the salary was due to be paid. Yet by dint of throwing staff at the problem, much hard work and long hours, every MP was paid on time. Had it been otherwise, brickbats would have been hurled. As it was not, it was taken for granted and certainly no thanks were forthcoming.

ON THE FRONTLINE

As regards how we functioned once we became operational, we struggled. For example, we had introduced a system for paying the MPs' claims for reimbursement which was entirely online. We did not accept pieces of paper on which were scribbled a request for payment. On one occasion, a very senior MP simply gave a member of staff a piece of paper on which was written a sum of £X followed by the word 'taxi'. When asked what we were expected to do with it, the reply was, 'Pay it.' Politely, it had to be explained (again) that submission of claims for reimbursement had to be made using the online system, followed by a receipt, and that, in any event, there were new rules concerning the reimbursement of the cost of taxi fares which he would need to show applied in the particular case, that is, that there was no other suitable form of transport available.

Some MPs struggled with the very idea of using an online system. Dennis Skinner, a member of very long standing, advised us that he had never used a computer in his life and was not about to change now[40] (I've omitted a number of words which were added to give emphasis to his view). On another occasion, pointing his finger at a senior member of IPSA's staff, he said, 'I'll never use your system.' My colleague forbore to comment that he wouldn't get any expenses

---

40   Perhaps of concern to constituents who live in, and wrestle with, the internet age.

paid if he didn't. Instead, we assigned a colleague who spent some considerable time with him and two other long-serving members, taking them, and more important, their staff, through the essentials of making a claim.[41] Another MP, equally not wholly at ease with a computer, made a claim and then pressed 'send'. But 'to make sure', he then sent the claim several more times. The end result was that, instead of one claim, it looked as if he was claiming several times for the same thing, which, if true, would have got him into hot water. This wasn't at all the case and we were able to rescue the situation, but it certainly caused us a headache. We were committed to transparency, and on its face, the record showed multiple claims. So, we decided that we needed to amend our processes to deal with honest errors. We introduced a grace period of three months during which errors and oversights could be corrected without being made public. And, in the meantime, as part of our outreach programme, we dispatched a number of trouble-shooters to help MPs with the system and urged them to appoint one of their staff who was, perhaps, more computer-savvy, as a proxy.

Another area in which we struggled initially, and still do to an extent, was in getting information to MPs about the rules and any revisions of them and how to operate the system. It was one thing to indicate what was required. It was another to get a sense of whether the message had got through. Of course, if a change in a rule or operating procedure was not picked up by an MP, it was always IPSA which was at fault, repeatedly lambasted for this or that failure. On occasions, especially initially, IPSA did fail to do what it should have done. But a large number of IPSA's failings proved in fact on examination to be errors on the part of MPs or their staff who simply had not followed the correct

---

41   The colleague was an ex-Royal Marine commando telecommunications expert, recently back from Iraq, who had a nice line in empathy and charm.

procedure. When this was pointed out, a fallback position was then deployed. IPSA was excessively 'bureaucratic' and got in the way of MPs
doing their job. I sought to make the point as often as I could that their
job included rendering an account to the public for the approximately
£160 million of funding that they received from the public.

Another example of messages not getting through concerned loans.
In our haste to put a system in place, we failed to address properly the
problem of cash-flow encountered by MPs (and especially those newly
elected) at the start of a parliament. Deposits had to be paid as part
of rental agreements for offices and accommodation, and equipment
and furniture had to be purchased. These start-up costs fell to the
MP and, for some, created significant difficulties. As soon as we were
made aware, we brought in a system of interest-free loans of up to
£4,000. We advised the respective Whips' Offices and wrote to MPs.
But communication was difficult.

There are none so deaf as those who choose not to bother to hear or
listen. Within days, one very senior MP berated me at a friend's son's
birthday party. She said that she was out of pocket because of start-up
costs, though she had been an MP for quite a long time, her office
was well established, she lived in a fashionable part of London and
represented a London constituency. Her husband joined the attack,
declaiming with the anger that a drink or three can induce that the
system was a disgrace and much more along those lines. I had been
to the ballet and had arrived late with one of my sons. Suddenly, I
was at the wrong end of a pretty heavy verbal onslaught. My son, a
good friend of the birthday boy, was shocked and appalled. He feared
that I might lose it. But I asked quietly whether, given the difficulties
being faced, the MP had applied for a loan.[42] This really set things off.

---

42   See Chapter 3. We introduced loans as soon as we were made aware of the difficulties that some
     MPs were encountering.

'What loans? There are no loans', and so on. I explained that there were indeed loans, that we had advised all MPs of this and perhaps, if the MP contacted my office in the morning, she would be able to secure one. The contact was duly made. The loan was effected. All that was missing was an apology.

These early days of IPSA had some of the qualities of a battle-ground. We were not always nimble enough and certainly did not always provide the level of service that we should have provided. But we were as new to the system as were MPs and their staff. We had not had time to pilot anything. We had been given 'an impossible task'. Unsurprisingly, we stumbled on occasions. What would have been of the greatest benefit would have been a degree of understanding on the part of MPs and particularly those who spoke for them. Such understanding could have taken the form of, 'This isn't working as well as it could, how can we work together to make it better?' Such an approach is not uncommon in dealings with regulators and if the regulator is prepared to listen, as we were, improvements can be made. After all, objectively, it was in the interests of MPs to work in this way since they were the ones being regulated. But we only got the first half of the conversation: 'This isn't working.' It was so hard to get what could be described as a mature, grown-up conversation. The silent majority kept their heads down. The naysayers kept up the attack. Right through to September we convened daily meetings at 9 a.m. to deal with the latest onslaughts and turbulence. We only half-jokingly dubbed it 'Gold Command'.

CHAPTER 7

THE SPEAKER'S COMMITTEE ON THE IPSA (SCIPSA)

Things came to a head a couple of months after the election of 2010. The scheme was in place and IPSA was inching forward. We had a temporary allocation of funds but now needed the funds to carry on for the coming financial year. Most agencies at arm's length from government are funded by the particular Department of State which created them (for example, the Healthcare Commission was funded by the Department of Health). This is an uneasy relationship, particularly if the agency does things which the relevant department does not appreciate. As chairman of the Healthcare Commission, I had been charged with assessing, independently and for the first time, the quality of healthcare provided by the NHS in England. Inevitably, from time to time (too often, in fact) this involved conveying bad news. The Department of Health was torn between taking credit for the vigilance of its regulator and insisting that things were fine and that the NHS was performing well. The department's response (prior to getting rid of the commission altogether and replacing it with a body with a softer touch!) was, year on year, to challenge and reduce the commission's budget. It was independent, but not allowed to be that independent! I spent five years battling for the resources needed to do the job, not least because 'the job' was routinely expanded to include additional areas of enquiry and concern while it was proposed concomitantly to reduce the funds made available.

How did IPSA deal with this? After all, the I in IPSA refers to 'independent'. I well remember a conversation with then Prime Minister David Cameron on one occasion which began with his saying, 'Ian, I know you are independent, but…' Defying protocol, I interrupted to say that you couldn't begin a sentence like that and then put a 'but' in it. Independence was like pregnancy. We moved on!

That said, any grown-up versed in the ways of Whitehall and Westminster recognises that independence is a complicated concept. I have often argued that it does not mean that the independent body must adopt some purist position, obsessed with defending itself against real and perceived threats. It does not involve people in my position getting up each morning committed to poking our fingers in government's eye. Rather, independence has to be negotiated every day. But the negotiation is against the background of certain propositions that are non-negotiable, lines in the sand, if you will. If, for example, you are asked whether you could delay publication of a report for a couple of days to allow government to deal with something that they regard as more pressing, it would be silly simply to say no to demonstrate your independence. Rather, you would be wise to explore the reason offered and the implications if the request is acceded to. Then, you make a decision. You are not there to obstruct government. You are there to act in the public interest, so you weigh the public interest.

IPSA's independence necessarily raised questions about how to manage our funding, given that we were independent of government, though ultimately resourced by government. The answer was to use the device only rarely deployed, for example, in the case of the Electoral Commission, which, by its nature, was created to make decisions which would affect Parliament and so should be made by a body independent of Parliament and government. The device for dealing with funding, since the money still has to come from public funds raised by the government through Parliament, is to have resort to what is called a Speaker's Committee. In IPSA's case, it is the Speaker's Committee for the IPSA (SCIPSA), a committee chaired by the Speaker of the House of Commons, with members drawn from all sides of the House. Funding, once decided upon, is a charge on the consolidated fund, meaning that it is not subject to the vote of Parliament. The device, however, in IPSA's case is only partly successful in ensuring independence. First, the legislation requires that the Treasury (the government) has to approve what is called IPSA's annual estimate (or proposed budget). Secondly, the SCIPSA was initially made up solely of members of the House of Commons. As such, the funds of the regulator, even if approved by the Treasury, were still under the control of the regulated.

For me, this was and remained a strategic and tactical challenge. On the one hand, SCIPSA (MPs) were, as some saw it, feeding the dog that was biting their hands. The less made available, or the more conditions that could be attached, the less freedom of movement IPSA would have in practice. On the other hand, the money allocated to IPSA was overwhelmingly for dispersing to MPs, to pay for their staff, their travel, their accommodation and so on. To reduce IPSA's budget, or mess about with it by laying down conditions, would be to cut off their own noses.

The only battle to be fought, therefore, was over that amount of the estimate which was needed for IPSA to meet its costs as a functioning organisation. The amount was initially in the region of £6 million, a drop in the ocean in terms of public finance, but the only thing that gave those opposed to IPSA any leverage. If IPSA was not given the funds necessary to do the job as it saw fit, the scheme could not be operated. This was precisely what some wanted. Starve IPSA of funds and we would have to abandon the system we were putting in place. We would simply have to distribute such funds as were deemed appropriate by the SCIPSA by giving each MP a lump sum and invite them to get on with spending it. This would be an even more lax system than that which had given rise to the expenses scandal in the first place. It would be 'anything goes'. Without appropriate funds for its own operation, IPSA would be a paper tiger, unable to regulate effectively. The reasons for the creation of IPSA would be undermined. Transparency and assurance would go out of the window. There were others, of course, who recognised that the public would not stand for this. IPSA had to be allowed to do its job, albeit under close scrutiny. What to do?

We had to appear before the SCIPSA in the early summer of 2010 to present and gain approval for our estimate for the forthcoming year, the first full year of IPSA's operation. The battle-ground would be IPSA's own costs. But it was also the opportunity for those who deeply resented IPSA's existence to give IPSA a thorough working over. They felt that they had been wrongly tarred by the scandal of 2008–09, that they had done nothing wrong, that they had been elected in 2010, and that this had wiped the slate clean. Some went further. Yes, there might have been the odd practices regarding 'allowances' that were unfortunate, but Parliament had panicked, and passed an unnecessary piece of legislation.

The selection of the membership of the SCIPSA was in the gift of the Speaker. Initially, it consisted of Mr Speaker in the chair and seven MPs: the Leader of the House (Conservative), the chair of the Committee on Standards (Labour), and five other members who do not hold ministerial office (two members of the Conservative Party, two members of the Labour Party and one Liberal Democrat). There were no members drawn from the wider public, though I and others had pressed that there should be, not least to bring a degree of independence from politics to the committee. In due course, towards the end of 2010, three lay members were appointed.

The Leader of the House, as the member of the government with whom I most closely liaised, was a member *ex officio*, as was the chair of the House's Committee on Standards. As for the other members, the Speaker left it to the whips of the then three main parties to sort out. This meant that the animus against IPSA tended to be reflected in terms of the appointments which were made. The cheerleader for this constituency was the Liberal Democrat, Bob Russell (later Sir Bob), who became increasingly ludicrous as time went on in his obsession with IPSA.[43] For him, a cheap point was never too cheap. His pursuit of IPSA was relentless albeit irredeemably ill-informed.

THE FIRST MEETING

We were advised that the first meeting of the SCIPSA would be a full-scale hearing in one of the principal committee rooms (in public, as all such hearings are). It would be televised and broadcast live. I as chair was to appear with the chief executive. Naturally, in addition to ensuring that we were on top of the figures and arguments, we spent some time by way of rehearsal being grilled by members of our staff. The aim was to prepare us for what was to come. Frankly, in the end, nothing could have prepared us!

We were kept waiting for close to an hour. We sat outside, fending off the media who had come expecting a show. As we waited, an MP, Phil Woolas, began to make a commotion. The director of policy went up to him and asked if he could help. Mr Woolas stared at him and

---

43   I was told that whenever the Liberal Democrat MPs met together in the House, he would launch into a tirade against IPSA at the earliest opportunity.

exclaimed, 'I hate you!' He then added by way of qualification, 'Not you, the IPSA board.' It turned out that he was worried about whether the budget set by IPSA would cover the cost of certain expenditure. The director told him that, if he was in difficulties, he should apply to draw on the contingency fund which we had set up. Mr Woolas said that there was no such fund. The director said that there was and that we had written to all MPs about it. 'No, you haven't,' he replied. As it happened, the director had a file with him which, among other things, contained a copy of said letter. When he was shown it, Mr Woolas replied, 'Ah.' He was encouraged to contact us and sort things out. His anger briefly subsided.[44]

When we were called in, the seats for the public were full. Sitting immediately behind the seats at the table allocated to the chief executive and myself were a number of MPs. I recognised them as among the less well-disposed to IPSA. The atmosphere was one of significant expectation. This was going to be Romans versus Christians, with no prizes for guessing who the Christians were!

The session was scheduled to last an hour. It went on for more than two hours. I had made it clear to colleagues beforehand that the sole purpose, from our perspective, was to secure our estimate for the year. Whatever may be thrown at us, this was the prize that we should keep our eyes on. Much was thrown. The Chancellor of the Exchequer had announced after the election that public spending would fall by 5 per cent in each of the five years of the life of the current parliament. The first question put to me was what I intended to do in the light of that announcement. Thinking on my feet, I committed IPSA to similar

---

44   He later reverted to type and was one of the chorus of shouters whom I refer to below. He lost his seat on 5 November 2010 when an electoral court found that he had knowingly made false statements: https://www.independent.co.uk/news/uk/politics/former-minister-phil-woolas-loses-his-seat-2126251.html

savings, in the knowledge (or assumption) that if I did not do so, the committee would do it for me anyway.

Then, the questions began in earnest. They were rightly challenging, seeking to understand the arguments underpinning our estimate. But they were both aggressive and dismissive. Members were expecting, indeed demanding, a perfectly smoothly operating system, ignoring the fact that we had been established at breakneck speed. One theme pressed on us was: how could we justify a bid for our operating costs of several million pounds when all we were was a glorified payment office? It was pointed out that, in fact, our primary role, as specified in the statute, was that of a regulator, developing from scratch a scheme of expenses. We were, therefore, not a glorified sort of cashpoint, as was being suggested. We had a far more serious task. It was to introduce probity and accountability into the distribution of taxpayers' money to MPs. A quick change of tack produced the question, 'Why are you appointing a communications director?' Wasn't this an unwarranted waste of taxpayers' money, or, as the egregious Bob Russell remarked, a device for undermining MPs? We replied that, in fact, we had one press officer and one assistant. It was their job to communicate with and inform our various audiences – MPs, their staff, the media and the public. It was, I said, a considerable challenge, as the current proceedings demonstrated.

Bob Russell chose to attack me personally for presiding over an organisation which, by comparison, made Cafcass (a public body which had become a notorious basket case) look good. I thought this a bit rich given that we had been in business for less than two months. Remembering my own admonition that getting the estimate approved was the aim of the exercise, I decided to sit there and take it. But it got worse. Mr Russell asked how could we presume, by issuing the scheme of expenses, to dictate how he ran his affairs. Here we got to the nub of the perceived slight. Shades of article 9 which I referred to at the outset[45] were hovering in the wings. By regulating 'his' money, I was controlling what he said and did. Did I not realise, he asked, that he had a mandate from the people who elected him? I reminded him wearily that we had a mandate which Parliament voted for and which we were fulfilling.

Desperate to land at least one punch, he even demanded to know how we had got to the meeting from our offices half a mile away, hoping no doubt for an admission that we'd come by the taxi denied to him. I was about to suggest to the Speaker that this might be somewhat off the subject of our estimate, when my chief executive replied simply that we had walked. Mr Russell deigned to approve. (On a subsequent occasion, Mr Russell railed against our 'lavish' offices, which, as far as I'm aware, he had not visited. IPSA was based, in fact, in bog-standard offices in a high-rise building near Victoria Station, which was also home to a number of other organisations. To attract possible tenants, the reception area looked swanky when viewed from the street, but it was all for show. There was nothing swanky by the time you reached our floor.)

Throughout this ordeal, the Speaker was not particularly effective. It was his job to keep order, but he seemed to have decided that MPs on his committee wanted their pound of flesh and he wasn't going to get in the way. Apart from remarking that there was so much noise that he could barely hear what I was saying, he did nothing about the extraordinary behaviour of the group of MPs sitting directly behind us. Throughout the answers that we offered they maintained a chorus of 'Fucking liar' in the case of the chief executive and 'Bollocks' in my case, sufficiently loudly for all to hear. My chief executive sailed on

---

45   See footnote 3.

serenely. I did what any person who is rather deaf would do: I took out my hearing aids.

When it was all over, the Speaker indicated that they would let me have a decision on the estimate in due course. He added, darkly, that there might be a need for a further meeting. What happened next was instructive. Our appearance before the SCIPSA had been televised. The reaction of those who watched, I was told, was one of amazement. Social media echoed with attacks. 'They still don't get it' was a commonly expressed view, the 'it' being that the reputation of MPs and Parliament had been seriously damaged by the expenses scandal and was not going to be repaired by attacking with varying degrees of self-importance those who had been appointed to put things right according to a statute that most of them had voted for.

When we were called back for the further meeting, it was held in an upstairs committee room on a back corridor in the House of Commons rather than in one of the grandstanding arenas of Portcullis House. Only a couple of journalists were there. The questioning was much less aggressive. The meeting did not last very long and very shortly thereafter the estimate was approved. The message had got through. If MPs were going to take on IPSA in public, IPSA was likely to garner the greater sympathy and support.

Thereafter, IPSA's annual appearances before the SCIPSA were always in committee rooms on the back staircase, with no television coverage, save on the parliamentary channel, and attended only by in-house journalists. And since everything would appear in Hansard, everyone minded their Ps and Qs.

CHAPTER 8

COMMUNICATION, CONTACT, COMPLIANCE

IPSA's early months were spent trying to bed in the systems which had been created in such a hurry and to establish a protocol for our dealings with Parliament. One example arose early on. How should IPSA be held accountable to Parliament (or at least the House of Commons)?

One day, I became aware that a question had been asked about IPSA in the House. One of IPSA's senior staff, following his civil service training, had drafted a response which was to be passed to the Leader of the House for him to use in answer. Perhaps my antennae were more attuned to the notion of independence, but I immediately convened a group of senior staff and advised them that we would not be doing this in future. I explained that it would not be proper for us simply to brief a minister who would then speak on behalf of IPSA. Certainly, IPSA was funded from the public purse and so must render account ultimately to Parliament. But the mechanism for doing this was through the SCIPSA. In every other respect, we were independent and must act as such, including speaking for ourselves.

I proposed that, following the example of the Electoral Commission, we should ask the House, through the Speaker, to designate someone who would respond to questions raised in the House about IPSA. Our responsibility would be to liaise with this MP and supply him with a written answer which he would then report to the House. He (Charles Walker MP[46]) would not take questions, but would serve as a conduit for further comments back and forth. The system worked very well. But it grew out of the vigilance necessary to preserve IPSA's independence, oftentimes in contexts where MPs and others, rather than seeking to undermine it, simply did not think in the right terms about where IPSA sat in the new constitutional arrangements.

A LIAISON GROUP

The aim of facilitating communication between IPSA and MPs (and their staff) also persuaded me to urge from the outset that a group be established which would meet regularly to exchange views. I suggested it be called the 'liaison group'. Though the idea was accepted,[47] it was many months before the MPs who would serve on the group were chosen. Following established practice, they were selected through the 'usual channels', that is to say that the Speaker, in his capacity as chair of the SCIPSA, approached the Whips' Offices of the various parties. It was agreed that I (on behalf of IPSA) and one of the MPs (on behalf of the group) would take it in turns to chair meetings. I tried to ensure that meetings should rotate between IPSA's office and the House of Commons, but only one meeting was actually held at IPSA. I also agreed that IPSA would provide the secretariat.

The idea was a simple one. The MPs would listen to and comment on our plans; we would listen to and comment on their observations about how we were meeting our statutory duties – what was working

---

46 A member of the SCIPSA and vice-chairman of the Conservative 1922 Committee.
47 The then Leader of the House referred to the desirability of such a group and that he was working on organising it at our first meeting with the SCIPSA in June 2010.

well and what was not and how the project might develop. The ambition was for the group to serve as a forum for the exchange of views away from the cockpit of politics; to think strategically about the development of regulation and support for MPs in this new and very unfamiliar environment. To underline the importance that we attached to the exercise, each member of the board plus the chief executive and director of policy attended.

It would not be an exaggeration to say that the group was a total failure. Edward Leigh MP, the chairman of the MPs' group, made no secret of his view that the whole notion of IPSA was folly. Though he always expressed himself with great courtesy, it seemed to me that in his view IPSA was to be tolerated in the short term but dispensed with when MPs had served sufficient penance. For the rest of the MPs who were members, meetings were increasingly taken over by a litany of what I have called 'war stories' – how this MP's claim had taken too long to settle, how that MP could not get through on the telephone on a particular day, and how all of the MPs found the online system 'clunky' and an unjustified intrusion into their time. Of course, when particular issues were raised, we usually had no notice of them. All we could do was to offer to look into them, which was often judged to be feeble.

Any effort to turn the conversation to overarching challenges, such as the provision and cost of accommodation in London, or how many staff MPs needed, or whether it might be possible to develop a job description for MPs, disappeared in a mass of further 'war stories' about having to pay deposits on office premises, or problems with the cost of TV licences. In the end, it was clear that the group was not seen as a group but as two sides, with the MPs polite, but never far from boiling over. It was even clearer that, as a sounding board for policy, it was not working. After a couple of years, I decided not to convene further meetings till I heard from the MPs. Silence followed.

That said, I did not give up on the notion of liaising with and learning from MPs. Instead of the liaison group, we invited in mid-2013 a separate set of MPs to meet us, all of whom had entered the House in 2010.[48] They were not part of the previous scandal. They had only known IPSA and our systems as being the way to gain access to funds. Refreshingly, they all took the view that they could not understand the opposition to a system of submitting claims for costs and expenses and working within budgets, because this was the world that many of them had known before coming into Parliament. So, with that out of the way, we were able to explore the various observations and suggestions that they offered.

The meeting was judged a success. But, as in all dealings with MPs, it is hard to maintain their interest. Sadly, they did not take up our offer of further meetings. But that said, building on what we had learned, we decided to convene ad hoc groups of MPs and, importantly, their staff, who have a particular interest in aspects of the working of the scheme, to listen to their views and to encourage them to take part in pilots where we could test proposed developments. It took far too long to get this level of engagement. Some of the responsibility for this rests with IPSA. But, at last, real progress in effective engagement was on the cards.

COMPLIANCE

When Parliament first passed the statute creating IPSA, one of its features was to give IPSA responsibility for receiving and addressing complaints that MPs had breached the standards laid down by the House governing the behaviour of MPs. As the Constitutional Reform and Governance Bill was making its way through Parliament in 2010,

---

48   Two members, Nicky Morgan and Sarah Wollaston, were particularly helpful.

this responsibility was removed to avoid IPSA's being dragged into disputes over parliamentary privilege. In addition, the opportunity was taken to tack on to the bill a number of other provisions relating to IPSA. The two most important were the decision to pass responsibility for setting MPs' pay and pensions to IPSA and the revision of the provisions relating to MPs' compliance with the scheme.

I will get to the story of pay and pensions later.[49] But here I am concerned with compliance. What the CRAG Act did, once passed by Parliament, was to give IPSA a much more limited role than previously envisaged, focused on ensuring compliance with the scheme laid down by IPSA. What would this entail?

We had no idea what might happen once we began operations after the election of 2010. On the one hand, the toxic fallout from the expenses scandal would suggest that compliance would be a high priority for post-2010 MPs and non-compliance would be rare. On the other hand, MPs are an unpredictable group. Many are not risk-averse. So, to signal our intent yet not go over the top, we set up an office consisting of a compliance officer and two assistants. This seemed about right, given that IPSA is a small outfit (at the outset there were around sixty-five staff).

The compliance office by statute is independent of IPSA: independence within independence. The budget for the compliance office is a separate heading in IPSA's estimate put before the SCIPSA. The compliance officer was answerable to me as chairman and thus to the board. The procedures to be followed in responding to complaints of non-compliance are laid down from time to time by the board. But in other respects in carrying out its functions, the compliance office acts independently, underscored in the statute by the fact that the

---

49   See Chapter 16.

compliance office has the authority to look into decisions made by IPSA about claims if asked to do so by an MP, as well as look into complaints against MPs.

It soon became clear that MPs were keeping to the rules. Indeed, if anything they were under-claiming, that is to say not claiming for expenditure which would have been allowed under the scheme. In the beginning, given the risk that a particular claim may not be allowed and that this fact would become known to the public, some MPs erred on the side of caution and did not make a claim. Meanwhile, the compliance officer was busy liaising with the executive and the board who were responsible for drawing up the rules and procedures which would govern the way in which he (it was a he) would operate. This took time and was the subject of consultation. So, all was relatively quiet on the compliance front.

Once work on the rules was completed and in place, it became clear that the demands on the compliance office were going to be much less than initially predicted. Against this background, I was surprised to learn that the compliance office was about to publish its first annual report in which it named over thirty MPs as being in breach of the rules. I asked to see the report, as I'd had no part in it. It was immediately clear that the compliance office had adopted a somewhat inflated notion of their role and independence. They had worked as if in a bubble, with little or no real interaction with the rest of IPSA. I could see that there were problems. First, the report was not well written. And secondly, it had not been checked by, and thus not informed by, the various teams in IPSA. Once the senior executives had learned of it they had alerted me – any release would have to be carefully managed, given that relations with MPs were particularly poor.

A new compliance officer had recently been appointed, replacing the initial temporary appointment. I asked that the publication of the report be held back so that it could be reviewed by the relevant teams in IPSA. For example, there was concern within IPSA that many of the examples described as breaches of the rules were due to administrative errors on the part of MPs, still trying to come to terms with a new world. Further, and much more disturbing, I was told that the staff in the compliance office, in the absence of complaints and thus in the absence of much to do, had decided to take their own action. The office had gone through every MP's website to see whether there was any breach of the rules, not least as regards the ban on using taxpayer-funded websites for party-political purposes. Some few, minor breaches had been found.

The approach adopted raised serious questions. Instead of reacting to complaints raised by the public or IPSA's staff, the compliance office was looking for work. It was adopting a model of regulation which may be appropriate in some circumstances, but was inappropriate in the case of IPSA. It was the model of the regulator as police officer. That was not IPSA's role. And the situation was made worse by one particular case. As part of the trawl through websites, an MP had been advised that his website breached the rules about political statements because it had the emblem of a red rose at its head. The MP in question pointed out, in pretty acerbic tones when contacted by the compliance office, that the red rose may be the symbol of the Labour Party but it was also the symbol of the county of Lancashire where his constituency was (and that he was a Tory MP!).

I asked that there be a pause before publishing the report. Despite my request, the publication went ahead. Much work had to be done to repair relations. The compliance officer was replaced. His staff was pared down to just one part-time assistant.

For the future, it was clear that the relationship between the compliance office and the board, particularly the chairman, was crucial.

Mutual trust and sensitivity to circumstances were the important features of that relationship, rather than some abstract notion of independence. Once the initial hiccups in establishing the role were overcome, everything went very well. The principal reason for this was the personality and skill of Peter Davis, the new compliance officer. An ex-chief superintendent in Durham Police, he brought tact and good judgement to his role. The understanding was that, operationally, he was free to act as he chose. At the same time, he kept me informed of matters which he understood I might need to know about. He introduced a different and more mature approach to addressing complaints. He worked with the policy team whose job it was to revise the rules from time to time. Crucially, he injected a level of judgement and discretion which allowed him to winnow out complaints which lacked substance and to concentrate on the relatively few which warranted enquiry and investigation. The conduct of the compliance officer was in my view exemplary during the five years that he served IPSA, combining mature judgement with rigour. He also won the respect of MPs, no mean feat for someone in his role.

His job was to examine complaints made both against MPs and against IPSA of non-compliance with the scheme of expenses. He developed a separate section on IPSA's website setting out, among other things, his role and how to make contact. A large proportion of the complaints that he received concerning MPs were either frivolous or politically motivated by local political rivalries. Having sought a response from the MP involved, he was usually able to dismiss the complaints without further ado. When they warranted more examination, he and his assistant would enquire further. If he found that there was no breach of the scheme, he would advise both the MP and the complainant that the complaint would be dismissed. On occasions, he would decide that he was not satisfied with the response received from the MP concerned and that the complaint should be looked at further. In such a case, he would open what was formally known as an investigation. On average, there were about three or four investigations going on at any given time.

As regards complaints against IPSA from MPs, the compliance officer followed a similar procedure. There were not very many such complaints, but a number were upheld, in which case, his decision was published on IPSA's website and appropriate action taken.

There were two features of the procedure that attracted attention. The first was that, until he decided to open an investigation, nothing was in the public domain, though, of course, it was open to anyone to make public the fact that a complaint had been made. The board debated the question of openness raised by this approach on a number of occasions. On the one hand, it was argued that IPSA's duty to have regard to transparency meant that IPSA should make public the fact that a complaint had been made and, if it was dismissed, we should publish this and the reasons for dismissing it. On the other hand, it was easy to make a complaint. The reputation of the MP concerned was at risk of being harmed, whatever its merits. This risk of harm had to be weighed in the balance, given the lingering history of the scandal of 2008–09. The board's discussion mirrored similar debates about the publication of the names of those accused of misconduct in other professions. After lengthy consideration, the board decided that only when an investigation had been opened into a case should the complaint be made public. This did not suit some elements of the media, but I think it was the right decision.

A second feature which raised concerns related to the role that the compliance officer played. He was there to determine whether a breach of the scheme had occurred and then, crucially, to recover any money on behalf of the taxpayer that had been improperly paid to an

MP. His role was not to identify criminal conduct and bring prosecutions. If he took the view that a crime may have taken place, his role was to liaise with the Metropolitan Police and hand over the case to them. Equally, it was not his role to determine whether an MP had, through any breach of the scheme, also breached the code of conduct governing the behaviour of MPs and overseen by the parliamentary commissioner and the House's Committee on Standards. Again, if he considered that there might be such a breach, he would report it to the commissioner.

I have said that his role was to recover money for the taxpayer. Ordinarily, when challenged concerning particular conduct, MPs were content to concede that they had breached the rules of the scheme (almost always through some oversight) and that money should be repaid. If this was agreed without the need to open a formal investigation, the fact that the MP had repaid the money in settlement of the complaint was not made public, just as the fact that a complaint was being looked into was not made public. This approach attracted adverse comment from some quarters when, at the request of the compliance officer, we consulted in 2014 on whether to continue the practice. The compliance officer's position was clear: until an investigation was opened, nothing was in the public domain, including the fact of paying money back. Elements in the media, ever alert to the possibility of a return to snouts in troughs, and ever ready to wheel out the charge of 'cover-up', urged that the compliance officer's approach was in breach of IPSA's duty to act transparently. The compliance officer pointed to the procedures under which he operated, which were set down by the board. The board had revisited the matter from time to time and decided to maintain its position. The view was that the punishment which MPs would suffer if the complaint or their settlement of it became public would be disproportionate to the wrong committed. Of course, if the infraction was deemed sufficiently serious or an MP refused to cooperate, the compliance officer could open an investigation and everything would then be in the public domain.

Before leaving the work of the compliance office, a couple of other points are worth making. In those cases in which there was a possibility that a crime may have been committed, the compliance officer reported the matter to the Metropolitan Police in London. This may seem odd, given that IPSA's jurisdiction extended to the whole of the UK. But there was a special unit within the Metropolitan Police which dealt on a national basis with cases such as those raised by IPSA.

Our experience in dealing with the police was frustrating. Cases dragged on for months and little or no feedback was forthcoming. There can be little doubt that this is a small example of a larger story of an over-stretched police force having to make judgements about priorities and where it deployed its resources. But it was not fair to MPs or complainants who wanted to know where things stood, especially as the issue may have found its way into the public domain.

Secondly, there were times when we had to deal with the parliamentary commissioner. In the revision of IPSA's role set out in the Constitutional Reform and Government Act of 2010, the responsibility for dealing with alleged breaches of the MPs' code of conduct was handed back to the House's Committee on Standards, but supplemented (rather like IPSA's compliance officer) by the addition of an independent parliamentary commissioner. It was established that she (the first appointee was a woman, as was her successor) would receive complaints and investigate them, reporting to the House's committee. There was some concern from the outset as to whether the commissioner could really be independent, given the context in which she worked and the cases she had to deal with. For our part, just as with the Metropolitan Police, the compliance officer agreed a memorandum of understanding with the parliamentary commissioner on behalf of IPSA. The terms were that should we come across circumstances which raised a question about whether an MP was in breach of the code of conduct, we would advise her. She for her part would advise us if she was made aware of a case which might also involve a breach of the scheme of expenses. While we referred a number of cases to her, no case was ever referred to us. Indeed, I was moved to remark, in a comment which attracted considerable attention, that it was difficult to have confidence in a system ultimately in the control of MPs who were, in effect, 'marking their own homework'.

CHAPTER 9

OPEN AND CLOSED

TRANSPARENCY

Regulators use the word 'assurance' to refer to ways whereby the public can assure themselves and be assured that the organisation and people being regulated are keeping to the rules. Alongside IPSA's concern for assurance in the form of written evidence to support claims, there was a further mechanism of assurance – perhaps the most important of all. I had indicated from the outset that IPSA would work in the open. The word of the moment was 'transparency'. IPSA would be transparent.

Of course, much depends on what you are going to be transparent about. During my early conversations with groups of MPs as we were setting up IPSA, it had been put to me several times that transparency was 'the answer'. It was the only thing necessary to make the new post-expenses scandal world work. It was the key to the new kingdom. I'm afraid that the vestiges of the lawyer still lurked in me. I demurred a little. Didn't it depend on what you were being transparent about, I asked? This didn't dampen the MPs' enthusiasm. My question tended to be brushed aside. I explained that it would fit the label of transparency to declare that MPs were to receive £X and leave it at that. This indeed was what many MPs had in mind. Operating that model of transparency would take us right back to the old system with two added flaws. We would be giving MPs the money with even fewer questions asked and we would be doing so while claiming that the system merited the description transparent.

So convinced were some that this thing called transparency was all that was required that a duty to be transparent was laid on IPSA when the Parliamentary Standards Act of 2009 was amended by the CRAG Act of 2010. It wasn't necessary in fact to legislate for it; we had decided from the outset that IPSA could only win over a sceptical public and media if the process whereby taxpayers' money was transferred to MPs was open to scrutiny. But, that said, I welcomed the fact that it kept us on our toes and gave legislative backing to the way in which we proposed to operate.

A crucial step regarding transparency was the board's decision in the early summer of 2010 to publish all claims for reimbursement made by MPs and IPSA's response to the claims. We announced that we would publish the first tranche of claims as soon as we could be sure that the information was accurate, given its sensitivity. Thereafter, we said that we would publish claims every two months. The frequency of the publication was, of course, a significant strategic decision. What we were aiming for was the arrival of a time when the publication of MPs' claims and IPSA's settling of them would be so routine as no longer to attract the currently avid attention of the media. This was part of a larger strategic aim of taking MPs' remuneration off the front page, as an indication that the historical issues had been resolved, regulation was working, MPs were complying with the rules, and the media could safely move on to other topics.

The publication of the first set of data in December 2010 covered claims made since the general election in the previous May when IPSA began operations. It was greeted with great interest by the media. Journalists were sent by their editors to pore over the claims.

There were no duck houses, no bottles of 'Bolly', no flat-screen TVs (claimed under the old system at a cost of over £8,000 by Gerald Kaufman by virtue of his membership of the Select Committee on Culture, Media and Sport).

This was not what was supposed to be going on. The picture was one of MPs being careful, even parsimonious. But weren't MPs supposed to be on the take? A slightly desperate press, especially the local press which saw itself as holding their MP to account, adopted a posture of faux outrage in their 'exposure' of claims for paper clips and the like. Was there no limit to the greed of these MPs – paper clips, whatever next! To any normal observer, these were just claims for things you need to run an office and such expenses were well within the scheme. But these were not normal times. You can imagine the entirely unwarranted apoplexy (or mirth) when IPSA's first publication of claims in December 2010 revealed that an MP had submitted a bulk claim for toilet rolls.

Some MPs felt that publication every other month would create a continuous barrage of much ado about nothing, while at the same time making their lives miserable. They pressed for twice-yearly publication if we continued to insist on publishing claims at all. They were also concerned that, because we published all claims made and IPSA's response to them, there would be occasions when we published the fact that a claim had been made but had been rejected as being outside the scheme. This was disliked by MPs. The system was complicated, they felt (it wasn't and isn't, though it was initially somewhat laborious), and mistakes were made. These later appeared, they said, as claims which had been made and denied which in turn made it look as if they were trying it on. In response to these concerns we had created the grace period of three months that summer during which errors in claiming could be corrected without being published later, even though technically, as a matter of public record, the claims had been made. And, secondly, we offered further training to any MP or member of staff who felt that they could benefit from it in dealing with the system.

As regards the proposal that we move to twice-yearly publication, we rejected it. We reasoned that, with such a delay, each publication would be an 'event', provoking a feeding frenzy of journalists ransacking the data for the slightest deviation from the primrose path, given the interest that the media continued to show in MPs' expenses. The interest had continued because of the succession of cases coming before the courts of MPs who had fiddled their expenses under the old, pre-2010, system. Try as we might, we could not get across to the media that these cases referred to the old system which IPSA had replaced. The distinction was unwelcome. It did not square with the proposition that 'all MPs are crooks', which was the prevailing (and deeply unwarranted) narrative.

We made it clear that publication was a central aspect of our duty to be transparent. We also made it clear that we thought that publication every two months was about right. We firmly believed that by the third or fourth tranche of published claims, with continued evidence of very high levels of compliance with the scheme's rules, the initial prurient interest would die away and publication would be a routine matter. At the same time, our regular publication of their claims served as a constant reminder to MPs of what might happen if they chose to try to avoid or evade the rules. Some few did breach the rules and had to deal with the publicity which followed. Our prediction that interest would wane was borne out. By the third round of publication, interest among the national press and broadcasters was minimal: there was nothing to report except compliance. The local press kept up their vigil, thereby, quite properly, playing a part in holding MPs to account before their constituents.

IPSA's long-term objective was to publish claims virtually in real time, for the benefit of the taxpayer and the MP. The technology being used did not allow for this, not least because it could not ensure that all the necessary checks before publication had been made in as timely a fashion as was required. But it was an aspiration, part of a more general ambition to enable MPs to keep on top of all aspects of their expenditure, rather like banking online, once the limitations of IPSA's information technology could be dealt with.

As regards carrying out the necessary checks, IPSA had made it clear that, in publishing claims, it would ensure that certain information relating to the MPs making the claims was not disclosed so as to safeguard their privacy and security. There was a balance to be struck. Taxpayers and the media legitimately sought the greatest possible transparency, in the light of what had surfaced in 2008–09. IPSA for its part had to weigh this claim against the equally legitimate concern for the privacy of MPs and their families and, of ever-growing importance, their security. The precautions taken by IPSA included not publishing all the details of an MP's travel arrangements. Equally, only the first part of the postcode of an MP's home address was made public, to provide evidence of the area where the MP lived and the context in which claims might be made, but not the particular address. Even this proved problematic when the postcode referred to only a very few dwellings. The details relating to local suppliers of goods and services to MPs were also removed from claims and, of course, an MP's bank details were not made public. As a further check on the system for removing such information before claims were published, IPSA routinely sent MPs an advance copy of what was due to be released in the publication programme. This gave an MP's office an opportunity to check that all was well.

Despite these measures, IPSA ran the risk of making mistakes.

Information which should not have been disclosed could be made public. We regarded this as a very serious matter. To mitigate this risk, three distinct checks were put in place before data was published.

SECURITY

Concern about security grew as time went on. An MP, Stephen Timms, was stabbed in his office in east London in May 2010. Terrorism was a constant threat. MPs had a budget to meet the cost of what were regarded as standard security measures, such as alarms and locks. Claims for such expenditure were not published as a separate item but rolled into general office costs. Except in special cases, any further security measures had to be applied for and would only be agreed by IPSA if the MP seeking funding provided an assessment from the local police that additional security measures were called for.

Towards the end of my period of office, it became clear that MPs, quite rightly, were increasingly exercised about their and their families' security and that the existing arrangements for meeting the costs of appropriate security measures needed to be revised. I wrote to the Speaker and the Clerk to the Commons proposing a meeting. At that meeting in December 2015 a new approach was agreed. The Serjeant-at-Arms and the chair of the House of Commons' Commission agreed to draw up, after taking advice, a standard range of security measures which all MPs could apply for. The measures would be more extensive than those previously in place. I undertook that these costs would be met as a matter of course by IPSA. In accordance with existing practice and as a necessary part of our approach to MPs' security, the expenditure would not appear as a separate item when IPSA reported MPs' expenditure, so that the level of security for any particular MP would not be known. Where an MP considered that even more measures were called for than those agreed, a claim would have to be accompanied by a report from the police or the security services.

MPs quite rightly were concerned not just for themselves but also for their staff in constituency offices, and for their families. As regards staff, where MPs requested it, provision was made for extra locks and surveillance cameras, and staff could get personal alarms. As regards MPs' homes, the statute stipulated that funds be made available for the performance of the MPs' parliamentary duties. A question was raised as to whether measures to protect MPs' homes when they were away in Westminster could properly be paid for out of the public purse. I took the view that, while at home, an MP inevitably was working for at least some of the time on parliamentary business. Thus, to that extent, the cost of any security measures clearly fell within the statute. As regards the time when the MP may not be at home, we decided that it would be silly to suggest that security measures such as lights or cameras be removed and reinstated depending on the movements of the MP. So, we concluded that the cost could legitimately be met, and should be met, by IPSA. As these deliberations were taking place, the horrific murder of Jo Cox MP took place, making it starkly clear how vulnerable MPs are and how important it is for IPSA to support them.

CHAPTER 10

MEETING MPs

POLITICAL PARTIES

From the outset, even before IPSA began to operate, I held meetings regularly with various groupings of MPs. I was usually accompanied by the chief executive and sometimes by the director of policy, both extremely able and seasoned ex-civil servants. I represented the board. The other members of the board attended only a couple of such meetings, not only because they were not usually available, but also because dealing with an often angry group of MPs calling for blood (even if the anger was manufactured, as it usually was) had not been part of their previous working lives. I was attuned to it, as were my executives, though we were all surprised sometimes by the venom in the air.

My initial meetings with the three main parties took place during the months leading up to the general election of 2010. They were designed for me to meet MPs and explain our thinking in general terms, to listen to concerns, and to answer questions. My first meeting was with the Conservative Party's 1922 Committee. The meeting was in the room of the then chairman, Sir Michael Spicer. I had given a speech a couple of days earlier in which I had said that the scandal that we had just lived through had led people to take the view that MPs were on the take. I had hardly sat down when the ordinary niceties of hospitality were abandoned in favour of Sir Michael asking me somewhat aggressively whether I liked MPs in light of the views I had recently expressed that they were all on the take (he had not been at the event). I pointed out that this was not actually what I said, but that, in any event, my views were neither here nor there. I was reflecting on the mood of the country. What mattered was that there was a complete breakdown of trust and it was my job, with their help, to begin to restore trust. This was the cue for another member (there were four of them round a small table) to launch into a fierce and personal attack. The thrust was that I was victimising MPs and seeking to make their lives impossible (remember, IPSA was not yet operating). I tried to move the conversation on in the (vain) hope of obtaining advice as to how to create as good a system of regulation as possible. But the perceived wounds were too raw and the emotions too strong. They felt beleaguered. The irony was not lost on me (though it clearly was on them) that Sir Michael was someone who under the old system had claimed from the taxpayer £620 for a chandelier in his country home, £5,650 over nine months for gardening, £1,000 for servicing an oven and £609 for cutting a hedge around a 'helipad' (the helipad was, he said, a 'family joke'). He had announced, perhaps wisely, that he would not be standing for re-election.[50]

As I left the meeting, the MP who had been most vociferous in his criticism of me and IPSA, Charles Walker, stopped me at the door and apologised for his anger, observing that I had been given a thankless task and that his colleagues felt very sensitive. This was a form of behaviour that I came to be familiar with, not just in the case of this particular MP, who became an important link between IPSA and MPs, but of MPs generally. In front of their peers, they fell into

---

50   He was subsequently elevated to the House of Lords.

tribal behaviour, scenting whatever was the mood and reflecting it. In private, they could be courteous and charming (with the exception of Bob Russell, who could never even bring himself to acknowledge me as we passed in corridors). In this mode they would be understanding and commiserate with me regarding the cross I was asked to bear. But at the next meeting…

My first encounter with the Liberal Democrats was again to seek advice while we were still preparing to launch IPSA. It was chaired by Nick Clegg, who seemed only just to have control over the group (of around thirty-five). They did not appear to have a consistent view on anything and argued as much among themselves as with me. I was pressed by Mr Clegg to indicate what IPSA was going to do on a variety of matters. The final exchange amused the group. Mr Clegg said that he would be failing in his duty as leader of his party if he did not ask me again what IPSA planned to do. I replied that I would be failing in my duty as chairman of IPSA if I described plans which were still in the making and had not yet been made public. We parted relatively amicably.

Amicable would not be the word, however, to describe my initial meeting with members of the Parliamentary Labour Party. Acrimonious and nasty would be better descriptions of a pattern of behaviour that did not vary over the years when we met members of the party in conclave. The Scottish contingent was the most vociferous. They embodied a sense of entitlement and of bitterness at being held to account by some regulator. Most were, of course, veterans, who had been elected time and again to such an extent that they seemed to take their membership of the House, and what they saw as the perks that went with it, as an entitlement. It was not surprising when they were all swept aside in the carnage of the Labour Party in Scotland in the election of 2015. They seemed just to take everything and everyone for granted and reacted badly to being crossed, as they saw it. I remember one particularly vociferous member of the group saying that if he were a trade union leader (as he had been) and was presented with the package of pay and conditions that I was talking about, he'd bring the workforce out on strike. It was with some difficulty above the clamour of approval that I explained that IPSA was still in consultation mode (that was why I was there) and that I was sure that he knew that we had no jurisdiction over pay (at that time). Neither of these points seemed to carry much weight. We were there to be abused, and abuse was what we got.

Thereafter, there were regular meetings with groups representing the various political parties, but I largely delegated these to the executive. In addition, the chief executive also maintained regular contact with the Chief Whips of the various parties. The brief in holding these meetings was to report actions and plans; explain, listen, and then report back to me and the board. The meetings were useful in explaining developments, though bruising on occasions. I remind you of the report in the MailOnline which memorialised a meeting held by the director of policy as follows:

> A meeting with IPSA policy director John Sills and Labour MPs was so stormy that one MP said: 'If there'd have been a rope handy, we'd have used it'.
>
> A subsequent meeting was cancelled.[51]

As chairman, once IPSA was up and running, I decided that it would be more productive for me to schedule regular meetings with one or two strategically important individuals rather than with groups.

---

51   For an account of this meeting, described by the director of policy as 'the worst meeting ever',
      see Appendix II.

So, with my chief executive, I would meet the Leader of the House, who was the member of the government charged with maintaining contact with IPSA, the shadow leader, the chair and deputy chair of the 1922 Committee and the chairs of the Parliamentary Labour Party and of the Liberal Democrats. By and large these meetings were helpful. They were conducted with courtesy and respect – and sometimes things even got done.

LEADERS OF THE HOUSE

IPSA had to have some formal link with the House of Commons to serve as a two-way means of communication and consultation. That link was with the Leader of the House, the member of government who is responsible for managing the business which comes before the House. The first leader whom I dealt with was Harriet Harman. This was before the election of 2010, while IPSA was still in shadow form. I found Harriet, whom I had met previously on a number of occasions, helpful and considerate. She recognised the difficulty of the task facing IPSA and was keen to ensure that we were able to organise ourselves and get on with things. One of the happy consequences of our meeting was the ability to strike up a relationship with the senior official in the leader's office. This official was an immensely helpful source of advice over the coming years. He reported concerns to us and reported our concerns to his boss. He understood what we were about and, quite rightly, recognised that he was there to make things work. I was distressed, though not surprised, that he was moved on to another job in the House when Chris Grayling became leader. Being helpful, particularly to IPSA, was apparently not a valued trait. I formed a poor opinion of Mr Grayling, as I will describe later.

The election of 2010 ushered in the coalition government with Mr Cameron as Prime Minister and Mr Clegg as Deputy Prime Minister.

Sir George Young became the leader. Because it was a coalition government, he met me with the Liberal Democrat Deputy Leader of the House, at first David Heath and then Tom Brake. David Heath did not say a great deal in meetings but was warm, polite and helpful. Mr Brake was more spiky. He was one of those who regarded IPSA as at least an irritant and was never slow to show his antipathy, usually with some petty criticism. He did not seem to measure up to the office he held. Sir George, by contrast, was a long-serving Member of Parliament who had always been something of a hero of mine because of his anti-smoking stance when junior health minister, a stance which got him sacked by Mrs Thatcher.

The scheme of expenses came into operation on the day of the election. He and I wrestled with the teething troubles that IPSA was going through and the tea-room hostility which he was reporting to me. By and large, Sir George sought to continue the approach begun in my dealings with Harriet Harman of sharing concerns and seeking to improve things against the difficult background of the first years of IPSA. He was charming and delightfully courteous, as befitted an Etonian of the old school. But there was a problem: it was one of my confidence in him. At critical points I was not confident that he could deliver what he might want or had suggested might happen. I did not think he had enough power or political will to stand against those who would harm IPSA. I was constantly having to work out and plan against alternative scenarios. I often found myself in the world of the 'dark arts'.

The worst example of the uncertainty surrounding IPSA's relationship with MPs and the government was the sudden and completely unexpected re-emergence (or resurrection) of a committee of the House called the Committee on Members' Expenses (previously 'Allowances').

The genesis had been a debate on a motion put forward by Adam Afriyie in December 2010. He is a rather self-important Conservative

MP who made a lot of money in IT and made much of the fact that he made little use of IPSA. He also made much of the fact that he saw no purpose in IPSA, that it was all a terrible (and inefficient and expensive) mistake and that a return to something that looked like the old regime was the only way forward to restore the rights and standing of MPs. IPSA had just published the first tranche of receipts to support claims for reimbursement and there had been the predictable (though unnecessary) nervousness among MPs. Mr Afriyie saw it as the opportunity to launch a broadside against IPSA. In proposing the motion criticising the complexity of the scheme and urging IPSA to simplify it, he asserted that IPSA was 'frustrating' the work of MPs. He called for IPSA to:

> get a grip on a system that is taking MPs' time away from constituents and is costing the taxpayer far too much.

Of course, there is another position that says that a relatively limited time taken to render an account to taxpayers concerning what was being done with their money was entirely appropriate given what had gone before. Indeed, there is a powerful argument that this is not taking MPs away from their constituents but rather enabling them to be connected more closely. As for our cost to the taxpayer, it was less than the previous system, and our budget had to be approved in detail by both the Treasury and the SCIPSA.

Mr Afriyie was not finished. He asserted that IPSA's scheme favoured wealthy MPs, a view that I had not heard before from his side of the House and which was plainly not the case. The reason he offered, however, had nothing to do with the wealth or otherwise of MPs. It had to do with transparency:

> If a Member does not have sufficient resources to subsidise

themselves in their role, they are then ensnared in a vice-like grip which is designed to bring them into disrepute with every single receipt that's produced for every single personal item.[52]

Underneath the hyperbole, there was a real point about cash-flow. But it was a point that we had already addressed in large part through extending loans and by plans to introduce payment cards as soon as we could responsibly do so. That apart, it was nonsense on a grand scale. What he was talking about was a system of producing receipts and claiming reimbursement, with payment being made on average within around five to eight days. Making claims in this way was something familiar to millions up and down the land, although the speed of reimbursement by IPSA was considerably faster, with many only receiving payment monthly. But to Mr Afriyie, apparently, MPs were different, even when it came to accounting for spending other people's money.

Other MPs piled in, but David Blunkett appealed for a calm and considered approach, taking account of the forthcoming review of the scheme that IPSA had proposed. And John Mann attacked what he called a 'special Westminster club with its desire for a special status in society'.

He rejected the suggestion that MPs were unable to do their jobs under the new system, remarking that he could do his job 'as well as I did in the past'.[53]

Unsurprisingly, Mr Afriyie's motion was passed and this is how what had previously been called the Committee on Members' Allowances came to be revived. The committee had been created by the House in January 2009. Its role had been to bring forward an interim

---

52   www.bbc.co.uk/news/uk-politics-11885613
53   Ibid.

system of 'expenses and allowances' in response to the scandal of 2009. It was thought that, with the creation of IPSA, the committee had been wound up, since the role of determining the basis on which MPs might receive funding from the taxpayer might be thought to have been passed by statute to IPSA. But no. Committees seem to enjoy a kind of twilight existence – not dead until formally killed off. This committee had not been killed off. It merely lay dormant. In July 2011, it was renamed the Committee on Members' Expenses to reflect IPSA's rejection of the term 'allowance'. It was wheeled out by IPSA's opponents as a vehicle for holding hearings on IPSA in the context of the wider question of the payment of MPs' expenses.

MPs hostile to IPSA were queueing up to get on to this committee. Procedurally, although apparently the committee could be resurrected, it had to be formally commissioned by the House before it could carry out any inquiry into IPSA. I urged Sir George to nip it in the bud by getting the House to oppose any such commission. He sympathised with my position. He understood that this was an existential crisis for IPSA. But, nonetheless, the government took no action and the House voted to commission the committee to conduct an inquiry into the operation of the Parliamentary Standards Act (in other words, IPSA) and report to the House on options for the future. Worse, it approved the appointment of Mr Afriyie as the chair.

I was both disappointed and dismayed. The government knew that this would give the head-bangers an opportunity to declare open season on IPSA. The government knew that IPSA was the only game in town and that their interests lay in helping us to succeed rather than pandering to the naysayers. The government also knew that the media, and the public fed by the media, would not accept a return to the old ways. But, when I challenged George, he replied that it was regrettable but that he did not have the votes to stop the head of steam generated in the House in favour of the committee.

I understood the politics (or at least I think I did). The calculation was that Afriyie could have his committee but the government would make sure that nothing would come of it. But the distraction the committee caused, the extra work it provoked when we were stretched to the limit, the life it breathed into the diehards, and the assault on the very *raison d'être* of IPSA were a high price to pay. I was left to hang out to dry as the politicians, with George at the centre, played their games. Another case of honeyed words but less than honeyed action!

I will describe later my dealings with Mr Afriyie's committee. Here I will merely say that the committee was a thoroughly third-rate exercise from start to finish.

Despite the Afriyie distraction, when he stepped down from government, I wrote to George, as I did to all MPs who from time to time had some sort of responsibility for IPSA, thanking him for the help he had given to IPSA as it sought to establish itself. Typically, he wrote back in very generous terms, commiserating with me for having taken on what he called, with some hyperbole, the hardest job in public life. He is a very nice man. But he is a politician.[54]

The next Leader of the House whom I dealt with was Andrew Lansley. I knew him a little from his time as Secretary of State for Health, given my involvement in health policy. He had been appointed as leader in what many saw as a step towards the exit door of government because of the turbulence caused by the changes and upheaval ushered in by his legislation on the NHS. He conducted himself throughout impeccably. He understood that his role was to convey the views of government and to some extent his colleagues, but that he was not a

---

54   Now deploying his skills in the House of Lords.

shop steward for the disaffected. He also knew that he could expect me to brief him on matters which would be coming up so as to take account of his views.

Throughout my dealings with the various leaders we operated a policy of 'no surprises', meaning that we always gave advance notice of reports, statements or actions so that the government would not be caught unawares. It was supposed to be a reciprocal arrangement and ordinarily worked well, though there were a few exceptions on the government's side. It was particularly important that it should work well during my dealings with Mr Lansley as IPSA's board wrestled with the issues of pay and pensions. As I will describe, MPs' pay was a particularly sensitive issue given the Chancellor's austerity programme which condemned those working in the public sector to a limit of 1 per cent in any pay rise. Mr Lansley relayed the government's position clearly. He also totally respected my position, as having a brief to determine MPs' pay independent of government. It was a good and grown-up relationship.

One poignant feature of the relationship with Mr Lansley was that it was clear that he greatly missed being the Secretary of State for Health and was almost in mourning. I well remember one meeting at which we were discussing pensions. It is a complex and some might, euphemistically, say a 'dry' area. But Mr Lansley's eyes lit up as he pressed us on relatively arcane points. He was full of references to the negotiations he had had with nurses and doctors. For a moment, he was back in the Department of Health.

Mr Lansley was followed as leader for a relatively short time by William Hague. We contacted his office to see whether he could squeeze in a meeting with me before the summer recess of Parliament which was a few days off. He agreed to see me at noon. He had just been moved from serving as Foreign Secretary. Major issues of international affairs were still swirling around him. His office asked us to wait as he took a call from the Prime Minister of Australia, who was keen to catch Mr Hague before going to bed (the Prime Minister, not Mr Hague – there being eleven hours' time difference!). After about twenty minutes we were ushered in. I explained that this was a courtesy call and apologised for the fact that dealing with me would be something of a let-down after his meetings with film stars.[55] After a few exchanges, another overseas telephone call came through. Clearly, foreign governments had been slow to keep up with shuffles in the coalition government, or they preferred to deal with someone whom they knew. We left him to it.

We had a further meeting in the autumn. Mr Hague was well briefed and courteous. I set out the matters which were occupying IPSA, not least the issue of pay and pensions, in keeping with the policy of no surprises. He was grateful and helpful. I had gathered that he had a reputation among civil servants as being respectful and good to work with. He certainly was in my dealings with him.

His successor as leader was Mr Grayling. My intelligence was that he was of the old school, was unsympathetic to IPSA and was a magnet for hostile tea-room gossip. My first meeting was at a time when IPSA had inadvertently, and for only the second time in nearly six years, released personal data about an MP which should not have been released. We reported ourselves to the information commissioner and apologised to the MP concerned. It was not a bad error but this was not important. Equally unimportant, save in mitigation, was the fact that the information involved had been sent to the relevant MP for checking (as was our practice) several months earlier and we had received no comment. It was still a serious breach of our rules.

---

55   He had worked extensively, for example, with Angelina Jolie while he was Foreign Secretary and she was a United Nations Special Envoy for Refugees.

I began the meeting with an apology for the breach. This was received and acknowledged. Mr Grayling did not dwell on it. Instead, he broadened the issue to IPSA's overall ability to preserve the confidentiality of information. Clearly, this was something that had been put to him by colleagues. IPSA had recently lost a case in the Court of Appeal concerning our obligations under the Freedom of Information Act. The issue was whether, in the case of an MP making a claim supported by a receipt, we were required to publish the actual receipt, or a summary of all the pertinent information. We did the latter. The Court of Appeal decided that we must do the former.

Publishing receipts had an ominous ring for MPs. Would all personal details be redacted prior to publication? This required manual intervention. Given the volume of receipts accumulated since 2010, if we had to publish them all there was a real risk of human error – of mistakes being made. But, even more important, it seemed, were MPs' concerns that if a receipt that they submitted referred to items bought for personal as well as business use, unless IPSA was vigilant in redacting the references to personal items, the media would descend on the offending item and we'd be back in 2008 with stories of duck houses and bottles of 'Bolly'. Mr Grayling declared himself unpersuaded as to our ability to avoid this. He raised the spectre of another expenses scandal, this time of IPSA's making. And, he went on, it was a 'make-or-break' issue. We assured him that we recognised the importance of what he had raised and had already put in place appropriate measures. 'Well,' he went on, 'I'm not trying to threaten you...', but I should realise that if there were even a hint of another expenses scandal, MPs would not stand for it. I should understand, he said, that it was open to the government to bring in legislation which could get rid of – or reshape – IPSA and that the government would not shrink from doing so. There was a bit of a frisson in the room. My chief executive, Marcial Boo, who had recently replaced Andrew Mc-Donald, my private secretary, his private secretary and Thérèse Coffey MP, the deputy leader, were all studying the top of the table. I realised that I was in the presence of a bully. Mr Grayling is a big man. I am on anyone's view a small(ish) man. I was used to bullies and could see them coming from some distance. I simply replied that I knew, of course, that he was not trying to threaten me, but that if he was, he should know that I didn't give in to threats easily. As regards the matter he had raised, I went on, he had my assurances.

I did not go on to add that both he and I knew that the threat was empty. There was no way that Parliament would ditch IPSA, given that they would never take back the responsibility for their own pay and rations. If we were removed, they would simply have to replace us with another body which would just be IPSA Mark II.

Thereafter, my dealings with Mr Grayling were workmanlike, though there was always a mild note of hectoring just below the surface. When issues were raised, his position routinely was that the answer (to the particular matter raised) was simple. This was never the case, but I suppose it looked that way if your point of departure was that regulation was a pain and that getting between MPs and 'their' money was an unnecessary complication.

When I stepped down as chairman I wrote to each of the leaders with whom I had dealt to thank them for working with IPSA. Only Sir George replied.

SHADOW LEADERS

As part of my intention to demonstrate IPSA's independence and even-handedness between the various political parties, I sought to see the shadow leader in parallel with the leader. My chief executive maintained contact with the smaller parties and the Whips' Offices.

The first shadow leader with whom I dealt after the election of 2010 was Hilary Benn. I found him immensely gracious. We had never met. He had clearly asked about me and by way of introduction said that he had heard that I believed in straight talking and so he would do the same. IPSA was in its infancy and 'war stories' were reaching him. He relayed them to me. I explained what might lie behind some concerns and undertook to look into others and report back. We were delighted when he accepted our invitation to visit the office and talk to staff. This was unique in my experience. Mr Benn was one of the few MPs who understood that the rules of the game had changed,[56] that I and he had a job to do, and that, rather than wishing IPSA away, it would be more productive to try to make things work. I welcomed this. Mr Benn was a pleasure to work with: professional, diligent, tough, but fair.

There was, however, one incident during my dealings with him that created tension, and it took some hard work to smooth the feathers that had been ruffled. An MP had broken her arm. She contacted the office for confirmation that she could use a taxi to get to and from the House and claim the cost under the scheme. The relevant staff member, taking perhaps too literally the proposition that MPs wished to be treated like their constituents and deciding that ordinarily a constituent would continue to take public transport and soldier on, told the MP that IPSA would not pay for a taxi to and from Parliament unless we had evidence in the form of a medical note that taking a taxi was necessary. It was a matter of minutes before this found its way to senior members of the party. The story quickly went round the tea rooms. Here was just another example of IPSA behaving bureaucratically and obstructing MPs as they went about their

---

56   Though the director of policy reported that on his initial visit to the office he remarked that IPSA was there to serve MPs, a view that he was quickly disabused of.

challenging and time-consuming job. I was contacted by the Whips' Office and Mr Benn on a Friday evening (why is it always a Friday evening?!). He asked if I could 'fix this, please, as it was doing IPSA considerable harm and was badly affecting the MP concerned'. I had a word with the relevant senior executive and reassurances were given that the claims would be met. I could see both sides of the argument. But I could also see that it is wise to pick the fights you want to fight. This was not one of them.

Mr Benn was replaced as shadow leader by Angela Eagle. I was tremendously impressed with the way she managed relations with IPSA and with me. If she had concerns, her office would raise them with us and give us notice and enough time to respond. Equally, I briefed her regularly on IPSA's activities and what she should be aware of. The success of the relationship was particularly crucial because for over two years we were wrestling with MPs' pay and pensions. I was very grateful for her preparation and that of her staff, her even-handed approach and her kindness. It was a pleasure to deal with her.

LEADERS OF THE PARTIES

I sought to have regular meetings with the leaders of the three main parties. In the case of the Conservatives, this meant meeting the chairman and vice-chairman of the 1922 Committee in the chairman's room in Portcullis House. As with most meetings, I would go with one or two members of staff. We would advise the office of whomever we were seeing of the matters that we wished to raise, usually addressing concerns which had been raised with us and detailing coming developments. In the case of the 1922 Committee, the meetings were usually fruitful, only occasionally descending into what I have termed 'war stories'. For the most part, we tackled both fairly detailed matters such as pensions, in which Charles Walker, the vice-chairman, was particularly interested, and strategic questions, such as the extent to which and the pace at which IPSA could begin to relax its prescriptive approach in favour of allowing MPs more discretion. This was – and remains – a continuing debate, as IPSA seeks to steer a path towards greater room for manoeuvre for MPs as regards their budgets, while not relaxing the accountability that the taxpayer both demands and is entitled to.

I found the chairman, Graham Brady, somewhat enigmatic. It was clear that he would have preferred the old ways. He always took the opportunity to put in a pitch for greater freedom of action for MPs as regards the money that they received. But he did so in a manner which suggested that he was saying what he had to say but understood very well that there would be no going back. His interventions reminded me of the advice I received from Archie Norman, a businessman who had sat as an MP. He had tired of opposition and gone back into business, as chairman of ITV among other things. When I approached Archie for advice, I found him wise and full of insight. He told me on one occasion that most MPs knew that they would not get their hands on power. That being so, they craved the approval of their colleagues. This was gained more by speaking than in any other way. They realised that what they said would not carry the day. But they would be heard and, of course, reported in their local media. That was enough.

I think that it was in this spirit that Graham Brady made his observations (although, of course, he had gained power, albeit not as part of government). And I listened. He had said his piece and it was important for him to do so. But he was also a pragmatist and knew what was what. The meetings were always cordial. We had a good working relationship, even if, as was often the case, both Charles and Graham were, in varying degrees, out of sympathy with IPSA. And the relationship was maintained by Charles Walker and IPSA's CEO through regular contact to mutual advantage.

As regards the Labour Party, I met the chairman of the Parliamentary Labour Party, Dave Watts, two or three times a year. He was an old-style trade unionist, keen to identify concerns and negotiate favourable terms. But he was also pragmatic and realistic. As time went on, given his union background, he identified strongly with IPSA's preparedness to consider a pay rise for MPs. He thus became a helpful channel of communication to the leader of the Labour Party, Ed Miliband, who, whatever may have been the wishes of the majority of his party, was dead set against any pay rise while the coalition's policy of austerity remained in place. Dave used all of his persuasive skills, largely to no avail. I grew to like and trust him and was upset to see how his wife's lingering illness affected him; wanting to be with her in Lancashire, but having to be in London.

When Dave Watts announced that he was standing down, John Cryer was elected the new chairman. I was only able to arrange one meeting before the election of 2015. After some searching, he found a space at the end of a corridor where we were able to speak as people came and went, surrounded by discarded tables and chairs stacked in corners. This, for me, served as a metaphor for the increasing disorganisation of the Labour Party, as Ed Miliband fought with his advisers on policy and, as far as IPSA was concerned, on pay. Mr Cryer was clearly not briefed. He listened while I set out the matters which I thought he ought to be aware of and sought his views, but he made little or no comment. His mind was on other things.

After the election, Mr Cryer was replaced by Chris Bryant. He was a breath of fresh air. Although not a fan of IPSA's arrangements, he accepted that in our dealings we both had a job to do and would do it best if we were respectful of each other, shared information and worked with a light touch. A joke or quip was never far away. I enjoyed working with him and his able deputy, Melanie Onn.

It was perennially difficult to arrange meetings with the chair of the Liberal Democrats, either because IPSA was not high on their list of priorities or because they were not well organised. It was probably a bit of both, though as regards the importance of IPSA, the regular diatribes of the egregious Bob Russell were probably enough to turn his colleagues off any further reference to us. As it happens, in contrast to my experience, our senior executives reported that, while meetings with other parties were not particularly useful (and often positively unhelpful in the case of Labour), in their meetings from time to time on practical issues they found the Liberal Democrats constructive and respectful of what IPSA was seeking to achieve.

This may be the moment to mention one of the high points in Sir Bob Russell's crusade against IPSA. It arose from his zealous scrutiny of the minutes of meetings of IPSA's board. The minutes reported that, at one meeting, two of the members of the board participated by speakerphone, being out of London. This may be a common practice in modern business. But not to Sir Bob. During Business Questions to the Leader of the House in the regular Thursday morning session in the House of Commons, he asked the Leader of the House for a debate on IPSA. He had 'discovered', as he put it, that members of the board had claimed their full daily allowance even when their participation was by telephone.

It was depressingly clear that, though he had served on the SCIPSA from the outset and therefore regularly scrutinised our accounts, Sir Bob seemed not to have acquainted himself with how members of the board were in fact reimbursed. Members of the board did not receive an allowance of any kind. Thus, they did not receive a daily allowance. They were and are paid on the basis of a daily rate. They were and are paid only for the actual time spent on any given day on IPSA's business, whether by being present at meetings or participating by telephone. They had to submit an account setting out the time spent on IPSA's business which was made public. Sir Bob's intervention was further evidence of never allowing the facts to get in the way of a smear.

MR SPEAKER

At the centre of IPSA's dealings with the House of Commons was Mr Speaker, John Bercow MP. He reserved to himself the final say as to who was appointed to the board and he chaired the SCIPSA, the body responsible for allocating IPSA's resources through the annual estimate.

His approach to IPSA was riddled with ambivalence. He was passionately of the view that MPs should never again have a say in their own pay and rations. But, as a self-styled champion of backbenchers, his was a ready ear for the many complaints and horror stories that did the rounds early on. My first dealings with him were in the very early days, when the media were in full cry against me. He telephoned me late in the evening and was keen to offer support. I was grateful. The next encounter was the first meeting of the SCIPSA, where, so far from chairing the meeting even-handedly, he actually indulged members of the committee in their feeding frenzy. Why, if he supported IPSA in principle, did he throw us under a bus? It also was a discourtesy which made relations difficult. An afternoon's fun was not worth the damage it did.

One of the members of IPSA's original board was Ken Olisa,[57] a banker and businessman. Ken is extremely bright and articulate. He also, quite rightly, saw the board as representing a new regime in relation to expenses based on the central principle of openness. Of the four members of the board besides me, the statute required that three

---

57   Now Sir Kenneth Olisa, Lord Lieutenant of Greater London.

be drawn from particular communities: the senior judiciary, auditors and ex-MPs. The fourth member, Ken, was therefore effectively the representative of the other 55 million or so of the population!

Ken took this responsibility seriously and was not slow to express his views, whether in private meetings or through the media. This attracted the fire of MPs and, through them, the Speaker. Commenting on a story in the *Evening Standard* reporting Ken's views on IPSA and its dealings with MPs, the Speaker criticised Ken in less than fair terms. At the heart of his attack was the suggestion that Ken did not understand the world of Parliament, was ignorant of its way of working and was biased against MPs. Ken is exceedingly able. As someone operating in the world of IT and finance, he prefers evidence to bluster. And, of course, one person's bias is another person's straight talking. Ken was put out and anxious to write to the Speaker. I asked him not to do so, not least because our relations with the Speaker were already very fraught. Ken pressed a couple of times more as it became increasingly clear that he and his fellow members of the board were being poorly treated through that very particular Westminster system of rumour and briefings.

I persuaded Ken to hold back on the basis that I would arrange a meeting with the Speaker, ostensibly about pensions, and take Ken along. In advance of the meeting, I said to Ken that we would deal with the business at hand first and then he could say his piece. We met in the Speaker's grand office. He was accompanied by an adviser. As the meeting drew to a close, Ken expressed his concerns about the Speaker's comments. The Speaker dropped into performance mode. He chose to lecture Ken on his lack of worldliness and ignorance of the ways of Parliament and politics. I was seriously unimpressed – as was Ken. Moreover, the Speaker adopted a style of discourse which I was becoming slowly familiar with. He did not so much talk as declaim, rather loudly and in orotund phrases. It was clear that to the Speaker we needed to be taught a lesson and reminded that we were lesser mortals. I was sufficiently surprised and offended by the Speaker's remarks that I put it to him that they were out of place and unwarranted. The meeting was not a success. We left very angry.

In the corridor outside, I turned to Ken and said that he should write his letter. There followed an exchange of correspondence; two letters on either side. Ken made it clear that there was a difference between commenting critically on the ways of MPs and being ignorant of them. He also revisited the concerns that I and he had expressed about the appointment/reappointment of members of the board, which I will touch on in a moment. For his part, the Speaker, aware that the letters would enter the public domain, contented himself with bland assurances.[58]

Prior to this meeting there had been a long-running argument, played out in public through letters, about the continued service of the existing members of the board, given that their initial term of office was drawing to a close. I had been warned in conversation by a senior official in the House that I should bear in mind that when politicians take against someone they can be utterly ruthless. I filed the warning in the back of my mind. Proof soon appeared.

Apart from me as chairman, the four other members of the board were all appointed for a three-year period.[59] Such a decision was odd because it meant that all of the members of the board would cease to serve at the same time, unless reappointed. On its face this was a bad idea. The corporate memory was put at risk. The continuity of thought and action, which in the early days of such an organisation was so important, would be undermined. But it fitted in well

---

58   See Appendix IV for the exchange of letters.
59   My original term of office was five years.

with another objective. There had always been a school of thought that IPSA should be a temporary measure until the storm had blown over and things could go back to how they were, or at least there could be a less exacting regulator. Three years had been mooted as the suitable period for penance. While this was never said publicly, the three-year period of appointment reflected this approach. The Speaker, guided by MPs, could then take stock.

Of course, I and colleagues on the board had pointed out to officials from the outset that the arrangement that all members of the board should cease to serve at the same time was inappropriate in terms of what is known as 'succession planning'. But the various communications and letters which we sent elicited no response.

By the time that the initial period was drawing to a close, it was clear to all but a few that IPSA was here to stay. I had made a number of speeches in which I specifically asserted that IPSA was there 'for the long haul'. So, if there were to be a taking stock of IPSA, it could not mean getting rid of it. But it could mean getting rid of the board (except for me). They had earned MPs' disfavour and the Speaker was listening. The move was unexpected but ruthless. In mid-2012, the four other members of the board were informed that their term of office was due to expire in January 2013 and that if they wished to continue to serve, they would have to reapply and subject themselves to the formal process of appointment set out in the legislation. They were as shocked as I was. The long-established practice in similar public appointments was that members of such a board would be reappointed for a further term, should they wish to serve, unless there were clear grounds not to appoint them. There were no such clear grounds nor were any cited by the Speaker. Instead, when I wrote to him objecting to the decision to require my colleagues to reapply, the Speaker took refuge behind a legal opinion given at his request by counsel.

From my point of view, the legal point was not a knock-out and the Speaker could certainly have taken a different view, as could his counsel. But it looked like one of those examples where you get the answer you are asking for. I wrote again urging the Speaker to reconsider the position, not least because of the real damage his removal of the whole board would do to IPSA's independence.[60] At a stroke, IPSA was being reminded that it served at the whim of the Speaker and MPs. This was not how an 'independent' body should be treated. All four of my colleagues declared that they would not reapply for appointment.

I was extremely concerned. So were others who regarded the cleaning up of Parliament as still a 'work in progress'. Under the headline 'Bercow and his bullies bring shame on our Parliament', Peter Oborne wrote in the *Daily Telegraph* of 15 November 2012 that:

> Bercow has tolerated a series of vicious and unscrupulous assaults on the expenses watchdog.

He noted that four members of the board were leaving. They were, he argued, 'victims of a power-grab engineered by Bercow'. He drew a parallel with the case of Elizabeth Filkin, who, as Parliamentary Commissioner for Standards, 'incurred the enmity of MPs'. She was, he wrote, 'invited … to reapply for her own job, which she rightly refused to do'.

Of course, my colleagues on the board could have accepted what was being done and reapplied. But they each decided to have nothing to do with the process for two reasons. First, they saw the departure from usual practice in favour of reliance on a particular interpretation of the statute as self-serving and dubious. Secondly, they had no

---

60   See Appendix V.

confidence in the procedure for appointment, not least the role that the Speaker would play, even though they had every confidence that the process before the Speaker's involvement would be impeccably fairly run by Dame Denise Platt (as indeed it was). So, they all decided not to reapply. IPSA had to set off again with an entirely new board. The MPs had taken their revenge, through the medium of the Speaker. It had no effect on IPSA's determination to seek to serve the interests of the taxpayer and of MPs, but it left a nasty taste. It also prompted the four members of the board who were leaving IPSA to write a foreword to the report on our first consultation on pay and pensions, which I was also happy to sign up to, in which they made their dissatisfaction abundantly clear.[61]

I had a further meeting with the Speaker around this time. It was an attempt to clear the air and indicate that we had to do business together so we should do so in as professional a manner as possible. I found the Speaker in declamatory mode again. He was supportive, but in a rather strange manner. The clouds of the recent past had not quite dissipated, such that he still felt the need to advise me on the ways of the world. I was particularly struck by his remarking that I was 'too clever' on occasions. Not knowing what he might mean, I ignored it. I reflected later that it was probably better to be thought too clever than not clever enough, though the latter condition may have been preferable from the point of view of those I dealt with.

As time went on, my dealings with the Speaker became easier. Indeed, on a personal level, I found him a kind and sensitive man, albeit that I was sometimes taken aback, indeed shocked, by his aggressive dealings on occasions with his staff.[62] But he was always an

---

61   See Appendix VI.
62   And with a member of IPSA's staff who only later complained to me when no longer working at IPSA.

inch away from dropping into performance mode. And this concern of his about me seemed never to go away. In his otherwise gracious and generous remarks when I appeared before my last meeting of the SCIPSA, he was still moved to comment that from time to time I had, perhaps, been 'abrasive' and had an 'obvious confidence' in my views.[63]

---

63   Minutes of public meeting of the SCIPSA, 2 March 2016. Mr Speaker described me as 'very tough-minded ... even perhaps – dare I say it – quite an abrasive fellow'. He said that he explained to his colleagues that it was my demeanour: 'He has an obvious confidence in his own views and judgement.' But he ended generously by thanking me for 'what IPSA had achieved'.

CHAPTER 11

INDEPENDENCE

One word which runs – literally – through the core of IPSA was independence. I sought to impress both on those outside IPSA (MPs, the media, commentators) and on those inside (the board and members of staff) that IPSA's legitimacy depended on its being and being seen to be independent. IPSA claimed to act in the public interest. Yet, members of the board were not elected, were not recallable and were not formally accountable to anyone. But we regulated people who *were* elected and accountable and who *could* be voted out of office. IPSA's legitimacy, its standing, its authority, therefore, depended on its being judged as independent of any interest except for the public interest. Moreover, it would retain this legitimacy only as long as it relied on evidence and reasoned argument in reaching its decisions about where the public interest lay.

The greatest test of IPSA's commitment to independence was during the nearly two years in which we wrestled with the issue of MPs' pay and pensions, which I will describe in due course. But a relatively early test grew out of the programme of austerity as regards funding in the public sector which was introduced by the coalition government immediately after the election of 2010.

As regards their salary and any annual increase in pay (until we had carried out our comprehensive review), IPSA opted to regard MPs and their staff as if they were public sector employees such that they fell within the government's austerity measures. As a consequence, after initially freezing their pay for two years, we announced that we would reflect the government's policy on pay and limit any annual increase in the pay of MPs to 1 per cent and also reflect this percentage in the budget made available to pay staff.

As regards pensions, the government further declared that the contribution to their pensions from public sector workers would be increased along a range from 1.3 per cent to 3 per cent for the forthcoming and subsequent years. But even if we regarded MPs as if they were public sector workers, dealing with their pensions was more complex. IPSA was under a statutory duty to ensure that the fund from which MPs' pensions were paid was protected. It was a relatively small closed fund, that is, contributions were made solely by MPs and the Exchequer and invested to meet MPs' pensions. There was considerable debate among those advising us as to what would be the effect if we were to increase MPs' contributions to the fund. One argument was that the contributions were already high as a proportion of their total income[64] such that increasing them further might cause some MPs to withdraw from the scheme. Then, at some point, if enough MPs stopped paying into it, the fund could well be put at risk in terms of being able to meet its current and future obligations.

Any matter having to do with changes in the remuneration of MPs had to be consulted upon. The process of consultation on the hugely complex and politically fraught issue of pay and pensions that we were planning to carry out would take some time. What should IPSA do in the interim, given the government's decision to increase contributions

---

64 As were the benefits.

as regards public sector workers? We published a short consultation document in January 2012. We put forward for consultation the proposal that on an interim basis we would reflect the government's position and increase MPs' contributions by 1.85 per cent. Internally, however, the board was divided as to whether this was the best course of action.

Would it not be better, some colleagues argued, to do nothing until all of the complex issues surrounding MPs' pensions could be carefully set out and analysed and opinions sought? Any interim arrangement would just be a distraction from what was an extremely detailed and complicated exercise and make more work for those who were already very busy. This disagreement soon reached the ears of Whitehall. The support for caution immediately provoked a reaction from government. IPSA, it was said, would be undermining the government's policy. If IPSA were not to increase the pension contributions of MPs when public sector workers would be paying more, this, we were told, would embarrass the government and make its battle to contain public sector pay that much more difficult. As the House of Commons had resolved, it:

> recognises the case for an increase in pension contributions made in Lord Hutton's interim report; and accordingly invites IPSA to increase contribution rates for hon. Members from 1 April 2012 in line with changes in pension contribution rates for other public service schemes.

We listened to these arguments. We pointed out that our responsibility was to make independent assessments and make our decisions in the light of such assessments and the evidence behind them. The government's policy and the programme of austerity were, of course, part of the background, but should not determine our independent judgement. The government responded very forcefully. It was clear that the politics – the apparent special treatment of MPs when everyone (at least in the public sector) was being asked to tighten their belts – rather than the economics, the sums involved and the stability of the pension fund – were the great concern.

Our internal discussions, the possibility that we would not introduce an interim adjustment, and the fact that the government was opposed and applying pressure, became an open secret in Whitehall and Westminster. MPs were interested because it was their pension contributions which we were talking about. And they were watching. Would we raise their contributions by 1.85 per cent or leave things alone till we had completed our work? For our part, we were keen to move slowly and carefully. We could understand the government's position. We could also see the arguments against making ad hoc adjustments which might create more problems than they solved.

A SUMMONS

At that point, I and my chief executive were surprised to receive an invitation (which looked a lot like a summons) to a meeting in the Treasury. On arrival, we were shown into the room of the Chief Secretary, Danny Alexander. He was not alone. Also present were Sir George Young as Leader of the House and link with IPSA and Francis Maude, Minister for the Cabinet Office. Once pleasantries were out of the way, we were treated to the usual 'We aren't seeking to put pressure on you as we accept you are independent, but…' They wanted IPSA to increase MPs' pension contributions in line with the increases in the contributions of those working in the public sector. I listened and replied that it seemed like just another day in the life of IPSA, since if it wasn't pressure from one source, as George would know, it was pressure from another. This seemed to surprise the other two. Busy as they were with the economy and the impact of the crash of 2007–08, IPSA was off their radar. It struck me that, rather naively, they just thought they would have me in, beat me up a bit and I would go away and do what was right.

The naivety lay in ignoring the history and context of IPSA, in not understanding the exposed position that IPSA found itself in. If I was seen to cave in (as it would be put) to the government, not only would MPs crank up the opprobrium, but IPSA's legitimacy as an independent body would be lost, never to be recovered. If we held to the other view, we would be exposed to a pincer movement from the media on one side and the government on the other. And Danny Alexander, rather crudely, made it clear that he would not be slow to attack us. He went so far as to threaten the chief executive that IPSA's accounts would not be signed off because his officials claimed that there was an irregularity. This was nonsense, but nasty nonsense.

I was troubled by the apparent lack of awareness not just of the challenges IPSA faced on all fronts but also of the particular circumstances and complexity of MPs' pensions. Clearly, they had not been briefed adequately or the meeting was just seen as making sure that we got their message and toed the line. I explained that IPSA had only recently been given the responsibility for pensions and then pay. The thorough review and overhaul that we planned must be done carefully drawing widely on evidence. Short-term fixes to meet political objectives were antithetical to such an approach. I also explained that the fund from which current and future pensions were paid was supported only by contributions from MPs, the Exchequer (the taxpayer) and returns on investments. The fund would be at risk if contributions did not meet its needs because a critical number of MPs decided to opt out.

As with all meetings, it's best to work out what's the best result you can get before you go in. Given that I was somewhat taken by surprise (we had no warning) by the heavyweights in attendance, I had to decide on the hoof. I decided that it would not be wise to take any decision there and then. I could, on occasions, take a decision as chairman without consulting the rest of the board. But I explained that this was not such an occasion. I would have to take the group's views back for consideration by the board. In doing so, I asked that the government confirm that the proposed increases in pension contributions would indeed extend across the whole of the public sector, such that to make an exception in the case of MPs would stand out like a sore thumb. I also asked whether some of the Chief Secretary's staff might work with IPSA's staff to assure us that the fund would not be put at risk if contributions were increased. We received such help and were reassured: in effect, the Exchequer assured us that, on behalf of the taxpayer, it would meet any shortfall should there be one.

As regards the extent of the increases across the public sector, while we were told that it was comprehensive, we discovered through contacts in the Treasury that one large group of public sector workers (over a million of them) would not, in fact, be paying more. So, the increases did not, in fact, apply to all public sector workers. MPs would not, therefore, be alone as being saved from paying the increases if we decided not to impose the higher contributions on them. The principal argument in the government's position – equal misery – was in fact unfounded. I was sufficiently angry on being told of this that I called Mr Alexander in his constituency in the Highlands of Scotland and indicated my concern at being misled, as I saw it. He expressed surprise that I might think this of him. But I did.

The question now was what should the board do, once I reported to them what was said at the meeting. We decided at the outset that we would stick to our principle that we would make decisions based on evidence and reason. We also agreed that, while it was a factor, the risk of upsetting or embarrassing the government of the day did not serve as sufficient reason, all things being equal, for changing our minds. We then asked whether all things were equal or whether there was anything further that we needed to take account of. We were advised by the executive that the research and advice from the civil servants in the Chief Secretary's office did change things. Their assurance, after discussions with the Auditor General's office, that the pension fund would not be put at risk, was new evidence. It dealt with our principal concern: that we would run the risk of destabilising the fund for a short-term fix. Furthermore, an increase in the level of contribution would be in line with our general approach, which was to regard MPs as if they were working in the public sector and, thus, treat them similarly to other public sector workers. In the light of this reasoning and evidence, we decided to increase MPs' contributions as a short-term, interim measure in advance of the review which we were just beginning.

The reaction was swift. It was put about that I had been leaned on by government and that IPSA had failed its very first test. Mr Speaker, lobbied by those opposed to the increases and always seeking to be the champion of the backbenchers, made his displeasure known to me. To those who would listen, we reminded them that we had heard the arguments and been persuaded. And, as I knew, MPs were not keen to make too much of a fuss because their constituents would not look kindly on what would clearly smack of special pleading. So, the episode closed and we moved on.

The reason why I have set out this relatively minor engagement at some length is because of what it illustrates. Most of all, ironically, it showed the strength of IPSA's bargaining power. While appearing to be under constant attack, and we were, I was always sure that, provided we argued our case and provided reasons – i.e. protected our legitimacy – those who would have got rid of us would be ignored. IPSA was the only game in town. It was in MPs' (and particularly in the government's) interests to support us, even though doing so might stick in their craw. Once MPs had decided that they should never again rule upon their financial arrangements, nor just give themselves a pot of money and be left to spend it as they wished, the pass was sold. IPSA, while needing improvement and falling short initially in several ways, was the only response.

Secondly, this example shows how IPSA could operate in a much more sophisticated way than it was given credit for. It could manage its independence and thus its legitimacy in a nuanced manner. We could accede to the reasoned arguments of the government concerning pension contributions, provided they understood that we needed arguments, not brickbats. Shouting and trying to bully us wouldn't work. They could have their way if they persuaded us. After all, it was no skin off IPSA's nose what contribution MPs should pay. IPSA was only concerned to get its approach right. The answer was less important. As for the media, the lesson for them was that we would not give in to pressure, from any quarter – including from them.

CHAPTER 12

SCIPSA AGAIN

The initial encounter between the SCIPSA and IPSA had been a bit of a car crash. At that point, three months or so into IPSA's existence, the SCIPSA consisted only of MPs. The requirement for there to be three lay members had been added to the Constitutional Reform and Governance Act of 2010, but no appointments had been made. They were appointed subsequently during 2010.

The membership of the SCIPSA is set out in the original statute as being: the Speaker, the Leader of the House, the Chair of the Commons' Committee on Standards, and five others, none of whom should be ministers. Following established practice, the five members were appointed by the Whips' Offices, and initially consisted of two members of the Conservative Party (Charles Walker and Laura Sandys), two members of the Labour Party (Rosie Winterton and Nick Brown) and one Liberal Democrat (Bob Russell).

The membership changed over time. There were several Leaders of the House over the period that I was chairman. Laura Sandys did not stand for re-election in 2015 and was replaced by Cheryl Gillan (who, somewhat ironically, had a number of run-ins of her own with the press[65] and Sir Thomas Legg[66] over her use of expenses prior to 2010). Rosie Winterton was replaced by Angela Eagle, the convention having been adopted that the shadow leader should take one of the two places for the opposition. Sir Bob Russell lost his seat in the 2015 election and was replaced on the committee by Pete Wishart of the SNP.

The procedure surrounding the approval of our estimate involved an initial submission to the Treasury and a meeting in private between officials and members of SCIPSA, which I did not attend. Prior to that meeting, the Treasury would iterate with my officials and then write formally to the Speaker. If they signalled that they did not approve the estimate, they had to give reasons. The Treasury never, in fact, withheld its approval while I was chairman. There then followed a public session to which I was invited. Ordinarily, the chair of public bodies would not expect or be expected to attend such meetings, unless specifically invited, because the accounting officer – the person responsible for signing off the accounts – is the chief executive. But the visibility of IPSA and the committee's desire to have the chairman appear before them led to my attendance.

On the appointed day, the SCIPSA would meet first in private and then we (I, the chief executive and the finance director) would be called in. We were questioned by MPs about certain aspects of the proposed estimate. But the occasion was also regarded, particularly in the early years, as an opportunity to complain about IPSA in general terms, its 'bureaucracy', its 'clunky' IT, difficulties in communication and so on. Much of the discontent was well-known and well-rehearsed and had been addressed in innumerable exchanges. But the opportunity

---

65   See, for example, *Daily Telegraph*, 11 May 2009.
66   He conducted a review in 2009–10 'to determine the validity of payments' of additional costs allowances (ACA) (for 'second homes'). In his report to Parliament on 1 February 2010, he described the ACA system as 'deeply flawed'. He decided that a number of MPs, including Ms Gillan (now Dame Cheryl), had abused the system and should pay back various sums of money.

to have another go at IPSA was not to be lost, particularly by Bob Russell. Occasionally, the estimate was discussed from a strategic perspective, but it was only occasionally.

One such example of a strategic discussion was when, at our second appearance, Laura Sandys pressed us as to whether we could separate the amount of money spent by IPSA on policy (the regulatory aspect of IPSA's role) and that spent on administration. This was an important challenge. The aim was to disaggregate our activities and then seek to examine whether either or both could be done more cheaply. The statute required IPSA to create a regulatory regime and then to administer the system which flowed from that regime. To some, this was anomalous. Organisations were either regulators or administered things. And, in the latter role, we were seen by some as just a cross between a back office, responsible for dealing with pay and rations, and a call centre. As such, we were compared unfavourably with call centres operating in the commercial sector.

There were several answers. First, as a matter of principle, there was no incompatibility, nor conflict, between having a regulatory and an administrative role. The regulation came first in the form of the scheme of expenses and the relevant rules and guidance. Then, the scheme fell to be administered in accordance with those rules and guidance.

Second, it was not plausible to suggest that IPSA's two roles could be split in some tidy way, allowing, for example, the administrative functions to be carried out at some distant and less expensive point, such as by relocating to Newcastle and thereby saving rent. This was because the operations team which administered the scheme were in constant touch with the policy team, the regulatory arm, not only through daily conversations, but also through meetings, so as to ensure that the scheme was being properly interpreted and operated by themselves and by MPs. Furthermore, if our operations team had been located in Newcastle, or even in Croydon, as suggested as a crowd-pleaser by David Cameron at Prime Minister's Questions on one occasion, staff would not have been able to make the hundreds of trips down the road to the House of Commons to help MPs and their staff with this or that problem.

Third, when it was put to us that we were just an expensive call centre, our director of operations, Scott Woolveridge who was deputising for the chief executive, was able to advise the SCIPSA that his previous employment had, in fact, included managing call centres. In his experience, which was extensive, he assured the committee that we were achieving considerably more for considerably less.

There was another theme which at least tangentially could be said to be strategic. It was always in the background. It was asserted that IPSA was 'too expensive' given the job it was doing. Well, from where I was sitting, the job that it was doing was not insignificant and was made that much more challenging by virtue of having to operate in a political cockpit.[67] As regards cost, the estimate that we submitted to the Treasury and the SCIPSA sought to pare down as far as possible the costs of administration. They mirrored the coalition government's programme of austerity in relation to spending in the public sector. When government announced on taking office in 2010 that there would be a saving of 5 per cent each year for the first five years of government, which would also be the first five years of IPSA's life, we made a commitment to do the same as regards our costs. This was notwithstanding the fact that IPSA's initial annual budget in 2010 was only about £6 million, roughly equivalent at the time to the taxpayers' subsidy of

---

67 We were also routinely criticised as 'bureaucratic', notwithstanding the fact that claims were paid on average within five to eight working days which compared very favourably with practice in the commercial world and the public sector.

the House of Commons' bars and restaurants. Indeed, in the context of government spending, we did not even appear on the radar.

SCIPSA's concern about our budget, however, was not straightforward. It was, if anything, highly paradoxical: we were too expensive yet did not spend enough on this or that. Two examples among many may suffice to make the point. First, our operations team typically received 150–200 telephone calls a day. We usually had four or five members of staff who specifically focused on calls, though they also had other responsibilities. The number of calls was not the only determinant of their workload. Many of the calls took some time to deal with, as MPs and their staff sought advice on one matter or another. Given the volume of the telephone traffic, calls were not always answered in as timely a manner as we would have liked. MPs routinely complained about being kept waiting or not being able to get through. We had two choices: employ more staff, which would have meant that we would overspend and risk our accounts being qualified by the National Audit Office, or control access.

Our research showed that the very large majority of calls from MPs and their staff took place in the afternoon. So, we announced in January 2011 that the phone lines would not be operated in the morning, freeing staff to deal with emails and the like. This went down very badly. We were failing in our duty to MPs in not operating a more comprehensive telephone system. Indeed, some urged that there be a 24-hour service. But such a service would be expensive. So, far from making the savings required of us, we would have needed more money. Eventually, we organised our operations team such that we were able to return to a service throughout the day. This was greatly welcomed, but I don't think the reasons for the initial limits were ever understood, let alone accepted. Nor was the incompatibility of asking for more by way of service while calling for cuts in staff.

The second example relates to communication: between IPSA and MPs and their staff – and more widely. When we initially created the various teams who were going to carry IPSA's work forward, we put together a team of one part-time and three full-time members of staff to constitute the communications team. One was to develop a website, the others were to respond to, and get our message out to, MPs and their staff, the public and the media. Within a few months, for reasons of cost and the urgency of other demands the 'team' was down to one and sometimes two.

We were routinely criticised by MPs about communication on a number of grounds. We did not provide sufficient information. Our website was not 'fit for its purpose' (true, but, again, it had to be created from scratch and needed to be adapted piecemeal as IPSA developed and the needs of others for information grew). So, at the same time and in the same breath (and this is the paradoxical point), MPs were saying that we didn't deploy enough resources to meet their needs while simultaneously attacking us for creating what was routinely called a bloated bureaucracy. Moreover, we made a bad job worse by choosing not to provide a proper service to MPs while creating a dedicated telephone line for enquiries from the media. So what little (not enough) we spent on communication we spent on the wrong things. We were spending taxpayers' money on 'spin doctors'. While MPs were made to wait to get through on the telephone, we pandered to the media and fed them stories.

In fact, we didn't have 'spin doctors' We didn't do 'spin'. Our activities as regards communication involved either informing those affected by, or interested in, what we did, or reacting to this or that question or complaint or request under the Freedom of Information Act, apart from the occasional foray into the public arena through a speech or an appearance before a committee. But MPs, or those who obsessed about IPSA, tended to judge us by reference to their own standards and approach to the world. Hence, we did 'spin'. The idea that we might be trying to fulfil our obligation to be transparent and open wasn't, in their view, the half of it. The high point of this position was when Ann Clwyd, under the cover of parliamentary privilege, used the debate prompted by Mr Afriyie's motion in December 2010 to attack IPSA's director of communications for allegedly leaking details of expenses to the press. She suggested that 'anti-MP' stories were being leaked by people at IPSA', adding that every time there was a debate on the expenses scheme a story would appear in the press the day before. This was a calumny of the first order. There was absolutely no truth in the allegation.

When I was made aware of Ms Clwyd's remarks and her baseless attack on a senior colleague, the debate in the House was still going on. I was so incensed that I sent a message to the minister, who later in the evening would be replying to the debate on behalf of the government. I told him that the accusation was false. The information which Ms Clwyd was referring to, as was made clear in the story in the press, had in fact been gained by the newspaper through a request made under the Freedom of Information Act to which IPSA was obliged to respond. I was pleased and grateful to the minister when, in his summing up, he referred to my note rebutting Ms Clwyd's allegation. I subsequently wrote to her inviting her either to let me know the evidence that she had relied on to make her claim so that I could take appropriate action, or to withdraw it. She did not reply, nor did she apologise. It was a shabby, indeed cowardly, performance, or as Peter Oborne put it, 'an attack [which] was especially low grade'.[68]

In short, therefore, as regards our approach to communication, the

---

68   *Daily Telegraph*, 15 November 2012.

incoherence that I referred to consisted of maintaining that we had a comms team that was at the same time too big (bloated and trading in 'spin') and not big enough (leaving MPs in the dark and giving priority to the media). From our perspective it was not big enough, but it was a question of funding. To stay within our budget we had had to pare down even the (very small) team that we had. They did a wonderful job of juggling all the demands made on us. But, as a consequence, the website was neglected and we were rightly criticised for that. We couldn't do everything but were in that situation very familiar to public sector bodies of being damned if we increased the comms team and damned if we didn't. The situation was only finally rescued when we began to ready ourselves, nearly two years in advance, for the general election of 2015. At that point, we were able to persuade the SCIPSA that a separate election budget was needed, an essential part of which was effective communication. The dedicated team was increased to four and attention began to be focused on getting the website into proper order.

LAY MEMBERS

Because of the peculiar constitutional arrangements whereby IPSA was to be independent, it was, of course, anomalous that the SCIPSA should consist entirely of MPs chaired by the Speaker. The anomaly was recognised from the outset.[69] After some several months' delay, it was accepted that the SCIPSA should be leavened by the addition of lay members. The number of three was hit upon. I don't know how or why, as I was not consulted or involved. Of course, to some this might

---

69   There is a parallel with the membership of the House's Committee on Standards. At first, the members were all MPs, prompting me to write on one occasion that their dealing with a complaint against a fellow MP was rather like marking their own homework. Eventually, lay people were added, but in a marvellous piece of political sleight-of-hand, the lay members did not have the right to vote on cases before the committee!

smack of tokenism since there were seven MPs and the Speaker. But it was better than nothing.

Given the less than happy relations between MPs and IPSA in the early days, mirrored in our dealings with the SCIPSA, we looked forward to the contribution that the lay members would make. They were not part of the factional tribes. They could see the world from the point of view of the taxpayer and perhaps be somewhat more understanding of IPSA's perspective. Largely, in the case of the first group of lay members, we were somewhat disappointed. Once appointed, a meeting was arranged between them[70] and me. It was clear from the outset that their prior meetings with the Speaker and members of the SCIPSA had disposed them to regard IPSA with suspicion. Sir Anthony Holland quizzed me about our communications team (the 'spin doctors' narrative) and criticised me for placing a story in *The Sun*. The story was merely a description of what IPSA was doing, but Sir Anthony seemed to suggest that we should not be talking to *The Sun*, and that by so doing were undermining confidence in MPs. I replied that *The Sun* was widely read, was routinely used by ministers (even sometimes by Prime Ministers) to set out policy, and was a good way of reaching beyond the Westminster bubble.

But the tone was set. We were, in some undefined way, hostile to MPs. The lay members were there to keep us in check and see fair play. The assumption was that otherwise we would not play fair. This was a pity. I and colleagues on the board realised that the appointment of the lay members was not the development that we had hoped for, whereby the antipathy of MPs would be offset by their more balanced (and informed) views. Instead, Sir Anthony was unhelpful. He seemed

---

70   These were: Dame Janet Gaymer, a distinguished solicitor and veteran actor on the Westminster stage, Sir Anthony Holland, a country solicitor who had served as president of the Law Society, and Elizabeth McMeikan, previously managing director at Tesco Express.

keen to be seen to be batting for the MPs. Dame Janet Gaymer maintained a severe approach. She saw her role, quite rightly, as being to probe. But the probing almost uniformly seemed to proceed from the premise that IPSA was falling short in this or that way or could do better. There was little by way of encouragement or of understanding the challenges that IPSA was facing, both operational and in terms of the overall acceptance of our existence. The third lay member, Elizabeth McMeikan, was more sensitive to IPSA's situation, but spoke only rarely. She did, however, work with the IPSA's executives behind the scenes to inform herself, which was welcomed.

Sir Anthony and Liz McMeikan were replaced after three years (Dame Janet's appointment was for five years) by Professor Monojit Chatterji and Ken Batty.[71] The two new members were very different. They seemed more obviously keen to hear and see all sides. By that time, IPSA had of course weathered the various storms and was settling in. These two new members recognised this and seemed to see their role as one of facilitating the consolidation of IPSA. While rightly pressing us on our continuing shortcomings, they understood and supported the proposals that we brought forward to introduce much needed changes in how we operated. This was very welcome.

---

71   Monojit Chatterji is a professor of economics at Cambridge University and Ken Batty has an extensive background in HR and IT on a global level.

CHAPTER 13

ORDEAL BY COMMITTEE

I have already described our earliest encounter with the SCIPSA, the Speaker's Committee on IPSA. The mechanism designed quite properly to oversee our expenditure of taxpayers' money also served in the early years as a vehicle for expressing the collective animus of MPs against IPSA. But the SCIPSA was not alone in this activity. In 2011–12, IPSA was subjected to scrutiny by a range of other committees. The scrutiny was unremitting, intense and, in my view, entirely politically motivated. IPSA cost the taxpayer about £6 million. It was responsible for designing and maintaining a new and challenging system of regulation. It was also responsible for the disbursement of around £180 million.

In the context of the public finances, the £6 million it cost to operate IPSA was barely noticeable. But that didn't affect the scrutiny. We were struggling to keep our heads above water and set up an entirely new regulatory body with concomitant administrative duties. But we were also routinely having to prepare for the next hearing of the next committee, with the accompanying need to pull together the relevant paperwork and organise internal meetings. The burden was very considerable and made heavier by the general hostility shown towards IPSA by MPs and their staff on the one hand and by the media, for different and often opposite reasons, on the other. Crucially, however, because the staff believed so strongly that what they were doing was really worthwhile and because of the leadership shown by the senior executives, so far from undermining morale, the noises off only served to harden the commitment to deal with whatever was thrown at us.

THE NATIONAL AUDIT OFFICE

Not long after we started to operate, I heard rumours that we were to be investigated by the National Audit Office (NAO). The NAO's brief is to examine the extent to which a body receiving public funds delivers 'value for money'. My immediate reaction was that it was a bit early, to say the least, to take a considered view. We'd only been in operation for a few months. The word I got back was that the NAO was being pressed by the Public Accounts Committee (PAC) and MPs generally to investigate IPSA and that this pressure began almost as soon as we opened our doors for business. The reason was clearly political: to embarrass IPSA (or worse) by a report from the NAO which painted us in a less than favourable light.

After some time, when the rumours had not died, I decided to telephone the auditor general, Amyas Morse, who led the NAO. He told me that there was indeed pressure being exerted for the NAO to carry out an investigation. He had resisted it on the ground that it was not common practice for the NAO to look into newly created bodies until they had been operating for at least three to five years. The reason was obvious. Until they had had an opportunity to settle in and establish a pattern of working, any judgement as to whether they provided value for money would be premature, un-reliable and unfair. He added that the request regarding IPSA was unique and confirmed that the pressure began almost from the first day. He also made it clear that, as a servant of the Public Accounts

Committee, it was ultimately the committee's decision, whatever he might advise. The implication was that he would not be able to resist the pressure.

The upshot was that he proposed that the NAO would carry out an investigation over the coming summer months, just over a year after we began operating, which would offer a snapshot of how IPSA was doing, without seeking to be determinative, and which would not impose too great a burden on the staff. This was the best outcome that I could hope for and I was grateful.

THE PUBLIC ACCOUNTS COMMITTEE

The NAO carried out its investigation and submitted a report to the Public Accounts Committee. Despite the disruption that the investigation caused, our dealings with the NAO were uniformly professional and, on their part, considerate. They recognised the situation that we both found ourselves in and the inappropriateness of conducting an investigation when we had hardly begun work. They concluded that IPSA did provide the taxpayer with value for money. The difficult circumstances in which we had been created and had begun operating were noted and progress in overcoming them was welcomed. Introducing the report, Amyas Morse wrote:

> Despite initial problems, IPSA has created an expenses scheme which safeguards public money and helps to increase public confidence. To improve the present uneasy relationship between the Authority and many MPs, both sides should make greater efforts to find common ground. In my view, IPSA is now in a good position to focus more on improving the quality of service it delivers.[72]

---

72   NAO report, 7 July 2011.

The NAO made a number of recommendations as to action that IPSA should consider taking.[73] They were all helpful. Most were already due to be introduced in the coming year and had been incorporated into our business plan. We made a commitment to report regularly on progress to the board and to the NAO. Otherwise, the report was very encouraging.

What would the PAC make of this? We were duly summoned. Not only was the chief executive invited but I was too as chairman. It is not usual for the chairman of bodies such as IPSA to attend because the accounting officer, the person responsible for the accounts, is the CEO. I formed the view that I was invited on the same Romans and Christians approach that had characterised the first meeting of the SCIPSA. So, I sent a message back that I would not be attending. There was then much toing and froing. The power of the committee to demand my attendance on pain of being held in contempt of Parliament was rehearsed. I was not persuaded, either, of the purported exercise of power or the existence of the penalty. However, I did not want my attendance or non-attendance to become the story, when the real story was IPSA's success. So, I showed up on the day with the director of operations, the CEO being ill.

The PAC was chaired by Margaret Hodge. She had acquired a considerable and deserved reputation as someone dedicated to holding organisations and people to account on behalf of the taxpayer. So, I was surprised by her first question. She asked me what I understood by 'value for money' (VFM). This seemed an odd gambit. It was either a serious question asking for a serious answer, or some way of demonstrating that whatever VFM might be, IPSA didn't quite get it,

---

73   That we should: improve our cost-effectiveness; adopt a more risk-based approach to validating claims; make clear that the scheme related to costs as well as expenses; seek to reduce the time that MPs and staff spent on the system; make our guidance regarding the scheme clearer; and review the remuneration of staff.

whatever the NAO might say. Or, of course, it might just have been a way of getting things started.

I chose to treat it as a serious question, not least because I had long been interested in VFM as a concept in the discourse of public policy, especially given my background as a regulator of the NHS. I explained that in my view the true meaning of VFM had been supplanted by a technocratic approach which concerned itself with cost and price rather than value. Value for money should, I suggested, be concerned with an enquiry as to whether the expenditure of public money achieved results which were of value to, and valued by, the public who provided the money. In that equation, the word 'value' was all important. And what the public valued was largely an empirical question, to be answered by the public by reference to the best evidence available, or by their representatives in Parliament. As regards IPSA, what the public valued was that the spending of their money by MPs should be regulated by an independent body committed to openness, and that they were prepared to see public funds allocated to IPSA for this purpose. Of course, IPSA had to spend their money wisely in pursuit of that purpose, but that was a second order issue which the NAO should examine against the larger background.

Mrs Hodge interrupted me to point out that what I was referring to was just one aspect of VFM – 'effectiveness'. She was, in effect, referring to what had become known as the 'three Es', the standard view being that VFM was concerned with economy, efficiency, and effectiveness (to which more recently there has been added a fourth 'E', equity). She said that my comments were addressed to only one of these. I replied that the three Es, while masquerading as objective, factual judgements based on evidence, were actually value judgements, a substitute for the single word 'value'. For example, the word 'efficiency' is not neutral. It begs the question: 'Efficient to what ends?'

and thus hides the choices which lie behind a particular conclusion. Thus, I suggested that VFM is a complex notion, warranting careful analysis. Amyas Morse was invited by the chair to bring things back to earth. Unsurprisingly he took us back to the three Es as the accepted basis for analysis and thereby reasserted the notion that VFM is a technical factual issue. But I had put down a marker.

The hearing then followed the usual pattern. The members had before them the NAO's report, which, if any of them was inclined to give IPSA a bad time, rather took the wind out of their sails. In response to most questions I was able to say how pleased I was at the NAO's assessment and how keen we were to address the areas warranting action which the NAO had pointed to. When it came time for one member to question me, she could barely conceal her disappointment, suggesting that I should feel pleased with myself, with the unstated comment that she was distinctly displeased in not having the ammunition she expected.

One member of the committee who was clearly displeased was Stephen Barclay. He began his questioning of me in combative style. When I referred to the fact that IPSA was a regulatory body and not just concerned with the provision of services, I was met with his assertion that he had worked as a regulator (he had worked for the Financial Services Authority for four years). Therefore, he declared, 'I understand regulation…' I wasn't quite sure where this was intended to take us. He then asked me 'whether IPSA has a duty to support MPs in the discharge of their duties'. It was clear that he thought that we did and that because a large proportion of MPs, including him, felt that we were not supporting them, I and IPSA were in breach of our statutory duty. Although he is a lawyer, Mr Barclay's understanding of the statute was wrong – and crucially so. I explained that our stat-utory duty was in fact 'to have regard to the principle' that we should support MPs. This meant that, as a regulator, we had to weigh how to reflect that principle in what we did, taking account of the interests of the taxpayer and public as well as those of MPs. If Parliament had wanted to say that it was our duty to support MPs, it could have done so, but it didn't. It gave us a different duty which required a balancing of interests. This left Mr Barclay, in his words, 'a bit confused'. He described my answer as 'nuanced', which is an odd way of describing a difference between what the statute actually says and his (inaccurate) version of it.

At one point in examining the cost of IPSA's administration, attention turned to the allocation of staff (and thus resources) to dealing with telephone calls. When we explained that we received anything between 100 and 200 calls a day, Mrs Hodge expressed herself as surprised if not shocked. Drawing, she said, on her experience in management consultancy, receiving so many calls was clear evidence that the scheme was too complex and that we were failing to communicate adequately with MPs. We had several goes at persuading her that the cost was justified. Few calls were, in fact, about the meaning of the scheme, we explained. Most were about matters of personnel, payroll and the online system. Secondly, the number of people whom we dealt with that she referred to so as to illustrate our inefficiency, namely 650 MPs, was wrong. It overlooked the fact that there were also over 3,500 members of staff in MPs' offices who telephoned us seeking a range of information or advice. Mrs Hodge seemed unmoved. It was ironic, therefore, to hear a fellow member of the committee, Mr Barclay, stressing the need for the telephone service and complaining about the reduction that we had introduced to save costs.

A significant issue raised by the PAC was the feedback that the NAO had received from MPs in a survey that they had conducted. The views expressed were overwhelmingly negative. We had complained to the NAO that the survey elicited very few responses, such as to make any conclusions at best hard to rely on. Moreover, in IPSA's early days it was almost *de rigueur* for some MPs, those most likely to respond to any survey, to condemn IPSA out of hand in the hope that it would be swept away on a tide of bad reviews. A further concern which we did not explicitly express was, of course, that regulators were routinely unpopular with those whom they regulate, in the same way that Christmas is not popular with turkeys.

The NAO understood the points that we made about their survey but went ahead and published the results in their report. They recommended that we should conduct an annual survey of MPs with the expectation that approval would increase over time. We accepted the recommendation and thereafter published an annual survey. There was some improvement over time, though the level of response was low. In the meantime, however, the results of the survey became 'Exhibit A' in the case that later committees before which we appeared in that hectic year would produce against us.

What lay behind the discussion of the survey was an observation by Stella Creasy MP. In putting a question to us, she began as follows: 'As your customers...' This troubled me, though I did not respond at the time; there were already a lot of hares running. Dr Creasy seemed fundamentally to misunderstand IPSA's position. Though we had an administrative role, as regards which MPs were in receipt of the services that we provided, MPs were not 'customers'. We were regulators. As such, we did not have customers. At best, we had clients. The distinction was not merely linguistic. It was a matter of principle. The customer is always right. By contrast, the regulated may object, but the last word, provided that it's reasonable, lies with the regulator.

This was something which needed to be dealt with. It was extremely important. The opportunity arose when I appeared later before Mr Afriyie's Committee on Members' Expenses, as I will explain.

In the end, our appearance before the PAC was helpful. We were able to set out our stall, address certain misconceptions and undertake to work together in the future with those MPs willing to do so on improving the system. Mrs Hodge was gracious in her introduction to the PAC's report, which was subsequently published on 23 September 2011. We were pleased to read that, notwithstanding the areas in which the PAC called for improvement (all of which we accepted), she concluded that within a year of our being set up:

> IPSA did a good job in introducing the new system for paying MPs' expenses. It came in on time, expenses have been paid within the rules and MPs have been reimbursed accurately. There is evidence that public confidence is starting to improve.

She added that:

> We were impressed by the constructive approach taken by all sides at our hearing. This bodes well for improved relations between IPSA and MPs in future. IPSA made a number of commitments to improve the system and we look forward to seeing the results.

THE LIAISON COMMITTEE

The Liaison Committee is a committee of the House of Commons made up of the chairs of each of the various select committees. It is, therefore, a committee of grandees. We met at their invitation in response to the consultation on changes to the scheme of expenses that we had launched in 2011. The committee sees itself as having some overarching responsibility for the operation of the Commons and IPSA is part of those operations. Another reason was, perhaps, to get a sense of what we were trying to do and put a face to a name. A further reason, perhaps, was to flex the House's muscles and show their authority. The hearing was conducted in a cordial manner, under the able chairmanship of Sir Alan Beith. The questions, as ever, were not strategic. They were not concerned with such matters as the new constitutional architecture represented by IPSA as an independent regulator or with developments in IPSA's role and operations. Rather, the various chairs rehearsed the usual 'war stories', and wondered what we were going to do about this or that. As ever, because we did not have notice of the issues raised, all that I could do was to offer the lame response that we would look into whatever was raised and advise in due course.

While it was not a particularly testing encounter, coming as it did on top of attendance at other hearings it was a further burden to deal with, given the preparation involved. It would have been disrespect-ful to the committee, as well as unwise, not to prepare as fully as possible. But preparation involved briefs relating to each member, noting in particular any interests which might touch on IPSA, plus any exchanges with IPSA and the outcome. It also meant rereading all our published documents so as to leave no stone unturned. And, as ever, there were at least two meetings with senior staff at which I and the relevant senior executives were grilled as if appearing before the committee. All of this, of course, takes place below the surface, but is demanding and time-consuming. I don't for a moment suggest that IPSA should not be held to account, but during 2011–12 it felt more like IPSA being held hostage rather than held to account.

COMMITTEE ON MEMBERS' EXPENSES (AKA 'ALLOWANCES')

It was not over. I was told that the House's Committee on Members' Allowances intended to hold hearings into IPSA. What committee,

I asked. Well, when the House was responsible for determining and managing distribution of taxpayers' money to MPs, there had been such a committee, the brief of which was to oversee the arrangements for doing so. But when this responsibility was transferred by statute to IPSA, surely, I thought, the committee had no standing and would have disappeared. I'm afraid that this was a case of 'beware the adverb', because it was not 'surely' at all. It appears that committees of the House do not die. They have to be put to death by some formal act of the House. And in this instance no one had put this particular committee to death. So, suddenly, out of nowhere, there was a motion before the House to sanction hearings by the committee into IPSA.

I have already described how I went to see Sir George Young, the Leader of the House, to urge him to stop this happening. The government could oppose the motion and make it go away. There was enough on IPSA's plate at the time without being exposed to some show trial, orchestrated by Adam Afriyie, the MP for Windsor, who did not hide his contempt for IPSA and his desire to return to the good old days when MPs got 'their' money and spent it, with little or no accountability. Sir George lamented the development. He recognised the pressure that IPSA was under and accepted that being hauled before another committee, especially this one, was at best unhelpful. But the next thing I knew was that the motion had been put and passed and Adam Afriyie had been elected the chair.

I was seriously unimpressed by the government's decision to stand by and let it happen and told Sir George as much. His response was that he (the government) did not have the votes to stop the motion so had to let it through. I felt that I and IPSA had been stitched up. While appearing to be sympathetic, the government's and Sir George's response had been entirely political. It was IPSA versus the mood of MPs in the House. It was no contest politically. So, the committee would be allowed to play in its sand pit. The government could always ignore whatever might emerge, while taking the credit from MPs for having facilitated a public working over of IPSA. In political terms it was a win–win for the government. And to call it cynical would be merely to forget the nature of politics.

I wanted more from the government, but understood the realities. So, while arguing with Sir George for what we saw as an appropriate way forward, we equally began to prepare for the worst. Time and effort would again be needed getting ready for hearings before a committee whose conclusion, at least on the part of the chairman – that IPSA be neutered if not abolished – was well-known before they had started. We were anxious to discover who was on the committee, apart from Mr Afriyie, whose views were well-known (though formed somewhat at third hand). He made only limited claims on IPSA, and these were mostly for staffing costs. He had made a fortune in IT and was keen to demonstrate that he did not need greatly to rely on the taxpayer. Though this may be admirable in itself, it rather insulated him from the circumstances of the 640-odd MPs who did. Our research showed that there was no one on the committee with whom IPSA had 'form', though one member, Nick Raynsford, had been in dispute on behalf of a fellow MP, based on a misunderstanding by that MP. The matter, I was told, had been satisfactorily resolved.

We had no idea what to expect from the committee. Its terms of reference were pretty wide. The committee was to report on the operation of the Parliamentary Standards Act with due consideration to:

a) value for money for taxpayers;
b) accountability;
c) public confidence in Parliament;
d) the ability of Members to fulfil their duties effectively;

e) fairness for less well-off Members and those with families; and

f) whether Members are not deterred from submitting legitimate claims.

It had taken evidence from a number of witnesses. The usual views were expressed: IPSA was bureaucratic, slow, inefficient, not 'customer-friendly' and did not provide a good deal for MPs. A few commentators from the media, think tanks, trade unions and public life were also called. Not surprisingly, attention was given to exploring other ways of remunerating MPs, with the recurring theme of giving them a set sum of money and letting them spend it as they thought fit, with limited regard for transparency or accountability. Interestingly, a GP and an occupational health professional were also among the witnesses to speak to the stresses that MPs encountered and to which the scheme of expenses was said to have added.

It was clear that these various witnesses were the hors d'oeuvre. The main course was the grilling of IPSA in the form of its chairman.

Our first appearance was on 13 September 2011.[74] I was accompanied by the director of policy. We were given no choice as to date or time. This created difficulties for me because I was required to be at another meeting in Whitehall. It was arranged that we would appear, but if we had not covered all the matters of interest to the committee by the time that I had to leave, I would come back for a further appearance. In the event, I was called back to appear on 25 October.

It was only mid-afternoon of the day before I was set to appear for the first time that my office received a list of close to fifty questions which the committee would be pleased if I addressed in my evidence. Even by the standards of relations between some MPs and IPSA this was extraordinary. It was beyond discourteous. We raised the matter

---

74   The oral evidence appears at https://www.parliament.uk/members-expenses-committee

with the clerk of the committee but got nowhere. At the time, we took the view that we were being hijacked. On reflection and after dealing with the committee, I came to the view that it was more cock-up than conspiracy. Mr Afriyie's lack of experience simply meant that the committee was not well run. That said, we were being asked to respond at the shortest possible notice to a large number of questions, many of which called for extensive research and preparation if we were not to mislead the committee, or which we would simply be unable to answer. We could, of course, have taken this latter route, but I was not keen for IPSA to appear to be ducking questions. So, my colleagues on the staff prepared a brief for me as quickly as they could and I reverted to the days of my youth and stayed up all night reviewing and learning the relevant information. As it happens, I did not think that the committee would go through the questions somewhat woodenly one by one, but I needed to be prepared for whatever might happen.

In fact, the wooden approach is precisely what happened. We were welcomed by Mr Afriyie. He then simply called on a member of the committee to begin going through the list of questions. I gave no indication of having prepared any answers. Indeed, at one point, I pointed out that I had only had less than a day's notice and so my answers might be less than complete, as some of them were. Of course, I had at my side the director of policy, whose knowledge was encyclopaedic, such that he could always bail me out if needed. And, as regards many of the questions, I could refer to the fact that the NAO and the PAC had already covered the same ground and published their reports.

I was surprised by how ineffective Mr Afriyie was. Here he was, realising an ambition of having IPSA answer to him, and yet missing the opportunity to conduct any kind of thorough and serious investigation. Perhaps, if his mind was made up, he didn't think it was necessary. There was little or no forensic engagement. There didn't even seem to be a lot of interest in the answers given. There was, instead, the impression of a committee which was not particularly well prepared, going through the motions, safe in the knowledge that – whatever I might say – they would have the last word and could recommend a new life after IPSA.

At the first meeting Mr Afriyie began by asking me whether I had found it difficult or challenging to implement the act. I could have gone on for some long time, but I chose to focus by way of difficulty or challenge on what Stella Creasy had said during my appearance before the PAC when she referred to MPs as our customers. To me, this went to the heart of the cultural change which IPSA constituted, even if some did not recognise it as such. The oft-expressed view of MPs and their staff was that we were concerned with 'customer care'. I explained that this was not an appropriate way of describing the relationship between IPSA and MPs. IPSA was not there to serve MPs. It was there to serve the public interest. There had to be a sea-change in attitude. MPs had to come to terms with independent, external regulation and all that it implies. There was no comeback, nor even acknowledgement of what I had said. The chairman simply moved to the next question on his list.

To me, the point was so fundamental to what IPSA was about, that after the hearing I went back and wrote two pieces for IPSA's website.[75] I dealt with the two issues that had concerned me in the hearing before the PAC: VFM and 'customer care'. I set out the views that I have just touched on. One member of the board, Ken Olisa, took issue. He did not see the point of writing some rather abstract analysis and said so. I responded that the pieces would be read and would serve as a background to further dealings with MPs and committees.

---

75   See Appendix VII.

This proved to be the case, not least in the acceptance that VFM in the case of IPSA required a more nuanced approach than that initially adopted whereby value for money was largely equated with cost, with the consequent view that the lower the cost, the greater the value.

At the second appearance in October I was accompanied by the chief executive and the director of policy. Members of the committee took the opportunity to go back over what had passed between us at our first meeting. It was all fairly straightforward until it was Mr Raynsford's turn to ask questions. Then the temperature rose significantly. Initially, he asked about value for money, which allowed me to rehearse my view that VFM is a complex notion, a point he accepted. He then pursued me about the principles which guided IPSA. He had persuaded himself that I was not sticking closely enough to the duties laid on IPSA by statute and was taking account of other matters. It was a bad point:[76] I clearly had to take account of a number of considerations in carrying out, and giving effect to, my statutory duties. I was surprised by Mr Raynsford's aggressiveness in asking his questions. Clearly, he was in 'beating up the witness' mode. In a series of exchanges he repeatedly pressed me as to whether I was surprised about criticism of various aspects of our operation and by the NAO's survey showing that many MPs were dissatisfied with IPSA. I refused to be riled. When he pressed again about whether I was surprised about the level of MPs' dissatisfaction, I fell back on the traditional response of 'With respect, Mr Raynsford'. No, I said, I was not surprised, but this did not mean that I wasn't concerned. The point I was making was that I was answering the question he had asked, rather than the unasked question: 'Wasn't it thoroughly disgraceful that MPs had responded in the way that they did to the survey?' Of course, if

---

76   As the minister made clear in his reply to the subsequent debate on the committee's report.

I'd been asked that, I would have made the points that I made at the hearing of the Public Accounts Committee: that the number of MPs responding was small, that we were still in the early days of IPSA and that regulators are routinely disliked by those whom they regulate. Mr Raynsford's largely cod outrage subsided and Mr Afriyie called an end to the session.

In due course, the committee reported to the House.[77] A motion was proposed by Mr Afriyie that the House accept the recommendations made by the committee in its report. Some members of the committee spoke in support of the report, as did the usual suspects, led by the indefatigable Bob Russell. Broadly speaking, the recommendations fell into two parts. There were those which followed on from the report of the National Audit Office and which IPSA had already undertaken to act upon at our meeting with the Public Accounts Committee. To that extent the committee was going over well-tilled ground and, to change the metaphor, was knocking at a door that IPSA had already opened.

Then there were the recommendations which in one form or another represented a full-on attack on IPSA's independence. Two stood out. First:

> IPSA's current administrative role should be carried out by a separate body, so that IPSA is not regulating itself, and the act should be amended to permit this. The best arrangement would be for that separate body to be within the House of Commons Service.

The administration of the scheme should, in other words, revert back to the House of Commons in the form of the old fees office. Secondly:

---

77   Hansard, 15 December 2011.

A body independent of both Parliament and IPSA be commissioned by the House Service to undertake a financial cost-benefit analysis to determine whether extending IPSA's current system of London and Outer London supplements to other regions in the UK could provide greater value for money for taxpayers, and an evaluation of the extent to which each of the aims for the act set out in 2009 would be achieved.

In not more than six months' time, the House should have the opportunity to consider the merits of that cost-benefit analysis and evaluation and to make a decision on whether there should or should not be a system of regional supplements instead of the existing travel and accommodation provisions.

The intended effect of these two recommendations was clear. No matter that the report began with a ringing endorsement of the need for independent regulation; the recommendations that followed were clearly intended to allow the House to retake control not just of the administration of financial support but of the principles on which that support was premised. Some MPs pushed back. It was inconceivable, they urged, that the House would get involved in expenses after the recent scandals. One member of the committee,[78] having clearly failed to persuade his colleagues on the committee, even went so far as to table an amendment to Mr Afriyie's motion. Rather than act on the recommendations, the House should, he urged, thank the committee and refer the report and its recommendations to IPSA for its consideration. This was a stylish form of castration.

When it came time for the government to reply, its response was straight out of the top drawer of political out-manoeuvring, even if

---

78   Guto Bebb MP.

Mr Afriyie was not a particularly formidable opponent. Clearly, the report was unacceptable to government. Whatever MPs might think in private, the government did not need the public relations disaster which would attend attempts to undermine or replace IPSA, even if MPs were to agree (which was unlikely).

First, Mark Harper, who was then the Under Secretary of State for Constitutional and Political Reform, responded on behalf of the government. I had previously had a number of dealings with him and always found him thoughtful, open-minded and often helpful. He understood what IPSA was trying to do and, while pointing from time to time to areas needing improvement, he was also prepared to support us. In giving his response, he referred the House to the fact that a number of recommendations were already accepted and being worked on by IPSA.[79] But there were others, he said, that embodied a contradiction that lay at the heart of the report. It talked of there being a need for an independent system for distributing taxpayers' money. But, at the same time, the committee was clearly proposing that control of the system should be vested in MPs. In the face of Mr Afriyie's increasingly ineffectual protestations, the minister, with a withering response, simply skewered him by referring him to the detailed recommendations which did so and thus were incompatible with IPSA's independence.

The amended motion merely thanking the committee and referring the report for IPSA's consideration was duly passed.

Then came a second step. Ordinarily, when a committee reports to the House, the government, after a debate, will publish a formal response. The consequence of this is that the committee can then go away and consider this response. It can decide to hold further hearings

---

79   IPSA's response to the committee's recommendations is on IPSA's website in the April 2012 review of the scheme, pp. 103–7.

or move onto another topic. Mr Afriyie's committee only had one topic: to consider 'MPs' Expenses'. If the government did not respond formally to the report, the committee would have no further business. This is what happened. There was no response. The government chose not to respond formally to the report. There was nothing more for Mr Afriyie's committee to do. By the careful use of parliamentary proce-dure, the government (in the form of the leader, Sir George Young) succeeded in seeing off an attempt to reopen the question which had been answered by the Parliamentary Standards Act 2009.

I saw this as a crucial point in the life of IPSA, a very important signal. The government was saying to MPs that IPSA was there to stay, as was the system of accountability that IPSA had introduced. Yes, we needed to improve. But there would be no going back. After a gruelling year of sustained ordeal by various committees, we felt that we had come through it and could now give our undivided attention to doing the job – and doing it better.

CHAPTER 14

FREEDOM OF INFORMATION

As a publicly funded body, IPSA is subject to the Freedom of Information Act 2000 (FOIA). We regularly received requests for information, usually from members of the public or the media. Responding was a costly and time-consuming exercise, but part of the price to be paid for having as open a system of governance as possible. By section 36 of the act, we could decline requests if the 'qualified person' judged disclosure would 'prejudice the effective conduct of public affairs'. Organisations had to nominate a 'qualified person'. We were fortunate in that we could nominate the judicial member of the board. He worked closely with the team and adjudicated on requests that they brought to him. Section 36 was not frequently invoked because we believed strongly in transparency and, of course, were subject to a statutory duty to operate transparently. If a decision of the qualified person was contested, an appeal could be made to me as chairman. I only remember a couple of such cases. If the person requesting the particular information was still dissatisfied, the case could be appealed to the information commissioner.

So, the FOIA served as part of the backdrop of IPSA's activities, but was never of any particular concern. Then we received a request from a journalist early in 2011 which took us into a long saga which finally ended in the Court of Appeal. The request was for the original receipts of claims made by three MPs in the year 2010–11. The MPs in question were John Bercow, George Osborne and Alan Keen, who had featured prominently in the expenses scandal and had subsequently died.

IPSA published information relating to claims on a regular, two-monthly basis, as I have explained. We did not publish the actual receipt, but rather all the relevant (as we saw it) information extracted from the receipt. If we were to publish the receipt in what might be called its raw form, we would have to remove or cover up any private and confidential information it might contain before releasing it. This process, called redaction, would have to be done manually. Not only would this be expensive, given the hundreds of claims and receipts processed every week, but it would involve human intervention and so raise the risk of human error. And a process which exposed MPs to human errors in the context of privacy or security was to be avoided if at all possible. So we operated a system of publishing a summary of the claim. Before introducing this procedure, we checked with the office of the information commissioner to establish whether such an approach would meet the requirements of the FOIA. We were advised that the example that we offered was acceptable. But the commissioner expressed no view as to the procedure as a whole.

So, when the journalist asked to see the claims made by the three MPs, we sent him copies of the information extracted from the receipts. He replied that he wanted to see the actual receipts rather than information extracted by IPSA from them. We resisted, arguing that our process provided the public with all the relevant information. He appealed. His appeal was rejected internally. He then appealed to the information commissioner. The issue for IPSA was, how should we respond?

On its face, a request for the receipts of three MPs was of no real consequence in terms of our protecting their privacy and security, notwithstanding the high visibility of the MPs involved. There were not so many and we could simply have checked and double-checked and triple-checked to make sure that no error had been made and then released them. But we were concerned at the deeper implications of the journalist's request. All receipts submitted to IPSA by MPs were retained electronically on a server. By the time of the request, IPSA had what might be described as a 'back catalogue' of around 800,000 receipts. Should the journalist's request be successful, just a few carefully crafted requests under the FOIA would mean that IPSA could be inundated with requests for receipts. This would mean that we would need to take on staff to carry out the process of redaction. Given that requests under the FOIA must be met within twenty days, we would also need to seek leave to delay the process of complying with the statute until we had completed the necessary redactions: a matter of several months, considering the care which would have to be taken to protect MPs' privacy. And, on that timescale, release of a huge number of receipts would coincide with the run-up to the next general election. There would be intense scrutiny of receipts for the discovery of any transgression of the rules. Although our evidence was that the rules were being scrupulously complied with, given the continuing distrust of MPs by the public and the preparedness of some sections of the media to play on and cultivate it, even the slightest breach could be seized on as proof that 'they haven't learned' and 'they still don't get it'. The possibility of undermining the still-fragile trust in our democratic institutions was plain to see.

The 'worst case scenario' of having to publish hundreds of thousands of receipts caused us to carry out some serious contingency planning. There were two central issues. What did we need to do operationally? And should we contest the application to the information commissioner?

Operationally, we worked out what would be involved from the point of view of staffing: what additional resources we would need, with what skills and level of supervision, and for how long. Then we translated the calculation into money. It was clear that on the basis of the worst case scenario we would need an injection of a further £3 million into our budget. The SCIPSA was advised. We explained both the nature of the potential challenge and our response to it. We also made clear that our request for additional funding was contingent. We wanted the SCIPSA's authorisation of a separate line in our budget to deal with claims for receipts from our 'back catalogue' under the FOIA. We would not draw down the funding, however, unless we failed to win the legal argument – that we already did enough to comply with the FOIA – and then received requests for copies of receipts in the numbers that we estimated were possible. The SCIPSA authorised the additional funding. Parenthetically, it's worth mentioning here that in doing so, a precedent was set whereby we were able to present our budget in subsequent years showing the agreed annual 5 per cent overall reduction in our administrative costs, while at the same time seeking increases in our budget to address 'one-off' issues. At the intervention of Andrew Lansley, then Leader of the House, we agreed to submit a detailed breakdown of expenditure under these separate 'one-off' budgetary lines, so as not to create elements of the budget which could not be adequately scrutinised. But it was an important budgetary device which stood us in good stead when it came to planning for the general election of 2015 and for updating our IT system.

Once we had secured contingency funding from SCIPSA, we addressed ourselves to the question of the appeal to the information commissioner that had been lodged by the journalist seeking the receipts. We decided to contest the application, both because we considered that our practice satisfied the requirements of the FOIA and because of the possible consequences of complying with the request. The reference to possible consequences is an example of what lawyers call the 'floodgates argument': that a flood would follow if the gate was not kept tightly shut. Tribunals and courts are usually unmoved by this argument, taking the view that they decide the case before them and are not there to deal with what might flow from it. But there are circumstances where it is right to point to the context in which a decision is being made and to its consequences. We thought this was just such a case (with the exception of the judicial member of the board, who was not optimistic of success).

The information commissioner decided in favour of the journalist. We decided to appeal to what is called the First-tier Tribunal, a court which forms part of the system of administering justice in matters relating to the decisions of public bodies.

Meanwhile, I was aware of discussions going on in government concerning the FOIA. The Conservatives in the coalition had always been ill-disposed to the act, whatever their public utterances, while their Liberal Democrat partners were enthusiasts. I went to see the Ministry of Justice's minister in the House of Lords, Lord McNally, a Liberal Democrat peer, who had responsibility for the area. I had known him since university days and had kept wicket to his unpredictable (even to him) slow bowling as part of the same cricket team.

Conscious of the fact that he was less of an enthusiast for FOI than others (perhaps because of his experience in government), I sought to explore options which might mitigate the challenge IPSA might face if we lost the legal case and faced a flood of requests for receipts. I knew that the government was considering consulting the public on a possible revision of the regulations relating to the FOIA. I sought to discover what progress had been made, what the possible time-scale might be, both as regards the consultation and any consequent change in the regulations and, specifically, whether the regulations might be changed to take account of the period of time it would take us to carry out the necessary redaction. At the time, the regulations allowed a public body to decline a request under the FOIA if the time taken to respond would be excessive (the time limit was sixteen hours). But, crucially, under the statute, the process of redaction was not regarded as relevant for the calculation of this time period. If I could persuade the minister to push on with the consultation on the regulations, include a change to bring redaction within the activities, which were time-limited, and allow us to resist publication beyond what we already published because of the excessive time taken for redaction, and do it all within the next several months, our position would be materially different. In particular, we would have a way of managing any flood of requests if the legal case was lost.

I also sought to explain that the implications of the information commissioner's decision were not limited to IPSA but would potentially have ramifications across Whitehall. The commissioner had decided that our summary of information was not sufficient to meet our obligations under the FOIA. We had to release the actual receipt, he said, because the receipt might have characteristics, such as a water mark or heading, or might contain material in addition to that which we had summarised that we may regard as irrelevant but others might not. What this meant across Whitehall would be that any comment, doodle, or marginalia on any note or memorandum must be revealed. As our chief executive, who had worked as a civil servant on the drafting of the FOIA, put it, the Freedom of Information Act would become the Freedom of Documents Act.

Given the possibility that the case could have wider implications involving government, I also asked whether the government would be prepared to support us in our appeal, whether by submitting arguments or by bearing some of the costs, or, preferably, both. The civil servants in attendance looked temporarily nervous. The minister might make a commitment before they had had a chance to brief him (and shoot the idea down). They needn't have worried. Lord McNally has been around a long time. He said that he would make enquiries about the regulations and otherwise consider what I had said. He encouraged my officials to maintain contact with his.

We did liaise regularly with officials from the Ministry but saw no movement on any front. When Lord McNally was replaced as junior minister some months later by Simon Hughes MP, another Liberal Democrat, I arranged to see him. As with Lord McNally, he was friendly, helpful and understood our position. He even agreed to offer assistance when I mentioned that the government might contemplate joining us in our litigation. There was a sharp intake of breath from his officials. Needless to say, once the meeting was ended with agreement to keep in touch, the officials must have taken him aside and explained the innumerable reasons why his offer of help, while understandable, was a thoroughly bad idea. There was no further mention of support.

Maintaining this twin-track approach of the political alongside the legal, we appealed first to the First-tier Tribunal. It rejected our argument. So, we appealed to the Upper Tribunal. It too rejected our argument. We then had to decide whether to appeal one more time, to the Court of Appeal. We decided to do so. We thought that the case raised important matters of principle concerning the meaning and intention of the FOIA. At the same time, we began to prepare for the eventuality of receiving a flood of requests if we lost the case. The general election of 2015 was still some months away, but we would need that intervening period to get our processes in place. On the timescale now in place, therefore, nothing would be released before the election, save the response to the initial request for the receipts of the three MPs named.

The Court of Appeal, speaking through the Master of the Rolls, Lord Dyson, agreed that the case was important and that it was appropriate for us to pursue the point even as far as the Court of Appeal. That said, the court decided against us. The focus was on the meaning of the word information. The court agreed that 'information' meant, in the context, the receipt in its raw form rather than what we had extracted from it.

The court also made it clear that, from their perspective, they were adjudicating on only the three requests that had been made. That there might thereafter be a flood of requests costing the taxpayer upwards of £3 million was not their concern. Although this was strictly true, it did look somewhat other-worldly. There are occasions when the courts will look behind the immediate circumstances of a particular case and recognise the larger context. And there are cases when the court won't. This was one of the latter cases. Plus, there was a different and wider context for the court also to take account of, namely the presumption that access to information should be as unrestricted as possible. Awkward as that might be in some cases, we recognised its validity.

The postscript to this chapter in IPSA's life is that, in fact, there was no flood of requests, no assault on the nearly a million (by then) receipts in the 'back catalogue'. Requests under the FOIA remained at more or less the same level. We were able to breathe more easily. We knew that the receipts would reveal little or nothing, since, as I have said many times, MPs almost universally complied with the rules and when they didn't it was usually because of some administrative error. Only very rarely was there a breach and when there was, it was pursued by the staff and ultimately the compliance office. What we were keen to avoid, particularly in the run-up to the general election, was the expenditure of large amounts of time and money in an exercise which, because it involved redaction, exposed IPSA and thus MPs to the risk of errors, with all the consequent damage such errors could cause. We were delighted, therefore, to return to the Treasury the money (£3 million) that had been earmarked for the possible fall-out from the original FOIA request.

CHAPTER 15

MONEY – FUNDING FOR MPs' STAFF

In Chapter 4 I set out a number of the elements which made up that part of MPs' remuneration that we called business costs and expenses. In what follows, I will consider one further part of the scheme: the funding for staff.

MPs need staff to help them to do their job. But what is it that the taxpayer pays for? The answer is – funding for staff to help MPs to carry out their parliamentary functions. By contrast, staff may not be paid from funds provided by the taxpayer for carrying out what can broadly be described as party-political activities. Enter immediately a definitional challenge. Frankly, to any politician, the distinction between the parliamentary and the party-political is a distinction without a difference. To them, they are the same. But the statute setting out IPSA's powers talks only of funding for parliamentary functions. How should IPSA deal with this?

One response would be to set out (or try to) what activities fall under each head. Anyone familiar with making rules will tell you that this is a non-starter. The lists will be never-endingly compendious, the terms used will be pored over to discover their 'true' meaning, and then something will crop up which no one has thought of. We decided to avoid that route. Instead, we identified activities which, by any reasonable understanding, could not easily be said to constitute fulfilling a parliamentary function. Initially, we only referred to two such activities: including party logos on a website (they were not forbidden, but the taxpayer would not pay for them), and campaigning for a candidate in a local election. By 2012 a longer list had emerged, including undertaking work on behalf of a political party. Initially, what we said took the form of guidance, but was then converted into rules, since many MPs preferred there to be a black-and-white ruling on such matters. This approach enabled us to give clear examples while not disappearing down some rabbit hole of details. It also reinforced the principle that our long-term aim was to leave such decisions to MPs' discretion, in the knowledge that any choice, when it involved spending taxpayers' money, would be made public.

Once that ground had been cleared, we had to decide two questions. The first was: how many members of staff does an MP need? The Senior Salaries Review Body, relying on the study carried out by the management consultants PwC, had determined three years earlier that MPs should receive such funds as to allow them each to employ 3.5 staff.[80] The second question was: what should MPs get by way of an overall budget for staff?

As for the first question, need is not the same as want. When we consulted MPs, some were clearly inundated with work of various kinds such that they felt that they needed and certainly could keep a dozen or more staff occupied. They were often MPs in metropolitan areas with significant numbers of residents needing advice concerning immigration or access to the welfare system. The level of work was, they reported, exacerbated by the disappearance of other agencies

---

80 Staff frequently worked on a part-time basis, such that the 3.5 (full-time equivalent) allocation might amount in fact to six or seven members of staff.

such as Citizens Advice Bureaux, which would otherwise have been able to offer help, as a consequence of the government's programme of austerity. By contrast, MPs in largely rural or suburban (and safe) constituencies indicated that they were largely content with the funding for staff. Indeed, a number of these MPs even indicated that they did not hold surgeries (which require staff to organise them) or did so much less frequently than others.

Faced with this difference in perceived and actual need, we looked for ways of developing some system of allocation which would take into account MPs' concerns and at the same time would be fair. One possible method was to allocate the number of staff by reference to the demographic nature of the constituency, metropolitan or suburban/ rural, less affluent or comfortably off. Whatever the logic, this was a non-starter. The Conservative Party pointed to the fact that the urban metropolitan areas were largely held by the opposition Labour Party. If these MPs were to receive more staff, it would, they argued, give them an unfair advantage come the next election. Their staff would be able to engage in a greater level of activity with a consequent increase in visibility (regardless of any purist view about staff only being enti-tled to support parliamentary functions).

After much discussion, it was clear that the only allocation that MPs would find acceptable was one which was even-handed as between all MPs. They should all get the same number of staff. To some MPs it would not seem enough, to others it might be more than enough. But in a world where the radar is exceptionally alert to the possibilities of others gaining an advantage, it was the only plausible solution. So, now the question became, what was the right number of staff?

We analysed the responses to our consultation[81] and reached two

---

81   The consultation was in November 2011.

conclusions. The first was that most MPs needed more than the 3.5 members of staff for whom they were currently funded. There was no doubt that many were struggling to meet the demands made on them, not least the demands generated by the explosion in the use of email and social media. Emails in particular posed a significant and growing challenge. Because communication was virtually instantaneous, the sender grew to expect a similarly instantaneous reply. The old ways of working whereby letters would be sent and everyone accepted that a reply would follow in a few days, depending on the vagaries of the post, were swept aside.

Then we decided that an increase to four staff per MP was appropriate, an increase of nearly 15 per cent, albeit in the context of small numbers. The increase did not reflect some finger-in-the-wind hunch. It reflected the considered conclusion of IPSA's staff in the light of the responses to the consultation and after interviewing a cross-section of existing staff and analysing a sample of the workload of MPs in various types of constituency.

The last step was to agree a budget. We took the view that, within the framework of four members of staff, it was for MPs to structure their offices as they wished. But, by way of guidance, we had already created in 2010 a template of an MP's office involving the employment of a senior manager assisted by others of varying degrees of experience. We established pay bands within which members of staff would be employed. Initially, we then took the mid-point of these bands, spread across what was then the 3.5 staff with differing levels of responsibility, and added up the resulting sum. This constituted the budget available to MPs for their office staff.[82] For the 2012/13 financial year, we calculated the budgets on the basis of four members of staff being

---

82   See Chapter 5 for the discussion of the particular arrangements regarding pay in the case of the employment of 'connected parties'.

paid at 60 per cent of the maximum. We also introduced a 5 per cent supplement to the budget for MPs with constituencies in the London area. Together, these factors resulted in increases of 20–25 per cent in MPs' staffing budgets.[83] We then took these proposals to the SCIPSA as part of the estimate for 2012/13. MPs on the SCIPSA did not, of course, need a great deal of persuading that the case for an increase in the budget was justified. It was duly approved.

While there was grumbling from those who wanted more (grumbling which never went away), at the same time there was genuine appreciation from MPs. It was the first time, as many MPs saw it, that IPSA had made an MP-friendly decision. They recognised that in a time of austerity a significant increase in their staffing budget was a clear recognition of the case that had been made. They also recognised that we had not ducked the issue but had argued the case at the meetings with the SCIPSA. For our part, we were keen to send a signal that, once again, if the evidence and the arguments supported a view, we would support that view, even if, as in this case, it meant an increase in the costs to the taxpayer. For those who were watching IPSA closely, it was a signal of what might be coming when we got round to MPs' pay.

---

83   The budget for staff in 2011/12 was £115,000 for all MPs. For 2012/13 it was £144,000 for London and £137,200 for non-London MPs – increases of 25.2 per cent and 19.3 per cent respectively.

CHAPTER 16

MONEY – REMUNERATION OF MPs

Now I come to the biggest challenge that IPSA had so far faced in its short life: MPs' pensions, pay and associated other forms of remuneration.

IPSA's duty is to make available to MPs such funds as will enable them to carry out their parliamentary functions. That's easy to say, but there are a couple of obvious problems. How much do MPs need and, implicit in that question, what exactly are MPs' parliamentary functions? Both of these questions hovered in the background as we addressed the issue of funds for MPs over the first parliamentary term, 2010–15. Neither has a ready answer. As for the first, MPs tended to ask for as much as they thought the system could bear, the system being both what IPSA was minded to make available and the political context in which IPSA was created and operated.

The answer to the second question – what MPs should be remunerated for – is even more elusive. Of course, on its face it is clear. MPs are to be remunerated, as we've seen, for carrying out their parliamentary functions. But what does this mean exactly? It might be a help if there were some kind of job description. But there isn't. Indeed, MPs have consistently resisted and continue to resist any attempt to devise one.

An attempt was made by a committee convened by the Speaker in 2007, but nothing emerged.[84] Instead, the mantra resorted to is that each MP does the job in his or her own way. As mantras go it's obviously entirely self-serving. It leaves it to the individual MP to equate whatever they might do with representing their constituents and then go on to say that it's for the electorate to judge how well they do the job (provided, of course, that the electorate knows what they are doing).

The most significant consequence of there not being any form of job description is that the discussions about what should be a proper salary end up as the question – how long is a piece of string. I'll explore this in more detail later when I deal with MPs' pay. I mention it here as being just one of the issues which lie beneath the surface when you consider how to remunerate those who are elected to the nation's legislature.

PAY AND PENSIONS
IN THE BEGINNING

It had become abundantly clear from the gallons of ink and miles of newsprint dedicated to the expenses scandal of 2008–09, that at least part of the explanation of why some MPs abused the system then in place was because they felt that they were not sufficiently well-paid. For decades the Senior Salaries Review Body and its predecessors had recommended that MPs' pay be increased. For decades the recommendations had been ignored by successive governments, always with the refrain that the time was not right. From the perspective of backbenchers toiling away on behalf of their constituents, it looked as if there would never be a right time.

In my early speeches and in conversations with ministers and

---

84 Report of the Select Committee on the Modernisation of the House, 'Revitalising the Chamber: the role of the back bench Member', 13 June 2007.

officials, I had regularly made the point that, to make sense of the idea that MPs' remuneration should be set by an independent body, IPSA must be given responsibility for MPs' pay and pensions as well as their costs and expenses. To his credit, the minister charged with bringing IPSA into being, the Secretary of State at the Ministry of Justice and Lord Chancellor, Jack Straw, got the point. By the Constitutional Reform and Governance Act of 2010, IPSA was handed this responsibility. It was to 'determine' the salaries of MPs (though not the salaries of ministers: any additional salary by virtue of being a minister was a matter for the government). IPSA was also charged with the responsibility of drawing up a scheme for the pensions to be paid to MPs when they ceased to represent their constituencies. So began a crucial chapter in IPSA's early life – perhaps its most crucial so far.

The CRAG Act transferred the responsibility to determine pay as of May 2011 and pensions as of October 2011. April 2012 was set as the point at which any new determinations could be introduced. Given the importance of the issues, we decided to proceed carefully. The context was that the scandals of 2008–09 were just a few years away and memories were sharp and feelings raw. Even to talk publicly about MPs' pay, save perhaps to reduce it drastically, was provocative. Also, the UK was in the throes of the worst economic crash since the 1930s, due to the irresponsible (and worse) practices of banks in the US which had infected much of the world's banking system. The coalition government had responded by seeking to cut public spending, choosing thereby to focus on (largely forlorn) efforts to reduce the nation's debt and deficit. One feature of this policy was the introduction in 2010 of a cap of 1 per cent on any annual increases in the salaries of those working in the public sector, the cap to remain in place for the duration of the parliament. Now that a law had been passed prescribing that each parliament should serve for a fixed term of five years, this meant that millions of public sector workers could look forward to this restraint on their pay for at least the next five years, regardless of any effect that inflation might simultaneously have on their disposable income. The cap did not, of course, apply to salaries in the private sector, over which the government had little control. These rose on average by around 2–3 per cent a year during those five years of the first fixed-term parliament. The salaries of senior executives in the private sector, even in the banking sector which created the crisis, grew by considerably more.

IPSA's response to its new role was to make it clear to everyone who would listen that our responsibility was to analyse all of the elements which, taken together, constituted MPs' remuneration and then to recalibrate them. So, the issue was not simply pay, nor just pay and pensions, but a number of other financial benefits that MPs enjoyed. Ideally, given the prevailing economic circumstances, the recalibration would produce a result that would be cost-neutral: in other words, it would produce a result whereby adjustments to the various elements of MPs' remuneration would end up not costing the taxpayer more. In fact, we achieved this result for the first year of the new arrangements: a significant accomplishment.

PUBLIC OR PRIVATE SECTOR?

We had a decision to make at the outset which was one of fundamental importance, but which had never previously really explicitly been confronted. In our analyses, where should we position MPs? Should they be treated as if they worked in the public or in the private sector? We had already acknowledged this point in making our interim decision about increases in pension contributions.[85] Now we needed

---

85   See Chapter 11.

to make a decision which would condition all that followed, given the coalition government's approach to those working in the public sector. The starting point was, of course, the fact that we had to argue by analogy. MPs are not employees. They don't work for the House of Commons. Nor can they be described as self-employed, not least because they cannot wholly decide what to do, how to do it and when to do it.[86] They are most properly defined as office holders, in that they occupy the office of MP, which exists independently of them. So where does this take us? (Remember that we were not seeking to resolve the question of MPs' status, but rather where should MPs be placed in the context of setting their remuneration.)

There is a case for treating MPs who have a budget to manage and staff to employ as if they are, in effect, running a small business. This might suggest that they should fall on the private sector side of the equation. On the other hand, they are seen and would see themselves as engaged in public service. This would put them on the public sector side. When we consulted with the public on this, we found they were in no doubt that MPs should be regarded as if they worked in the public sector. MPs, however, were torn. They saw the point about public service. They also saw the salaries earned in the private sector.

One device, of course, would be to fudge the answer. We could have accepted that they should be regarded as if they were working in the public sector, but then adopt the view that this meant high-end public sector, for example, chief executives of local authorities, head teachers, or general practitioners rather than those lower down the totem pole, as it was expressed, such as your run-of-the-mill nurses,

---

86 See the evidence of Dave Hartnett, Second Permanent Secretary to the Treasury, to Mr Afriyie's Committee, 27 October 2011.

teachers and police officers. Indeed, this argument was energetically pressed on us by many MPs.

But there's a problem with such assertions, something which seemed to me to have been perennially overlooked: the problem of comparisons – the chief executive rather than the nurse on the ward. The Senior Salaries Review Body in its reports and recommendations routinely used the device of what it regarded as important comparators when recommending what MPs should be paid. So did many of those whom we consulted. In addition to the head teacher and other such positions, the salaries of a brigadier in the armed forces or a senior police officer were regularly used as reference points. MPs should get what they get, it was said. But the question that I posed at one of our very early meetings was: why? Why should the rank of brigadier in the army be used as the comparator? Why not a sergeant? The answer is obvious. The comparator chosen is determined by a prior assumption as to what the 'right' answer looks like. A brigadier, the SSRB's preferred comparator, looked about right to them in terms of status and pay. But settling on a brigadier as the right comparator proceeds from a set of unstated and unargued premises: that MPs were like brigadiers in that most British of senses – they occupied a similar station in life (at least in their minds) and should be paid accordingly.[87]

IPSA was going to have to do better than this. We were going to have to keep to our defining principles. We were going to have to assemble evidence and reason our way through.

So, as a first step, we made a decision on where to locate MPs along the public/private spectrum. We decided to treat MPs as if they were public sector workers. Then, as we embarked on our analysis, we set our faces against simple-minded comparisons.

---

87   American lawyers describe this as 'conclusionary' reasoning whereby the conclusion comes first and the reasons are then marshalled to support it.

THE NAMING OF PARTS

We began work towards the summer of 2012. We identified the various strands of remuneration and discussed each in turn. The board's job was to identify the questions to be asked, so that the executive could draft a consultation document. A number of MPs objected to the idea that we should consult on their pay and pensions. What they meant is that they objected to IPSA's consulting the public rather than the small group (including MPs) referred to in the statute whom we were required to consult. The public were not consulted on the pensions and pay of GPs or head teachers, they argued. Why should MPs be singled out? Of course, behind these objections lay the real fear that, given the opprobrium in which MPs as a group were held since the expenses scandal, the public's view might be that MPs' remuneration should be less and certainly not more. For our part, we saw no reason to depart from our practice of consulting the public. Their views were a relevant element of the evidence. And, as I had made clear on all previous occasions, when we consulted we would have regard to reasoned argument. Conclusions without justification would not persuade us and nor would the more heady rhetoric found in the darker reaches of the internet.

MPs' remuneration took the following forms:

- a salary (£65,738 in April 2012);
- a pension;
- a resettlement allowance;
- a winding-up allowance (to meet the cost of winding up the office when an MP is defeated in a general election or does not seek re-election);
- assorted other benefits.

We would have to examine each of these in turn. Some we had already addressed, such as several of the ancillary benefits – the use of taxis, or the payment for meals while in Parliament (previously a £25 'allowance' but reduced to £15 and only on production of a receipt). But we recognised that we needed to revisit them if we were to carry out the comprehensive recalibration of remuneration that we regarded as essential.

As a matter of principle, we decided at the outset that each of the elements which, taken together, formed the package of remuneration would be examined in its own right and on its own merits. This meant that we would not make decisions based on what the overall bottom line would be. That's not to say, however, that we ignored the implications for the taxpayer of whatever choices we made. Nor did we ignore the notion that a solution which was cost-neutral would be ideal. It's just to say that these factors did not drive our choices.

Once we had some initial sense of the landscape, our thinking was that we should publish an initial consultation document asking for views. Then, having taken account of the views expressed, the staff would carry out further work. This would, in turn, enable us to publish a second consultation with suggested positions on the various issues. The responses to this consultation would then inform the board's final decisions.

TIMESCALE

The timescale was important. We intended to proceed carefully. We announced early on that although the statute provided that changes could be introduced from April 2012, any changes in remuneration would not, in fact, be introduced until after the next general election, due in May 2015. We made it clear, however, that we hoped to finish our work by early 2014 so that any changes (particularly if they involved an increase in MPs' pay) would not loom too large in the run-up to the election. We got the timescale right, but the hope that the world would move on and regard pay and pensions as settled was forlorn.

Our timescale was as follows:

- October 2012 – We published the first, wide-ranging consultation on MPs' pay and pensions and other elements of remuneration. It followed an extensive collection of evidence, including polling public opinion, and the use of focus groups and citizens' juries. The consultation paper was open-ended. It did not make firm proposals but asked questions about all aspects of MPs' remuneration.
- January 2013 – We published a report on the first consultation. It did not make recommendations on a package of remuneration, but set out a framework and the principles which would guide further work.
- July 2013 – Informed by the further work after the first consultation and by the views expressed, we launched a second consultation which contained proposals for MPs' pay, pensions, resettlement payments and some aspects of business costs and expenses.
- December 2013 – After the two consultations and our consideration of them, we published what we described as a modern, professional package for MPs' remuneration. The package was cost-neutral: in the first year of its operation it would not cost the taxpayer any more than was previously the case.
- December 2014 – The new pension scheme which we announced in December 2013 as part of the reforms was laid before Parliament.
- July 2015 – Immediately following the general election, we conducted a final consultation, as required by statute. On 16 July we announced our final decision on the package of remuneration for MPs which was to take effect in the current parliament.

MPs' PENSIONS

Pensions are complicated. They exist in an arcane world into which some wander never again to be seen alive and others besport themselves, never wholly to be understood by outsiders. IPSA was very fortunate in having Tony Stower as a member of staff; he became an expert but never lost sight of the need to communicate with the rest of us.

This is not the place to descend too far into the details of pension arrangements. Instead, I will set out in general terms the matters that we had to address and what we decided.

The vast majority[88] of MPs participated in a pension scheme (the Parliamentary Contributory Pension Fund) managed and operated by a board made up of current and past MPs, members of the House of Lords who had previously been MPs, and some external members.[89] The pension fund was a 'closed fund', meaning that it was open only to MPs and was funded out of contributions from MPs and the Treasury (the taxpayer). The board was responsible for ensuring that the fund was and would remain sufficient to meet the claims made on it, both at that time and for the future. IPSA, for its part, was under a statutory duty to ensure that, in any arrangements that we might make regarding MPs' pensions, we preserved the viability of the fund. That said, the Treasury had indicated in our previous dealings with them over pensions[90] that, all things considered, they would make up any shortfall there might be if MPs' contributions did not meet the fund's needs.

MPs could opt to pay pension contributions at different levels, expressed as percentages of their salary. Most of them paid at the highest rate, which, compared with the contributions of most people working in the public sector, was quite high. The other side of the coin was that the benefits paid out under the scheme were significantly more generous than those available in the public sector. There was, therefore, a

---

88   Some very few made their own private arrangements.
89   Including a representative of IPSA from 2012 onwards. This was very useful as it enabled excellent communication between the board and IPSA as we developed our plans.
90   See Chapter 11.

sense of gold-plated pensions which were not only generous in their own right, but were also heavily subsidised by the taxpayer.

Our deliberations focused on the contributions that MPs should be required to make, the benefits that they should enjoy and the consequent cost to them and to the public purse. In the background were the government's austerity programme and the recent report from Lord Hutton, commissioned by the government, which offered a road map for the future of pensions in the public sector.[91] Lord Hutton advised a movement away from what are called 'final salary' pensions, whereby the pension is calculated by reference to a person's salary in the final year of employment. He recommended that pensions for the future be based on 'career average revalued earnings' (CARE). Hutton's rationale was a concern about risk. Pensions based on final year salaries placed all the risk (of a downturn in the economy and a consequent need to meet any shortfall in income) on the provider of the pension (the state, in the case of those working in the public sector). The recipient was assured of the pension whatever the circumstances. Pensions based on career average earnings mitigated that risk somewhat, but not greatly. In the private sector, pensions based on final year's salary were no longer being offered to new employees. Instead, pension contributions were to be paid into a fund which the employee had to invest on retirement. In this way, all the risk of fluctuations in value is passed to the employee.

The issue for IPSA was where to position MPs' pensions along the spectrum of risk. A factor influencing that decision was the need to maintain the integrity of the fund. If the arrangements that IPSA decided on were thought by MPs to be too unfavourable, they might leave the scheme, which would place too great a burden on the

---

91 'Independent Public Service Pensions Commission: Final Report' (HM Treasury, March 2011).

Treasury if the scheme was to meet its future obligations. A further issue, assuming a sufficient number of MPs remained in the scheme to ensure its continued viability, was what contribution the taxpayer should make to the scheme when compared with public sector pensions generally.

We carried out a consultation in October 2012 in which we set out in detail various options. We also took expert advice. Then, we made a number of decisions. First, we replaced the system whereby MPs could make contributions at different levels as percentages of their salaries (13.75 per cent, 11.75 per cent, and 9.75 per cent respectively) with a single level of contribution (11.09 per cent). This meant that while some would contribute more, others who were paying the highest level of contribution would pay appreciably less. Secondly, we recalibrated the respective contributions of MPs and the taxpayer. Before our reforms, the respective shares were that MPs put in 37 per cent while the taxpayer made up the remaining 63 per cent. We changed these to 46 per cent and 54 per cent respectively, a significant reduction in the amount paid by the taxpayer. Thirdly, because previously there were different levels of contribution, there were also different rates of accrual – the proportion of their salary which MPs get for each year that they have served. The existing rates were 1/40, 1/50, or 1/60. We replaced them with a single rate of accrual of 1/51. Finally, we made two further decisions, both of which reduced the benefits enjoyed by MPs so as to bring them more into line with those in the world beyond Westminster. We reduced the lump sum paid if the MP died while serving, from four times the annual salary to twice the annual salary, and we reduced the pension paid to survivors from 5/8 of the MP's salary to 3/8.

The overall effect of these reforms was to put MPs' pensions on a more modern footing and to rebalance the relative costs and benefits as between MP and taxpayer. The board of the pension fund was helpful throughout. They saw the need to recalibrate pensions so as to reduce the burden on the taxpayer and bring the benefits enjoyed by MPs more into line with those enjoyed by others. A few MPs argued for greater variability in the contributions they might make, but we resisted, not least because of the administrative complications and consequent cost that it would give rise to. It was always open to them to make their own private arrangements if they wanted greater benefits on retirement.

The reforms to the pension scheme were announced in December 2013. The new Parliamentary Contributory Pension Fund Scheme was laid before Parliament in December 2014.

'RESETTLEMENT ALLOWANCE'

Prior to 2010, MPs who stood down (retired) or were defeated in an election were entitled to what was called a 'resettlement allowance'.[92] Depending on an MP's age and length of service, this 'allowance' could be up to a year's salary. Of all the 'allowances' that MPs granted themselves, this appeared particularly out of line with the experience of their constituents. Ordinarily, if you voluntarily retire from your job, you would not expect – nor would you receive – a sizeable pay-off (save, perhaps, if you were a banker or very senior executive). You've made the decision to leave and that's that. But for MPs, the 'resettlement allowance' kicked in. Equally, if you had lost your job, provided you hadn't been unlawfully or wrongfully dismissed, you might qualify for some form of modest, state-funded redundancy payment, but that would be it. But, again, MPs who lost an election were different.

---

92   Under the previous arrangements the House of Commons called it a 'resettlement grant', but we used the term 'allowance' to signal the fact that it was a legacy from the old system and would be phased out.

Though they were not even technically redundant, since the job still existed, they qualified for the very generous 'resettlement allowance', the first £30,000 of which was tax free.

The rationale, such as it was, was that MPs found it particularly difficult (the uniqueness of the 'allowance' would really suggest 'uniquely') to reintegrate into society and find another job if they wanted one. Some, of course, were by that time beyond retirement age and could call on their generous pensions. For the rest, the cold wind of possible unemployment called for the protection that the 'resettlement allowance' offered. There was very limited empirical evidence to support the claim about the difficulty of finding work. Indeed, empirical evidence was not deemed necessary, not least because it might challenge the assumption. By contrast, there was plenty of evidence of MPs moving effortlessly into the City or to consultancies. This was particularly so as regards the retiring MPs, who had had time to plan their next step.

It was therefore not surprising that, once made aware of this 'allowance', members of the public were suitably exercised. All the echoes of 'feathering their own nests' were there. In their responses to our consultation some MPs sought to defend the allowance, citing anecdotal evidence of this or that colleague who had struggled to find work, though how that was different from so many others who had also lost their jobs is not clear. Most MPs, however, recognised that this particular game was up. There was no place in the modern world for such exceptionalism.

IPSA decided to act as early as 2011 to address the issue. However, we took the view in our analysis of the scheme that fairness required that we should proceed in stages, not least so that MPs' expectations arising from the old system were not completely ignored and so that they would have due notice and could take on board the introduction of a new approach. The first step was to set out what would happen as a consequence of the next general election, due in 2015. The language was tweaked: we talked of a 'resettlement payment'. We made it clear that there would be no such payment any longer for those who voluntarily stood down. Only MPs who were defeated in the election would qualify. And the resettlement payment that these MPs would receive would amount to a month's salary for each year served, up to a maximum of six months. This mirrored the approach adopted by the National Assembly for Wales and seemed a fair first step.

The second step was to announce the arrangements which would come into operation from 2015 onwards and apply to elections thereafter. The payment was renamed the 'Loss of Office Payment' (LOOP). It was to be the equivalent of twice the statutory redundancy rate. As before, only MPs who had been defeated were eligible and they had to have served as MPs for at least two years consecutively.[93]

Our response to the 'resettlement allowance' was widely welcomed, save by some MPs who had served for a long period and would 'lose out', as they saw it, by virtue of the changes to be brought in as a consequence of the 2015 general election. Some, indeed, lamented that, if they had known what was coming, they would have stood down at the election of 2010. Instead, as a number put it to our staff, they were being punished for their 'public-spiritedness'. The cynic might argue that continued service as an MP which was motivated by concern for a 'golden goodbye' might struggle to pass a test of public-spiritedness. It sounded much more like a further echo of the culture of entitlement which was so embedded in the minds of many MPs, even those who had not fallen victim to the scandal of 2008–09.

From IPSA's perspective, our abolition of the 'resettlement allowance' reflected our overall aim: to establish a system of remuneration

---

93   LOOP was not intended to come into operation until the general election of 2020, but I am told that the calling of an earlier snap election in 2017 caused difficulties.

which treated MPs in a modern and professional manner. Though it did not form part of the consultation on pay and pensions (having been decided a couple of years earlier), it reflected the direction of travel and formed part of the jigsaw when it came to the subsequent overhaul of remuneration.

VARIOUS EXPENSES

Although the amount of money saved for the taxpayer was relatively insignificant, there was a symbolic importance in reducing or removing a number of financial benefits previously enjoyed by MPs. It helped to make the point that we were recalibrating the whole package of MPs' remuneration. A number of benefits had come to be expected when, in a modern, professional system, they were costs that MPs should properly bear for themselves. They included the purchase of TV licences, home insurance, travel by taxi except in certain circumscribed cases, and the subsidy for food while in Westminster. While most MPs understood and accepted the changes, this last item provoked an angry response from some senior Tories, causing one to storm out of the room (the meeting was in his room) and to describe me and my colleagues on the board as 'a fucking disgrace'.

MPs' PAY
SOME HISTORY

The argument about whether to pay MPs (and if so, how much) has a very long history, stretching back into the early Middle Ages.[94] From the beginnings of what could be thought to be Parliaments, it was the constituencies that Members represented which were expected to

---

94   I am grateful to Paul Seaward, director of the History of Parliament Trust, for the background papers he wrote and the seminar he gave for the board. I also rely on his article in *The House* magazine in November 2009 and the paper he presented to the members of the Committee on Members' Expenses in October 2011.

make some form of payment to those whom they sent to represent them, not the national government. At the end of a parliament the Crown would issue Members with a writ (the *writ de expensis*) which required local communities to pay. The first known example of this writ was issued in 1258. In 1327 the amount to be paid was fixed: four shillings per day for county Members and two shillings for borough Members, plus a travel allowance. These sums were not insignificant and in times of economic hardship sometimes went unpaid. Disputes were common between local communities and their representative Members, frequently leading to litigation. Some communities, resenting the financial burden, bargained for lower costs. Some chose to pay their Members in kind rather than in money, such as with farm produce, or, for example, in the case of Great Yarmouth, partly in fish.

Increasingly, over time, the ambitious and powerful offered to serve without payment. Typically, they came from local gentry for whom becoming an MP was a sign of increased status. By the end of the seventeenth century, the practice of payment had virtually died out. Most MPs were members of the local land-owning gentry. They could afford to spend time in London, paid for by the rent received from their land.

Samuel Pepys writing in his diary on 30 March 1668 recorded a conversation after dinner with his friends at which they regretted this development:

> The bane of the Parliament hath been the leaving off the old custom of the places allowing wages to those that served them in Parliament, by which they chose men that understood their business and would attend it, and they could expect an account from, which now they cannot; and so the Parliament is become a company of men unable to give account for the interest of the people they serve for.

The debate about paying MPs became sharper in the mid-nineteenth century. The Chartists made the payment of MPs the fourth of their six demands in the People's Charter of 1838.[95] The aim was to ensure a broader representation of the population in Parliament. By contrast, others argued that the only way to combat corruption was if MPs had independent incomes. John Stuart Mill, writing in 1861, strongly opposed the payment of a wage:

> The business of a Member of Parliament would therefore become an occupation in itself; carried on, like other professions, with a view chiefly to its pecuniary returns, and under the demoralising influences of an occupation essentially precarious. It would become an object of desire to adventurers of a low class; and 658 persons in possession, with ten or twenty as many in expectancy, would be incessantly bidding to attract or retain the suffrages of the electors, by promising all things, honest or dishonest, possible or impossible, and rivalling each other in pandering to the meanest feelings and most ignorant prejudices of the vulgarest part of the crowd.[96]

Gladstone also dismissed these concerns because so many people were willing to serve as MPs without payment, so prestigious was the status (leave aside the opportunities for self-advancement). But after the Third Reform Act of 1884, more MPs without independent means began to be elected. Various political parties responded. The Irish Parliamentary Party provided a basic salary for its Member and some working-class Members received a salary from trade unions.[97] The Liberal Party also adopted the principle.

---

95   That MPs should receive an annual salary of £500 and that, at the end of each parliament, their rate of attendance should be published.

96   Mill, *On Representative Government* (1861).

97   £200 per year from 1904.

In 1911, government finally acted. The catalyst had been the legal decision of the House of Lords in 1909.[98] The Lords had decided that it was unlawful for trade unions to use money paid to the union by its members to support members of the Labour Party. In the two elections in 1910, the Labour Party made significant gains. The Liberal Asquith government, through the Chancellor, David Lloyd George, responded. He took the first step in formalising the remuneration of MPs. He introduced an 'allowance' of £400. But he did so in a rather backhanded manner, urging that money be paid while at the same time also urging that it not be regarded as a salary.

> It is not a recognition of the magnitude of the service, it is not a re-muneration; it is not even a salary. It is just an allowance, and I think a minimum allowance, to enable men to come here, men who would render incalculable service to the State and whom it is an incalcula-ble loss to the State not to have here, but who cannot be here because their means do not allow it. It is purely an allowance to enable us to open the door to great and honourable public service...[99]

Even if it required what later might have been dubbed 'double-speak', the Rubicon had been crossed. They may be carefully chosen words, designed to usher in the new approach while simultaneously resiling from it, but there would be no going back.

Indeed, the resolution passed by the House that very same day highlighted the (perhaps intended) confusion. Was it, in fact, a salary, whatever Lloyd George may have said?

---

98   *Amalgamated Society of Railway Servants v. Osborne.* [1909] 1 Chancery Reports, p. 163.
99   https://hansard.parliament.uk/commons/1911-08-10/debates/36a91ce4-2902-4282-90c2-1720ac40077f/PaymentOfMembers

That, in the opinion of the House, provision should be made for the payment of a salary at the rate of four hundred pounds a year to every Member of this House.

As the social and economic backgrounds of MPs changed in the 1920s and '30s, pressure grew for a fair salary in addition to the amount for 'expenses'. But, in fact, the 'allowance' did not exceed £400 until 1937. Indeed, in the years 1931–34 it was actually cut (from £400 to £360). During the next three decades there followed a pattern of inaction resulting in increases which seemed on their face to be large only because they were playing catch-up; as salaries generally had grown there had been no concomitant changes in MPs' pay. The government of the day sanctioned increases in 1937, 1946, 1954 and 1957. But it was only in 1964 that someone external to government, Sir Geoffrey Lawrence,[100] was commissioned to undertake a review. His recommendation that there should be a significant increase in salary (almost a 100 per cent increase) from £1,750 to £3,250, of which £1,250 was to be for expenses, was accepted by the government. Lawrence also introduced a contributory pension scheme.

In making his recommendations, Lawrence referred to:

Members, of whom there are an increasing number not limited to one side of the House, [who] are forced to endure the discomfort, in spite of tax relief, of cheap and shabby lodgings in London; they cannot afford to use the Members' Dining Room; they have to submit to the humiliation of not being able to return hospitality even at the most modest level of entertainment; they are forced to impose considerable sacrifices upon their families and they find it

---

100 A distinguished lawyer and subsequently a High Court judge.

necessary to cut down the number of days on which they can attend sittings of the House.

Rail passes had been introduced as far back as 1921 and the rail scheme had been extended to cover travel to the MP's residence in 1945. A car allowance had been introduced in 1961. The next step, in 1969, was the introduction of a secretarial allowance, the forerunner of the office costs allowance. A much more significant step followed in 1971. The Top Salaries Review Body[101] recommended the separation of salary from expenses, and the additional costs allowance was introduced. Over the next thirty years, this allowance was to become the most prominent vehicle for extending the funding available to MPs.

While these changes and two major adjustments (from £1,750 to £3,250 in 1964 and from £3,250 to £4,500 in 1972) were intended to remedy the situation in which MPs found themselves, the high levels of inflation which prevailed in the late 1960s and the 1970s at the same time served to erode the real value of MPs' incomes. So, other reviews were carried out by the Senior Salaries Review Body (SSRB) in 1979 and 1983. Their recommendations resulted in staged increases during the period 1979–87 (from £9,450 in 1979 to £18,500 by 1987).

In 1988, the notion of tracking other public sector rates of pay was adopted. MPs' pay was set at 89 per cent of a Grade 6 civil servant, the most senior grade below the Senior Civil Service. This approach lasted until 1996 and had the benefit of certainty as well as building in an annual adjustment. It also had the effect of making a statement (ever so subtly by Whitehall) of just where MPs sat in the scheme of things.

In 1996, MPs voted against the government and in favour of the SSRB's recommendation of a 26 per cent pay rise together with

---

101   Later, the Senior Salaries Review Body (SSRB).

procedures for automatically uprating pay without the need for a separate resolution of the House on each occasion. In that same year, the anomaly that ministers were not allowed to claim their full parliamentary salary on the ground that ministerial work interfered with their work as an MP was removed and they received their full salary.[102]

Between 1997 and 2011, the House periodically voted on motions that their pay be increased. The motions were usually based on the regular reports and recommendations of the SSRB. Aware of the delicacy of the politics of voting themselves a pay rise, the amount of the increases was frequently less than that recommended. At the same time, MPs increasingly came to rely on 'allowances' to address the shortfall (a new 'communications allowance' of £10,000 was voted on in 2006 and 2007 and eventually introduced in April 2007). The benefit of doing so was that these 'allowances' were loosely regulated and were not readily in the public eye.

In a major review in 2001–02, the SSRB focused particularly on pay and pensions. In debates on the SSRB's reports, the focus was on pensions and allowances. Significant changes were made to both. A fundamentally different system of separate allowances replaced the previous office cost allowance and the terms of MPs' pensions were dramatically improved. The latter was particularly controversial given the difficulties being experienced at the time by private sector pension funds.

By January 2008, with the whiff of scandal beginning to swirl around the House,[103] the unease among some MPs at setting their own pay and pensions caused the government to ask Sir John Baker, a previous chairman of the SSRB, to carry out a review:

---

102 Salaries for ministers had been introduced under the Ministers of the Crown Act 1937 and are now governed by the Ministerial and Other Salaries Act 1975.

103 Through the use of requests under the Freedom of Information Act.

to examine options and make recommendations for a mechanism for independently determining the pay and pensions of MPs which does not involve MPs voting on their own pay.[104]

He reported back in June 2008. His principal recommendation was that MPs' pay be increased each year in line with the previous year's increase in public sector average earnings. He also recommended three annual uplifts of £650, 'to put MPs' pay at what the evidence suggests is the right starting level'.

He concluded his report by warning that the House's response to his recommendations would 'have a significant impact on the climate surrounding the issue and on the calibre of the people who decide in future to enter – and remain – in Parliament'.

Both his recommendations and his warning fell on deaf ears. The government opposed the £650 annual top-up payments. Instead, MPs voted themselves a 2.5 per cent pay rise. And, significantly for what was to follow, they rejected a proposal to replace what was called the additional costs allowance. This served as an ever-growing umbrella under which MPs' expenditure could find cover. MPs also rejected the idea of putting an end to the so-called 'John Lewis list', under which taxpayers' money was used to buy such items as kitchen and household goods for second homes without the need for receipts if the value was less than £300.

The planets were aligning.

Sure enough, everything changed when the *Daily Telegraph* published information about MPs' claims for expenses that it had obtained from a leaked computer disc. The paper began its drip-feed on 8 May 2009, with details of claims made by Cabinet ministers over the

---

104   https://publications.parliament.uk/pa/cm200809/cmhansrd/cm090630/debtext/90630-0013.htm

previous four years. These were followed by similar revelations about shadow Cabinet ministers and MPs from across all parties. Members were accused, among other things, of avoiding capital gains tax, claiming mortgage payments on a mortgage that had been paid off, and 'flipping' houses – claiming the costs of refurbishing a second home, as they were allowed, then changing the designation of their main home to claim refurbishment costs on that home also.

Lengthy criminal investigations into some claims were launched by the Metropolitan Police and continued into 2010. A number of MPs faced criminal charges. The scandal spread to the House of Lords with a Conservative peer charged with theft by fraudulent accounting. Three peers were suspended and ordered to pay back thousands of pounds for expenses which had been wrongly claimed.

The expenses scandal enveloped Parliament. The consequences were devastating. The public's trust in politicians and the parliamentary system reached an all-time low. Some MPs were de-selected by their constituents, others resigned, others decided not to stand for re-election. Many repaid the money that they had been paid for expenses that they had claimed for.[105]

IPSA was created. The Constitutional Reform and Governance Act of 2010 gave IPSA the power to set pay. As a mark of recognition that their world was about to change, even before IPSA acquired its powers in relation to pay, MPs voted for a pay freeze in early 2011. IPSA continued the pay freeze in 2012. In 2013 and 2014, MPs' pay was increased by 1 per cent in line with the coalition government's policy regarding public sector pay.

Meanwhile IPSA embarked on its in-depth review into MPs' remuneration, which resulted in a series of key proposals in July 2013.

---

105 Of their own accord, or as a consequence of a review of claims carried out by Sir Thomas Legg (see footnote 66).

COMPLICATING FACTORS

In carrying out our review, there were a number of factors which complicated the analysis.

ROLE/JOB DESCRIPTION

Ordinarily, when considering how much to pay people, you have regard to what they do. It's a pretty simple point. The usual approach is to identify the role and the responsibilities entailed and a corresponding job description. As we've seen, no such job description existed in the case of MPs. Attempts to agree one were strongly resisted, usually by reference to the proposition that all MPs see their job differently and that any form of job description would inhibit the freedom of action intrinsic in the role of MP.

It might be thought that this patently self-serving approach made it that much harder to hold people to account if it's not agreed (or clear) what they are accountable for. But IPSA had no statutory power to set out what the job entailed and MPs knew this. We were in their hands. We pressed on numerous occasions for something more helpful. We explained that, in our public consultations, people frequently asked, 'What are we paying for?' and were not impressed by an answer which to them was no answer.

One approach that I instigated was to suggest that, if it was not easy to set out in detail what MPs did, it might be possible to describe in general terms what MPs saw as the key elements of their role – things which all MPs should be doing. Examples might be attending a select committee, or managing dealings with constituents in an expeditious manner. Jack Straw, who as Lord Chancellor had established IPSA, accepted the merit of our position and offered to help. Indeed, he attended a meeting of the board to discuss how to take the idea forward. But nothing came of it

OUTSIDE EARNINGS

The question of outside earnings, of having another job, has long oc-cupied the minds of MPs. The two sides of the argument were aired in a debate in the House on 11 July 1979. In favour, the Leader of the House, Norman St John-Stevas:

> The tradition of this country is of unpaid and voluntary public service ... That tradition, although it is not sustainable in the con-ditions of today, dies hard. It influences public attitudes. It seems to me that the contemporary manifestation of it is that Members should be paid, but not paid adequately. That is not a principle of great logical merit, but it is a principle of powerful effect.

By contrast, his fellow Tory, Edward du Cann thought that:

> Some people believe that no Member of Parliament should have anoth-er employment ... A few hon. Members believe that there should be no increase in the salary of Members of Parliament. There is an irony in that ... The lower we artificially keep the remuneration of Members of Parliament, the more it is necessary for them to seek work outside the House. In addition, the allowances become more significant.

Each year MPs must declare, in a register of interests kept by the House, the earnings that they have received from activities other than serving as an MP. Even though the number of MPs declaring any income is quite small and even though the amounts earned are relatively low,[106] the annual publication of outside earnings attracts

---

106 In our consultation we referred to *The Times* of 22 August 2012, which reported that sixty-eight MPs had outside income of more than £10,000, eighteen recorded more than £100,000 and the rest earned less than £10,000 or nothing.

considerable attention from the media. The message, of course, is that they are still 'on the take', earning money from outside when they should be doing their job. Of course, the message is flawed from the outset as there is no agreement as to what their job is. And there are other points that can be made. It is not unknown for people in other walks of life to earn additional income from writing or public speaking. Moreover, even if an MP were to put in a sixty-hour week, this would still leave plenty of time to do other things which might be remunerated. And MPs' outside earnings must be reported so that the media and interested members of the public are aware. This can serve as a constraint against what some would regard as excessive. If it is deemed excessive, once it is in the public domain, the ultimate mechanism of accountability – an election – can allow the electorate to express their disfavour (or otherwise). One MP, Geoffrey Cox QC, routinely topped the earnings chart, earning over £800,000 as a practising barrister in one year and close to £500,000 in another, causing him to be away from Parliament and his constituency for weeks on end. These were by far the largest sums earned. Yet, his constituents seemed unperturbed and routinely re-elected him.[107]

During our consultations, we were regularly urged to put an end to outside earnings or to set a cap which would limit earnings to a modest amount. We set out the arguments and expressed the view that outside earnings were not a matter for IPSA. We took the view that it was a matter for the House, not IPSA. If the House wanted to take action, it could do so, by adjusting the House's Code of Practice relating to registering interests, or even by bringing forward legislation. Otherwise, IPSA's position was, as in many other areas, to rely on transparency: to ensure that MPs' financial affairs were known to

---

107   He was appointed Attorney General in July 2018 and declared that he would cease private practice.

their constituents and the media. Thereafter, it was a matter for others and ultimately the electorate.

PERFORMANCE-RELATED PAY

Performance-related pay is well-known in both the public and private sector. It was urged on IPSA that we should consider it as part of our reform of remuneration. It will not come as a surprise that we rejected the idea. There are two immediate stumbling blocks: what constitutes good (or bad) performance and, even if the relevant parameters of performance could be agreed, who would do the measuring? There is, of course, an echo of the problem of the job description and the discussions that we had about identifying certain basic activities which MPs were expected to perform, whatever else they may do. Once this initiative got nowhere, there was nothing to measure. So, once again, IPSA took the view that transparency – letting the electorate know what their MPs do – was the best way forward.

There was one other form of performance-related pay which was proposed by some senior MPs led by Jack Straw, who wrote a short submission on the matter. The suggestion was that there should be various levels of pay to reflect the time served in the House. This wasn't so much performance-related as reward for long(er) service, though if the transparency point is sound it can be said (just about) that the long-serving MP must have performed to the satisfaction of constituents by virtue of having been re-elected several times. We could see very little merit in rewarding longevity for its own sake. We rejected the proposal.

IMPACT OF PAY ON THE QUALITY AND DIVERSITY OF MPs

The question here was whether in making our decisions we should take into account what, if any, impact a particular level of remuneration might have on those who might put themselves forward to be MPs. It was suggested that if pay was not of a sufficient level (whatever that might be) only people with income from other sources would be able to serve as MPs. The opposite was also, of course, put to us: that the level of pay was so much higher than that available in many jobs in the public or voluntary sector that becoming an MP might appeal to some more interested in the income than the responsibility.

A number of the bodies which had engaged with the issue of MPs' pay had offered guidance on the matter. Their 'principles', while worthy, serve as an excellent example of the 'on the one hand, but on the other hand' school of policymaking.

In the view of the Lawrence Committee in 1964:

The salary for all members, whatever their type of constituency ... [should be] such as will enable those Members who are without private means or the opportunity to earn income outside the House efficiently to discharge the duties of the service without undue financial worry and to live and maintain themselves and their families at a modest but honourable level.

The Top Salaries Review Body proposed in 1971:

The salary should be sufficient not to deter people of ability and energy, particularly those with family responsibilities, who would not be able to call on other sources of income, and to ensure the adequate representation in the House of a wide range of social, occupational, and industrial groups.

The Senior Salaries Review Body offered the following in 1979, referring to the advice received from Hays Management Consultants:

[There is a] need on the one hand to provide a salary adequate to attract or at least not to deter suitable candidates from all walks of life, while on the other not setting it so high that it should be considered over-generous and of itself become a principal reason for seeking to enter Parliament.

There was no reliable evidence to test the various views advanced. Furthermore, selection of candidates (other than those from the fringes), was carried out by the various political parties at national and local levels in accordance with criteria that they regarded as important. It was not clear what influence, if any, IPSA, through its policy on pay could or should have on this process, particularly as there appeared to be no shortage of aspirants coming forward.

We took the view, therefore, that, while it was desirable that MPs should come from an appropriately diverse range of backgrounds and be suitably qualified, it was not for IPSA, particularly through the blunt instrument of pay, to seek to affect who should be an MP.

BEHIND THE SCENES

At the outset of our deliberations on pay, I and the chief executive took the decision that, in addition to all the consultations and meetings, there were two things that we should do away from the public gaze.

MEDIA

The first was for us to meet various editors of newspapers and of the news programmes on television and radio. The aim was simple: to explain that IPSA had been handed the responsibility of addressing an historically intractable issue – MPs' pay. We wanted them to be aware of this, how we were going about addressing it, and take on board their views. Given the attention being given to the issue, it was critical that our testing of ideas, sounding out opinion-formers and 'thinking aloud' could be done in private, away from the fevered atmosphere of Westminster. We never explicitly said that we were seeing them on a confidential basis; it was assumed. And none of them broke confidence over the succeeding year and a half.

There were a number of strands to the strategy. We wanted them to understand our approach based on evidence and reasoned argument. We wanted them to be aware of the facts — what MPs earned, how decisions on pay had been made in the past, the rise of 'allowances' leading to the expenses scandal, and the need to recalibrate remuneration in all its aspects, of which pay was but one item. Secondly, we wanted to ensure that through these contacts, any discussion of decisions that we might reach later would at least be based on understanding what we were seeking to achieve and might, therefore, be sympathetic, or at least not hostile towards the enterprise, if not necessarily the outcome. Thirdly, as regards newspapers, we met the editors of the broadsheets. We surmised that the red tops (the more populist papers) would be hostile to any pay rise given their limpet-like attachment to the 'MP as crook' narrative. The aim was that by pressing the case for reasoned argument and by sharing views we might prevent Fleet Street from adopting a unified position of hostility which some feared.

We received a fair and sympathetic hearing from most whom we met. One major newspaper opposed any pay rise, but the rest saw the case for an increase in the context of a wholesale recalibration of remuneration. Indeed, most argued for increases which were strikingly generous. One editor opted for a round number of £100,000. I suggested to him that, given that MPs at the time earned £67,060, his proposal would constitute an increase of 50 per cent, which in the context of a cap on public sector pay of 1 per cent might be stretching things a little. He got the point. But he was also illustrating one of the dilemmas: a significant increase in pay may be warranted on any rational analysis, but we were in the world of politics where reason does not always prevail.

Our strategy was largely a success. When we announced our proposals in July 2013, the leader in *The Times* read:

> The proposal by the Independent Parliamentary Standards Authority (IPSA) to award a large salary increase is politically impossible. It demonstrates a lack of regard for public opinion, for the problem it gives the party leaders and for the difficulties provided by current economic circumstances. And these are all things to be said in its favour … The proposals made by IPSA are not for a single year of pay. They are proposing a one-off change to pay as part of an overall reform of terms and conditions built to last.

The red tops went on the attack, albeit only for a day or so before moving on. The rest – broadsheets, TV and radio – were more measured. The hard work had paid off.

A SOUNDING BOARD

The second thing to be done away from the public gaze was the chief executive's idea. I readily bought into it. He suggested that we (he and I) should convene a small group whom we could meet privately and discuss pay in all its aspects. There were three in the group: an MP, a senior journalist and an ex-MP who was a very successful businessman. The businessman arranged for us to meet at his office. We met on several occasions, each meeting lasting about two hours. We wanted to test ideas and hear their responses. We also wanted their views. We were greatly helped by their insights, particularly as regards the sense of the possible when it came to pay, and the management of communications. We were also helped and immensely impressed that the confidentiality of the discussions was never breached.

I also took advantage of my friendship with Alastair Campbell, Mr Blair's director of communication from 1997 to 2003 and, thereafter, a significant commentator on the ways of Whitehall and Westminster, to sound him out in early 2013 about the politics of increasing MPs' pay. He was helpful as usual, but his conclusion was blunt: 'It'll never happen.'

THE FIRST CONSULTATION

The first consultation took place in October 2012. It did not make any firm proposals. Instead, it posed questions about all aspects of MPs' remuneration. The consultation was informed by extensive research and evidence. We set out evidence on how MPs' pay compared with that of other professions, with other representative bodies in the UK and overseas and with national average earnings over the previous 100 years.[108] For example:

- A comparison of the pay of legislators in a sample of eleven countries found that the mean average was £77,189 and the median £79,566 (Ireland) compared with the UK's £67,060.
- Data on the pay of other professions, which was central to our aim of creating a modern, professional approach to remunerating MPs, notwithstanding the absence of any job description for MPs and the inherent difficulties of using comparators, suggested a salary in a range from £75,000 to £85,000.
- As regards the professions identified by the SSRB as useful comparators, MPs had slipped from 85 per cent of their average earnings in 2007 to 80 per cent in 2013.

---

108   See also the graph at Appendix VIII showing the change in MPs' pay from 1911 to 2010.

- If the various previous recommendations made by the SSRB in the early 2000s had been accepted, MPs' pay would have been between £73,000 and £79,000.
- The 100-year average ratio between MPs' pay and national average earnings was 3.16. If MPs' pay was adjusted in 2013 to reflect this ratio, it would have been £83,430.

What this evidence suggested was that MPs' pay was too low. An appropriate figure on the basis of our various analyses seemed somewhere in the region of £75,000–£85,000.

The consultation, informed by this evidence, took a number of forms. There was a conventional online consultation which produced 100 written responses in October 2012, rising to 550 by the following July. We also conducted surveys online and hosted forums on IPSA's website. YouGov and ComRes, two specialist polling organisations, were commissioned to survey public opinion. ComRes organised four focus groups and two citizens' juries in Reading and Huddersfield.

To seek to promote as much discussion as possible, we also commissioned a series of essays by guest commentators which were posted on our website; we held seminars at the Institute for Government in London; and we convened a panel of academic experts. Senior executives held briefings with both the media and MPs and I gave a number of public lectures and interviews with the media, including radio phone-ins. Apart from discussing the issues, we had a larger goal in mind. We wanted to make it legitimate to talk about MPs' remuneration, *because of* rather than *despite* the expenses scandal.

One of the most interesting exercises was YouGov's confidential poll of an appropriately weighted sample of 100 MPs. The MPs were asked what they thought MPs should earn. All of them took the view that they should be paid more than the current salary.[109] According to the poll, Conservatives favoured a salary of £96,741, Lib Dems £78,361, Labour £77,323, and others £75,091. Controlling for MPs in each party, the weighted average of the MPs' suggestions was a salary of £86,351.

What did members of the public say? The online responses varied from no salary to one of £200,000. In the former camp was someone whom I spoke to on a radio 'phone-in' who put it to me that being an MP was a privilege and that this was sufficient payment in itself. Our two citizens' juries settled on an average of just under £50,000.

There was, therefore, a significant gap between the evidence from our research, the views of MPs and the views of taxpayers. It was our job to square that circle. Doing so was made that much more challenging because of the differences of opinion within IPSA.

IPSA

It was important for me as chairman to gauge what the board, the senior executives and the staff thought. Hearing their views would serve as a source of informed opinion because they were familiar with the evidence that had been collected. It would also tell me the level of agreement or divergence within the organisation. This was not unimportant because, ultimately, I had to get the board and staff behind a decision that they would be comfortable with and could support publicly.

Well, each of the members of the board had a different view. Some were on what might be called the more generous side, based on the evidence that we had collected. Others were much less generous, opting for a somewhat 'hair-shirted' approach, keen to reflect the austerity of

---

109 Something to bear in mind when I describe their responses to IPSA's subsequent recommendations.

the times and recent history. The executive were also divided. Most favoured the lower end of the scale; some were bullishly generous. Among the staff the general feeling was that, if one criterion for an increase in pay was that it was deserved, they were inclined against an increase. They, after all, were the ones who had to deal with MPs on a daily basis and consequently had a somewhat more jaundiced view.

The critical moment was the away day that we spent in a rather down-at-heel hotel in Croydon. The first-class preparation of the executive, and their skilful management of the proceedings, which were sometimes heated but never over-heated, allowed us to resolve all of the key issues. It was a tribute to everyone that we were able to reach a view that we could all live with. We did so through reasoned argument. Positions were respected. Everyone felt able to speak. And, crucially, we did not take a vote, we just kept on talking. It is not my style of chairmanship to put things to votes. Rather, I trust colleagues to speak their minds and, if they see that they are not winning the argument, to concede. Voting creates fissures which are often difficult to repair. The respectful give-and-take of argument is preferable.

THE SECOND CONSULTATION

In July 2013, we launched a second consultation. In contrast with the first, this one contained specific proposals about all aspects of MPs' remuneration – not just pay, but pensions, resettlement payments and other benefits. Here we are concerned with pay. We recommended that MPs receive a salary of £74,000 beginning from the day of the new parliament, after the general election due in May 2015. This constituted a 10 per cent increase in pay. As may be imagined, in a context of austerity where increases in pay for those working in the public sector were limited to 1 per cent, the recommendation attracted a great deal of attention. Much of the attention was condemnatory, some belligerently so. Some commentators, however, were sympathetic – a result, perhaps, of my careful courting of elements of the media.

There were several factors that were absolutely central to our presentation of the recommendation on pay. First, it was based on evidence, reasoned argument and the various views expressed to us. Secondly, it was a one-off settlement to remedy an historical anomaly. Thirdly, it was part of a package of decisions about remuneration which, taken together, constituted a complete recalibration of MPs' relationship with taxpayers. Fourth, in the first year of its operation, it would be 'cost-neutral', which is to say that increases in some areas would be offset by cuts in others. As such, it was a good deal for taxpayers, for MPs and for the body politic.

The point about 'cost-neutrality' was very important, both financially and psychologically. In a poll carried out by ComRes in September 2013, 66 per cent said that £74,000 was too high, while 24 per cent thought it was about right. But if it was part of a 'cost-neutral' package, which it was, only 45 per cent said that it was too generous, while 40 per cent said that it was about right.

Away from the more scientific approach to gauging opinion, the recommendation on pay in our July consultation fared rather worse. While the broadsheets and the BBC acknowledged that we had produced 'a balanced package', there was considerable opposition from the red-top end of the media spectrum. As is usual, I made myself available for interview to the television and radio stations. The opening line was almost always, 'How could you recommend such a pay rise at a time like this…?' My approach was to establish a number of points whatever question was asked. These were: that there was never a 'right time'; that, as a consequence of the time never being right, we had landed in the mess exposed in 2008–09; that IPSA was given the job of sorting things out; and that sorting it out involved a package of reforms of which pay was one part. By and large, this message got through. The interviewers were challenging but measured.

That said, neither I nor IPSA escaped the particular brand of opprobrium that is poured from a considerable height by those whose chosen platform is some form of social media. I avoided it, but I was advised that it was like a convention of shouty pub bores, united in their anger at the world. My younger son drew my attention to one such example (of, he said, very many) in which a person had posted a picture of me on his Twitter account and under it had written:

> This is a photograph of Sir Ian Kennedy who wants to give MPs a 10 per cent pay rise. If you see him in the street, throw faeces at him.

The response from MPs was muted. They were mostly silent in public, whatever they might think privately, and privately most supported what we were recommending. But what of the party leaders? When I went to see them to explain what we were doing, they each (Messrs Cameron, Clegg and Ed Miliband) in their own way signalled their opposition. It was a rerun of every occasion when the SSRB had recommended an increase in pay: 'The time was not right.' The issue to them was wholly political. It was about 'handling' – presenting a particular story in a way that reflected best on them. It was not about fixing once and for all the mess that MPs' remuneration in all its aspects had become. That was for dreamers. They lived in the here and now, beset by the countless struggles that they were engaged in. Well, we were not dreamers. We had a job to do.

In December 2013, following this second consultation, we announced our recommendations. The two elements which related to pay were a one-off adjustment in salary from £67,060 to £74,000, together with a system of indexation for the following years for the duration of the next parliament. This meant that there would be an annual, automatic adjustment. The adjustment would reflect changes in income in the whole economy.[110] Indexation had several objectives. The most important was that there did not have to be a consultation on pay every year, with all the raising of temperatures involved. Secondly, it tied MPs' pay to the success or otherwise of the economy. It meant that their income would be on the same footing as those whom they represented. Thirdly, it followed that their income could go down as well as up.

POLITICS

A crucial footnote to these arrangements was that IPSA is required by statute to review pay in the first year of each new parliament. This meant that, whatever we recommended by way of MPs' pay from 2015 onwards, we still had to review pay in the year 2015/16, after the forthcoming general election in 2015. In other words, we could legitimately postpone a final, final decision till after that election.

In terms of strategy, this was of very considerable importance. We had thought that by announcing our proposals in mid-2013, eighteen months before the election, we would take the sting out of opposition to a pay rise in the media and elsewhere, long before MPs and would-be MPs began their politicking. We were wrong. As 2013 became 2014 and the months wore on, it was increasingly pressed on us that MPs were meeting hostility on the doorstep from constituents who contrasted the circumstances of public sector workers with the impending riches of MPs. We were told that we were damaging parliamentary democracy and MPs by inviting the accusation that MPs were about to dive their noses back into the trough. We were told that the public did not understand that it was IPSA, an independent body, which was proposing the

---

110 The 'whole economy' refers to pay in both the public and private sector. We subsequently changed our decision (see Chapter 11).

pay rise – the public was convinced that it was MPs themselves. We were pressed to delay implementation till things got better (the old siren song), or simply to abandon the whole idea. The latter would mean, of course, that MPs would be less well-off all round, given the reductions in pension and resettlement payments, but this was shrugged off in typical short-termist, respond-to-the-moment fashion.

But we heard a different story. What we heard was unequivocal. Whatever might be claimed, MPs' pay, in fact, barely figured 'on the doorstep'. It was the populist press, not the electorate, which was making the waves. The public were much more concerned with their jobs, the National Health Service and what future their children could look forward to in a country then entering its fifth year of austerity.

But, to prevent the issue from gaining any further traction, I drew attention to IPSA's statutory obligation to review pay after the general election. If there were MPs who were encountering pressure from constituents about pay (despite our evidence to the contrary), they had the perfect response: pay was no longer for them to decide, and, in any event, nothing about pay had been finally decided yet, nor would it be until the consultation after the election. Should they be so minded, MPs could also indicate their opposition but say that the whole matter was moot until IPSA made its mind up after the election.

In my meetings with senior figures, I explained this strategy as a means of taking pressure (largely from the media) off MPs, while signalling that, although it was unlikely that we would change our minds about the remuneration package, we could legitimately and truthfully say that we would finally make our decision after the election in the light of the circumstances then prevailing. The Prime Minister, David Cameron, got the point immediately and thought it very helpful. The Deputy Prime Minister, Nick Clegg would not see us, but the Lib Dems generally were somewhat less persuaded, torn between the clear benefit of the proposed solution and the politics of the moment which saw their party being abandoned by supporters who held them to blame for being party to the coalition government's policy of austerity.

Ed Miliband, whom I knew a little and liked on a personal level, surprised me. He completely ignored the strategic point that I was making. He simply said that he was opposed to any pay rise and therefore was against any strategy, mechanism, call it what you will, that did not make his opposition clear in the run-up to the general election. No government of which he was head, he told me, would countenance introducing a pay rise for MPs in the current circumstances. I'm not sure whether he was poorly briefed or whether this was a triumph of rhetoric over reason, but it struck me as very odd. It was a kind of knee-jerk populism, though it may have been a refusal to be drawn into tactical manoeuvres in the face of a matter of principle, as he saw it. I suppressed the temptation to respond to his first point by suggesting that the prospect of his forming a government looked at best remote on current evidence. Instead, I pointed out that it was not for government (his or anyone else's) to decide MPs' pay. That was IPSA's job. We had been given the job by Parliament. MPs had voted for it. The pass was sold. We had to do what we thought was right. I acknowledged that he might oppose what we recommended, but, short of getting rid of us, he would have to live with it. All that I was doing was merely trying to find a way whereby candidates for election and re-election could fend off the question of their pay, over which they no longer had any say. He did not seem to understand what I was saying. He didn't change his position. We parted amicably, as ever, but, for my part, I was both surprised and disappointed.

As the general election grew closer, the media increased their pressure on MPs. In response, some MPs publicly attacked IPSA for forcing a pay increase on them when it was the last thing they wanted and was so divisive in a time of austerity. In one meeting with the Parliamentary

Labour Party, one MP was sufficiently overtaken by his own rhetoric to assert that the increase in pay was, in fact, a plot by IPSA to destroy Parliament! Meanwhile, the *Daily Telegraph* was said to have contacted every MP to ask whether they would be accepting the recommended pay rise after the election. Some few, often in marginal seats, went public and stated that they would not accept it.[iii] We were sympathetic to MPs who were confronting this kind of blackmail. We had hoped that by settling matters long beforehand, the election would be fought on the issues concerning the electorate rather than the obsession of some with MPs' pay (without any mention of it being part of a package). But we were wrong.

We made it clear to all who would listen that, in any event, it was not open to MPs to accept or reject whatever pay IPSA finally decided on. There was no opting out. They would be paid what IPSA decided. This was the new constitutional arrangement. Once we had reached a final decision, the relevant amount would be paid into each MP's account. Thereafter it was for MPs to decide what to do with it, including, if they were so minded, giving the amount representing the increase in pay to a favourite charity.

THE GENERAL ELECTION OF 2015 AND THE AFTERMATH

Immediately after the election, as we had indicated, we carried out the review of pay required by the statute under which we operated. We decided to allow only six weeks for the consultation since the issues at stake and the relevant evidence had all been well and truly ventilated. We decided to ask only one question: was there any change in circumstances such as to justify departing from the recommendations that we had made in December 2013?

---

iii   Charles Walker was one of those prepared to put his head above the parapet and say that he did support the proposed increase.

While there was the usual noise on social media, the consultation did not throw up a great deal by way of reasoned argument. In its response, the government repeated its position that the time was not right for MPs to receive a pay rise. Informally, we were advised that, if we persisted in going ahead, the mechanism for indexation would be particularly problematic. Choosing to reflect movements in wages across the whole economy would mean, on current figures, that MPs would receive an annual uplift of 2–3 per cent, while public sector employees would be capped to an uplift of 1 per cent.[112] This would be very unhelpful for government and could damage IPSA's relationship not only with government but also with a sceptical public.

The board was sympathetic to the government's position. We decided to adjust the recommendation that we had made concerning indexation so as to align annual increases for MPs to those paid to workers in the public sector rather than across the whole economy. This was the right thing to do on the evidence; circumstances had changed in that the government's programme of austerity was likely to last considerably longer than initially thought. The change also demonstrated that the consultation was not an empty exercise. We were prepared to listen and to be persuaded. We were even congratulated by the government for reaching a conclusion that all could live with.

While the consultation was going on, the more indefatigable elements of the media kept up their pressure on MPs. 'Are you going to take the pay rise?' was asked, particularly of those who had condemned the increase in pay when it was first recommended. Some said that they would not accept it. Aware that it would be paid to them anyway, they indicated that they would donate it to some cause or other. As a response, we

---

112   In fact, though the government claimed that public sector pay increases were capped at 1 per cent, the real rate of increase was around 1.7–1.8 per cent because a large number of employees were entitled to annual automatic increments, such as teachers and workers in the NHS.

asked all MPs whether they wished us to send them the relevant form so that money could be paid elsewhere (it is called the 'Give-as-you-earn' scheme). In the event, less than two dozen gave us such instructions.

We announced our final decisions on MPs' remuneration, including pay, on 16 July 2015. The annual salary was increased to £74,000, backdated to 8 May, the day after the election. Annual changes to the level of pay would be linked to changes in average earnings in the public sector for the life of that Parliament.

All that remained was for me to present myself for the ritual grilling on College Green.[113] I did thirteen interviews over a couple of hours, for both television and radio. As before, whatever the question posed, I made two central points: that IPSA was putting in place the final piece of the jigsaw relating to MPs' remuneration, thereby tying pay to the larger project of reforming all aspects of MPs' remuneration; and that MPs' pay had always been a toxic subject, but with our reforms in place we had put an end to this toxicity. To those who protested that the time was not right, I reminded them that there had never been, nor would there ever be a right time. That being so, we could either sit and wait for the next disaster to occur, or act. We had acted.

IPSA had successfully recalibrated the relationship between taxpayers and MPs. It was the culmination of over three years of dedicated hard work by IPSA's staff. It took courage on occasions. But the board, the executive and the staff never wavered, even when some disagreed. When I stood down as chairman, in his parting words to me, Mr Speaker referred to the issue of pay and said that he and his fellow MPs had thought that, in his words, I would 'fold' in the face of the relentless hostility from some quarters. There was never any risk of that.

---

113   The stretch of lawn opposite Parliament where the media conduct interviews (weather permitting).

UNFINISHED BUSINESS

There was one element of the reform of remuneration which ought to be mentioned for the sake of completeness. It featured in our recommendations but failed to gain much traction.

We recommended that MPs produce a report at the end of each financial year, setting out how they had spent the money from taxpayers disbursed by IPSA. We published the budgets received by MPs. We published the claims that they made. The third part of this cycle of transparency would be for IPSA to publish annually MPs' own accounts of what had been achieved in return for the modern, professional remuneration we had put in place – what MPs had done during the year in carrying out their parliamentary functions. This, we argued, would not only improve even further their accountability; it would also achieve what was probably an even more important aim.

We had been struck during our consultations by how little many of their electorate knew about what MPs actually do. Many of those whom we spoke to assumed that being in the Chamber of the House of Commons was their principal activity. Thus, when pictures on the television news showed a sparsely populated Chamber, as is often the case, it was assumed that MPs were sloping off and not doing their job. That they could be attending committees, seeing constituents or representatives of interested parties, attending other meetings, or doing a host of other things, did not seem generally to be appreciated. Partly, of course, this was due to the fact that many MPs did not make it clear what they were up to.[114] Our view was that if we could persuade them to write a report, this would serve to inform their electorate

---

114   I remember one MP telling me that a constituent had complained that she had gone to her constituency office to see the MP but he was not there. 'I was in London,' he had replied. 'Oh! What were you doing there?' she had asked.

and, over time, generate a greater understanding of what being an MP entails and a consequent increase in respect and appreciation.

IPSA had no statutory authority to insist on it. All we could do was to urge that MPs adopt what we recommended. The proposal was met with very considerable hostility from some MPs. The Speaker, among others, denounced the idea. It would, he said, be a mechanism whereby IPSA was seeking to hold MPs to account. This patently was not the intention. It was said that we would be providing the media and those opposed to MPs with a tool to ridicule and attack them. I struggle to see how this could be so. The Labour Party, reflecting this anti-transparency mood, went so far as to instruct its MPs not to have anything to do with the proposal. I found this redolent of old ways and deeply disappointing. What we were doing was simply giving substance to the idea, espoused so frequently by the Speaker himself and others, that Parliament should be more open, and, I would add, thereby better understood.

About forty MPs embraced the idea. Many of their accounts were very informative. For the rest, it evoked little response. One reason was that it was IPSA which was recommending it, and that inevitably provoked a negative response. Secondly, a number of MPs pointed out that they already published an account of their activities on their websites and elsewhere. We responded by saying that what we had in mind was a neutral description rather than something which was more designed to advance the status of the MP than to inform the electorate. To assist in achieving this we suggested that we might agree a template of matters to be reported so that there was a common form of submission, to which the MP could then add some free text. Significantly, we were then asked by many MPs whether IPSA would meet the extra cost incurred – a lesson that old habits die hard when it comes to scenting the opportunity for another 'allowance'.

Despite the hostility from some and an initial lack of support from many, it may be that this recommendation gains momentum over time. It would be a pity if the chance was missed to improve the population's understanding of the work of Parliament and parliamentarians.

CHAIRS OF COMMITTEES

Since the reforms advanced by Tony Wright in 2007 (then MP and chair of the Public Administration Committee and subsequently a member of IPSA's board, having stepped down from Parliament in 2010), select committees of the House of Commons have a chair who is elected by MPs. One of the aims of this development was to offer a separate opportunity to develop a career in the House other than seeking to be appointed a member of the executive/government. To signal a move towards a greater professionalism, chairs of select committees were remunerated.

There is also an institution called the panel of chairs. This panel consists of MPs who chair the committee stage of proposed legislation. The duties vary. They can be onerous if a bill is complex and substantial and occupies many days of debate and deliberation. They can be less so if the bill is simple and short.

As part of our review of remuneration, IPSA had to decide whether to make any changes in the arrangements for these two categories of chair.

We agreed that the chairs of select committees should be paid a supplement to their annual salary of £15,025 per year from 2015/16. There were at the time thirty-five chairs. We agreed to keep the matter under review should the number of chairs increase significantly. Thereafter, for the life of the parliament, they would receive the same indexed increase as applied to their base pay.

As regards the panel of chairs, there was a complicated system in place whereby there were four tiers of pay. Of the thirty-four members of the panel, seventeen were in the top tier and received £15,025 (the same as chairs of select committees), while fourteen were in the lowest tier and received £3,000. The rationale for this arrangement was that it was based on length of service. But it was apparent that someone starting out could well have to chair a committee dealing with a bill of great complexity, such that the pay regime did not necessarily reflect experience. We did not see the need for the differences in pay. After consultation, we decided to pay all of the members of the panel of chairs the same amount as chairs of select committees with the same arrangements regarding indexed increases.

CHAPTER 17

CARRYING ON

I was appointed as chairman of IPSA with effect from November 2009 for a period of five years. Towards the end of 2013, I was advised by the Speaker's office that the process of recruiting a chairman would begin soon, with a view to finishing the process by the late spring of 2014 in time for an appointment in the November.

I had to decide what to do. Chairing IPSA was a pretty thankless role. The personal acrimony did not bother me greatly, though it upset my family, but the daily uphill grind of dealing with some of the MPs was tedious. Playground bullies, smart-alecks always ready with a clever put-down honed from their days in university debating societies, the eternal plotters and the just plain nasty were routinely in my face. The very many (and there were very many) decent MPs who deplored the silly railing against IPSA kept too low a profile for my liking, but, of course, quite rightly, they had decided that there were more important and pressing things to spend their time on.

On the other hand, there was still work to do if I was going to get through the wholesale reform of MPs' remuneration and guide IPSA through the forthcoming general election. IPSA's work was important in reshaping a small corner of the nation's constitutional arrangements and I wanted to see things through.

There was no point asking the Speaker to follow the well-established practice of reappointing me as chairman for a further term unless there were strong reasons not to (and there weren't). He had already shown, in his insistence that the members of the first board reapply for their jobs, that he saw the statute as allowing him to ignore standard practice and make members of the board, including the chair, jump through the hoop that he controlled (although he wouldn't have put it like that!).

I ran the risk, if I applied, of not being appointed. This would be personally disappointing. It would also be frustrating to leave work undone. That it would be seen in the wider world as rejection and failure didn't bother me too much. I'd been raised on Kipling's notion of the 'twin impostors'.[115] If I didn't apply, I would feel that I had let down my colleagues and the staff at IPSA. I had a good relationship with them and knew that they wanted me to carry on and finish what we were doing.

I decided to take the risk and apply. I indicated that I wanted to finish what I described as 'Phase I' of IPSA and usher in Phase II, which was to address three principal challenges: simplifying the scheme of business costs and expenses, overhauling completely the less than efficient IT systems and improving the service provided for MPs and their staff.

The appointment procedure followed its normal course. I got on with the day-to-day work. I applied formally. I was shortlisted for the appointment, along with, I think, four others. Since it is standard practice to shortlist the incumbent (even though standard practice was not the most reliable guide), I read nothing into this decision. Then I was called for interview.

---

115   Kipling's poem 'If—' has the well-known lines:
'If you can meet with Triumph and Disaster,
And treat those two impostors just the same'.

It was the standard interview: a short presentation (in which I set out my thoughts on the transition from Phase I to Phase II) and then questions. In the chair was Dame Denise Platt, who had an enviable reputation for fairness and integrity and lived up to that reputation in the way that she conducted matters. She knew about the circumstances surrounding the decision to require the members of the first board to reapply for their jobs. She had chaired the panel which had appointed their successors and I had sat on that panel with her. She knew, therefore, that what was going on was not usual. Rather than ignore it, she acknowledged it and then began the interview. It was an impressive and reassuring performance.

The Speaker had insisted that one member of the panel be an ex-MP, which was entirely understandable given that the job entailed dealing with MPs. The ex-MP, whether by choice or as a device to test all aspects of my suitability, played the 'bad cop' routine: 'IPSA was unpopular with MPs because of your leadership. Isn't the best way forward to get rid of you and find a more measured chairman?' I demurred. One of the lay members of the SCIPSA, Elizabeth Mc-Meikan, was also on the panel. She had always impressed me by her preparedness to listen and learn. During the interview, she seemed to understand that I and my colleagues were embarked on an exercise which involved the day-to-day, but was also grounded in a clear set of strategic objectives. In response to the ex-MP, I remarked that IPSA's plan was to move from prescription to discretion in the way that we dealt with MPs and fashioned the scheme, though the pace of doing so depended in large part on the conduct of MPs themselves. This appeared to strike a chord with Ms McMeikan. She seemed to appreciate that there was a clear strategy which allowed the board to assess IPSA's progress.

Two days after the interview, Mr Speaker telephoned to congratulate me on my reappointment. I thanked him both for the news and for his kindness in calling.

So, after this rather strange hiatus, during which I had simply carried on, I went back to carrying on. We announced the news to the board and staff and there was general relief. Ironically, given the effort that I had put into ensuring that MPs' pay should be increased, my pay remained the same as when I began in 2009. It was set by Mr Speaker at a daily rate of £700 – not a great deal given the level of responsibility, but what one expects when taking the path of public service.[116]

My reappointment had one particular feature which I had proposed and to which Mr Speaker had agreed. It was that my term of office should not run for a further five years, but rather for eighteen months. The reason was connected to the legislation introduced by the coalition government providing for fixed-term parliaments of five years.[117] Unless the five-year cycle was broken, IPSA's chair would come into office just as preparations for the next general election were in full swing. This would not be a good time to have someone new to the world of IPSA take over the reins.

My appointment, therefore, ran from November 2014 to May 2016. It meant that I could see through the package of reforms relating to remuneration, lead IPSA through the challenges of the general election (which were many) and then map out the elements of Phase II before standing down.

---

116 I claimed for the number of hours that I actually worked, which were paid for as a fraction of a standard working day of eight hours and details of which were routinely published.

117 Shown to be something of an illusion by the Prime Minister calling a 'snap' election in May 2017 only two years into the life of the parliament.

CHAPTER 18

GENERAL ELECTION OF 2015

Planning for the general election of 2015 began in earnest in early 2014. We had, in fact, already done a fair amount of planning just in case the coalition government fell and there was a snap election. We were still dealing with the package of reforms relating to remuneration as well as meeting the demands of our day-to-day activities. It was clear that we needed to recruit a senior member of staff who could take charge of planning for the election and build up and lead a dedicated team of staff. The aim was to provide as good a service as possible to MPs and the public both in the run-up to and during the election, and in the aftermath. We had to identify the tasks that we would need to carry out, plan how to do so and deliver on those plans. We were extremely fortunate in securing in Judith Toland an outstanding project director who led the team. Together, they delivered and did us proud.

To build this new team (the GE team, as we called it), we needed additional funds. At our first meeting with the SCIPSA way back in 2011, we had agreed to reduce our overall running costs by 5 per cent a year. So how were we to meet both objectives? In drawing up our budget for agreement by the Treasury and then the SCIPSA, we resorted to the approach that we had previously used in the case of the requests for the publication of receipts under the Freedom of Information Act.[118] To meet the possible avalanche of requests, we had created a separate heading for what we called 'one-off' costs. The avalanche did not materialise, but the precedent was set. 'One-off' costs, we explained, were to allow us to pursue a particular project, which we costed in detail. Once the project was completed, the funding would lapse. We asked for, and were given, around £3 million for the GE project.

In the run-up to the election, we had to ensure that MPs' claims for reimbursement were met, their accounts were settled and money that had been loaned was recovered. We immediately came across a practice which echoed the past. We had decided in our early days that office equipment, though bought by the taxpayer, became the property of the MP. To decide otherwise would have drawn IPSA into recalling computers, mobile telephones and the like and then having to dispose of them, which would probably have cost more in terms of administration than the value of the items. As a consequence of this decision, we introduced a rule that MPs could not purchase office equipment, for example computers, after a date six months prior to a general election. The aim was to ensure that MPs, particularly those standing down, could not purchase a whole lot of IT equipment at the taxpayers' expense which they could then take with them. Predictably, there was a surge of purchasing in the days before the six-month deadline. Some MPs bought several laptop computers and mobile phones. The concern was that family members were being provided for. But we had no evidence. When we challenged the purchases, we were told, with varying degrees of outrage (faux or real – who could tell?) that the several pieces of equipment were for various members of staff.

---

118   And, first of all, to meet the costs of recruiting new members of the board in the estimate for 2012–13.

For the eighteen months or so of planning for the election it was clear that we would have a significantly increased workload. We hired close to thirty new staff. By early 2014 we had embarked on an extensive recruitment campaign. We were able to recruit an enthusiastic and switched-on group of recent graduates or post-graduates. Having these enthusiastic young people around created a buzz. They were committed to public service and were excited to be involved in breaking new ground, since this was the first GE that we had been involved in managing. I spent quite a lot of time moving round the various groups, welcoming them and impressing on them the importance of their work. While I had to hint to some that they shouldn't work too late – getting the work/life balance right was important – for most there was a stampede to the local pub at around 5.30 p.m. This helped further in creating a bond between them.

The director of operations introduced her music-led team meetings, which proved a great success. Equally popular was one of the ways of training staff in how to handle dealings with MPs through role-playing. On one memorable occasion, a senior and long-standing member of the team became so immersed in her role as an MP seeking help that she stormed out of the meeting when not given the advice she wanted. The sessions prepared the staff for the range of responses they might get from potential callers. As it happens, the director of policy reported that, in fact, most MPs were courteous and grateful for the help that we provided, which hadn't always been available in the past.

Over the months, our big conference room was slowly transformed. Every wall was covered by diagrams, flow-charts and yellow Post-it stickers. Dates, weeks and months were ticked off. A report on progress was a standing item on the board's agenda as a mechanism for assuring ourselves that we were on track to deliver. Looking beyond the myriad details which had to be addressed, there were three key concerns which were central to everything we were doing. The first was MPs' staff. The second was money – payment to MPs or recovery of money from them. The third was the need to provide MPs with an appropriate level of service.

STAFF

When Parliament was prorogued (the official term used to describe the end of a parliamentary session), MPs and their staff continued to receive their salaries and MPs could still claim for costs and expenses until the election. Once it had been held, there was then a two-month 'winding-up' process for those MPs who had not sought re-election or had not been re-elected, for which MPs received a specific 'winding-up budget'. As regards their staff, the non-returning MPs had to declare them redundant. IPSA offered to assist MPs in the process. This was appreciated by many. But there was a determined group of MPs who decided to play the system on behalf of their staff. While the loyalty to their staff was commendable, the manoeuvring was not. It sailed far too close to the wind. It revolved around what is known as PILON (payment in lieu of notice). PILON exists, as the name suggests, to allow an employer to pay an employee a sum of money for the time equivalent to that period of time otherwise required as a notice period, without the need to serve the notice period. If the employer (MP) delays giving notice, the member of staff may no longer have a job and so may not be able to serve a period of notice. PILON then kicks in.

Some MPs, of course, may have delayed giving notice simply because their minds were elsewhere, notwithstanding their obligation to protect the public purse. But this may not always have been the case. Two separate issues arose. As regards MPs who were retiring, the date of the election had been known for some long time. They could have wound up their offices in good time before the election. But many didn't. So staff needed to stay on (and get paid) to help with the process of winding up. Secondly, and this was the case as regards both MPs who were retiring and those who were not re-elected, some MPs delayed giving notice to their staff until late in the process of winding up in order to maximise the opportunities of staff to take advantage of PILON.

This was a clear breach of the trust owed to taxpayers by those MPs who purposely played the system. As part of the review of our performance in delivering the GE that the board requested, I was particularly concerned that IPSA should identify how much this activity cost the taxpayer. The review was still under consideration when I stepped down as chairman, but clearly there were lessons to be learned.[119] Equally clearly, there were disturbing echoes of previous preparedness to put the interests of MPs (and their staff) above those of the taxpayer.

MONEY

The next area to be addressed was money. The issues were complex. First, MPs had to submit all their claims for reimbursement and we had to settle them. Not only was this challenging in operational terms (namely, getting MPs to do things in a timely manner), but there were questions of accounting because the relevant period of time straddled two financial years.

Then there were loans to be paid back. At the start of IPSA's operations in 2010, we had extended a significant number of interest-free

---

119 The review, called The General Election Assurance Report, published after I had left, found that IPSA paid out £648,000 of PILON of which between £380,000 and £435,000 could have been avoided through timely notice. Even more concerning was the £743,000 of payments for holiday time not taken: http://www.theipsa.org.uk/media/184539/general-election-2015-administrative-lessons-report-version-published-on-website-apr-16.pdf

loans to MPs to deal with such matters as deposits on property or the purchase of equipment. At the end of 2014, we reminded MPs that the loans would have to be repaid before they stood down. This came as a surprise to some who had either forgotten that they had taken out the loan or hoped that we had forgotten. We hadn't. It was not an easy exercise to gather in the money owed, but it was done. For those who dragged their heels, we made it clear that we would withhold any money owed from the payments that they would otherwise receive on standing down or from their salaries or budgets in the next parliament. The money was ultimately recovered, but it took tact, toughness and perseverance in equal measure.

Next was the question of what had previously been known as the 'resettlement allowance'. We had announced the phased ending of this 'allowance' in our package of reforms in July 2013. Those standing down and not contesting the next election would no longer qualify for any payment. For the election of 2015, those who stood for re-election and lost would receive one month's salary for every year served up to a maximum of six years. From 2020 onwards, MPs who stood but were not re-elected would receive what we restyled as the Loss of Office Payment (LOOP). It would amount to twice the statutory redundancy pay, provided that they had served at least two years as an MP.[120]

A further tranche of money which was included in our package of reforms was called the winding-up payment. This was a budget amounting to two months' worth of MPs' combined staffing and office budgets. As the name suggests, it was intended to enable MPs to do all the various things that have to be done in winding up their activities as MPs, such as closing down their offices and moving out

---

120 This proved to be problematic when the Prime Minister called a snap election in 2017. Though two years had just about elapsed since the 2015 election, it meant that one MP received nothing and quite a few got very little.

of their rented accommodation. Included in the package was a return trip to Westminster. Some MPs complained that the money made available was not enough, though the subsequent assurance report on the general election[121] showed that MPs on average spent only 57 per cent of the available budget.

SERVICE

The further area of concern to IPSA was that In the run-up to and during the election we should provide as good a service as possible in what were challenging times for MPs. The GE necessarily produced three categories of MP for whom IPSA had to be concerned: those not standing for re-election, those standing but not re-elected and those re-elected. There is, of course, a fourth category, the new MP, but we would meet them only after the election.

The aim was to meet all of the MPs who had declared that they would not be standing for re-election and take them through the various matters which had to be dealt with. The number grew over the weeks as the GE approached; from the mid-thirties initially to the final total of ninety. Arrangements were made to meet each of them individually, brief them on what needed to be done and offer support (for example, as regards pensions). The plan worked very well. Problems were ironed out. Many of the MPs involved expressed their thanks. It was a good example of IPSA moving into the mode I had described as Phase II, of which the aim was for IPSA to provide the kind of service that MPs were entitled to expect.

It was significantly more challenging to deal with the second group of MPs – those who were not re-elected. They were, of course, hugely disappointed. Not unnaturally, IPSA and its concerns were the last

---

121   See footnote 119 and the report: http://www.theipsa.org.uk/media/184539/general-election-2015-administrative-lessons-report-version-published-on-website-apr-16.pdf

things on their minds. Moreover, expecting or hoping to be re-elected, they had usually made no arrangements for the other option. We made every effort to reach out to them, to explain what needed to be done, and to brief them in one-to-one meetings. But, unsurprisingly, things did not always go smoothly. The lessons to be learned by IPSA – and there were a good number – were set out in the review that the board commissioned. They were intended to inform IPSA's approach to sub-sequent general elections.

As for the newly elected MPs, IPSA arranged for each of them, whether returning or new, to receive a package of information. Obvi-ously, in the excitement and euphoria of the moment, IPSA was not on their minds. What we had to do was to draw attention to the fact that they would need, and be entitled to receive, funds which were available through IPSA. We also had to make it clear that they had to present themselves in Portcullis House so that we could take them through the process of induction and collection of their details so that we could pay them. Beyond that, they could read all the information about the scheme of expenses and other IPSA-related materials at their leisure.

Several days were set aside for this process. IPSA worked closely with the administration of the House of Commons so as to coordinate operations. Previously, relations with the House were not always easy, as IPSA was regarded with suspicion. A feeling of resentment – that they had unfairly been blamed for the expenses scandal (though not by us) and that IPSA had taken 'their' work – simmered below the surface. Through the outstanding leadership of the director of the GE programme and the wholehearted commitment of officials from the House, hatchets were buried and cooperation flourished. This was a significant breakthrough and one which greatly helped MPs in their navigation of the complex, even arcane world that they were entering.

To signal to the staff how important these first few days of contact with MPs were in setting the tone for future dealings, I asked colleagues on the board to try to attend one of the various inductions – groups of around thirty MPs were given a time to attend. MPs were each assigned a member of staff who took them through the details of what needed to be done. On day one I was told that 170 of the 182 new MPs were seen, a remarkable achievement. I went to a particularly memorable early afternoon session. MPs were slowly trickling in.[122] Then, suddenly, the peace was broken by the appearance of close to thirty-five of the newly elected SNP MPs. They were in high spirits. They'd already been up in the Chamber challenging protocol by taking selfies. Now they were ready for us. They had none of the shadows of the previous scandal hanging over them. They were an immensely generous and happy bunch of people. They went through the process of induction with patience, good humour and courtesy. For a while, at least, they were a pleasure to deal with...

---

122 Boris Johnson showed up in regulation cycle helmet and clips and was shown to his election contact. He was soon on the telephone – he hadn't brought any of the relevant details.

CHAPTER 19

PHASE II

I began to use the expression Phase II (or IPSA 2.0) from the middle of 2014 onwards. It signalled that once we had settled the package of reforms relating to remuneration and dealt with the significant operational challenges represented by the general election, IPSA would move into Phase II. With both of these done and dusted, what did I have in mind?

In short, reference to Phase II was intended to indicate a new start. It was as much rhetorical as practical. It was a signal that IPSA was now a mature organisation. It would behave accordingly. This meant learning lessons and making changes as well as building on what had been achieved. By the middle of 2015, IPSA had gone through one entire parliamentary cycle. It was important to analyse our performance and ask others for their views. There were lessons to be learned and we needed to identify them.[123] This would provide the bridge to Phase II.

As for Phase II, we created a programme which we called IPSA 2017. It set out what we planned to achieve by the end of that year.[124] We

---

123 Hence the assurance report referred to in footnote 119.
124 Which would be eighteen months after my stepping down. I was concerned to lay the groundwork.

deployed Judith Toland, who had made such a success of the general election programme, to take charge and drive it forward. There were three key elements:

- simplifying the scheme of expenses;
- updating the IT systems;
- providing a better service to MPs, their staff and the public.

SIMPLIFICATION

The director of policy had long been calling for a systematic review of the scheme of expenses with a view to making it simpler to understand and operate. There was no doubt that it was too complex. Decisions made in the early days when we felt the need to be prescriptive (and many MPs preferred having some rules to follow), combined with additions to plug this or that gap or make this or that adjustment, had contrived to produce through a process of accretion a scheme which demanded far more time for reading and study than MPs and their staff should be expected to devote.

The scheme needed a root-and-branch overhaul. This also allowed us to get rid of some rules which had outlived their usefulness or were creatures of their time. The director of policy attacked the task with enthusiasm. He and his team were the ones who had to guide the operations staff in IPSA through the sometimes labyrinthine rules. They also had to field many of the questions and complaints from MPs and their staff.

The result of his work was a very significant simplification of the scheme. The rules relating to reimbursement for travel were a particular target. Initially, not least because of pressure from the National Audit Office, which insisted (quite rightly) that money was properly accounted for, the rules were detailed and complex. A number of changes were made. For example, the rules on travel by members of staff were brought into line with the rules for MPs; MPs could claim for travel by their spouses, a change which was much appreciated by Scottish MPs; the definition of travel to Europe was simplified and the cap on the number of journeys removed; and a number of somewhat pettifogging restrictions were removed, such as placing a limit on the cost of a journey by taxi in circumstances where the journey was allowed by the rules (the simplified approach was that if you needed to get home by taxi, you needed to get home by taxi). Another area of simplification was the decision to allow MPs greater discretion in claiming for office costs by being less prescriptive in policing the boundaries between the parliamentary and the political. The underlying principle of transparency – that claims for expenditure would be published – had become such an entrenched feature of the scheme that IPSA had the confidence to make these and a number of other wide-ranging changes.

This process of simplification has been welcomed both internally and by MPs, although the preceding consultation document was not universally well-received. In the spirit of open-mindedness and to ensure that a broad range of options was at least put forward for consideration even if it might not meet with widespread approval, the document reopened some old issues such as the provision of accommodation for MPs and the employment of relatives and 'connected parties'. It also offered one or two radical solutions. This is what consultations are about, but I am told that in a particularly bad-tempered meeting, one MP described the document as the 'literary equivalent of a punishment beating'. *Plus ça change*!

UPDATING THE IT SYSTEMS

IT systems and the public sector have become almost a music-hall joke. Projects are abandoned at great cost. Budgets rise and rise.

Things routinely don't work as they were supposed to. The inept civil servant, unworldly in the ways of commerce, is pitched against the wheeler-dealer salesperson, adept at making snake oil look like champagne. And so on, and so on.

We were aware of this background. I had some experience, having delivered an IT system for the Healthcare Commission which was on time and within budget and which, most importantly, did the job, and we did so again in setting up the first online system for IPSA (even if it was a bit clunky). I was very keen that we husbanded the taxpayer's resources and did things with due care. We were forced to act in haste in setting up IPSA's IT system – hence the clunkiness. This time, I wanted us to get it right.

But things were not going to be straightforward. Central to the design of a new IT system was a clear understanding of the tasks which it would have to perform. This meant that we needed a clear understanding of the scheme and its future operation. So, in theory at least, there were two approaches that we could adopt. We could wait until all the deliberations and consultations on changes to the scheme had been completed before redesigning the IT systems to reflect the new way of business. This would mean that we would have to operate the new scheme using the existing IT systems for however long it took – perhaps two or three years – before the new IT system was operational. This would be problematic. The whole point of a simplified scheme was that more and more could be routinised, depending on data and the analysis of norms or patterns of behaviour and deviations from them. This would be several bridges too far for the existing IT systems. The alternative approach was to begin the redesign of the new IT system in tandem with the redesign of the scheme of expenses. This would be a risky exercise calling for careful leadership and constant communication. It could only work if those responsible for the IT system were given some comprehensive view, at least in outline, of what the system would have to do for the scheme to operate. Otherwise, there would have to be some sort of step-by-step approach which simply would not work in the context of designing a whole new IT system. The conundrum was slowly being resolved as I left.

PROVIDING A BETTER SERVICE

Phase II was intended to signal that IPSA was now a mature regulator and was keen to build an increasingly mature relationship with MPs and their staff, in which distrust (and even dislike) could be replaced over time by mutual respect and understanding. The history of the previous five years suggested that this would not be easy, but times had changed. IPSA had achieved the two principal challenges that we were set: a scheme of expenses that regulated transparently the expenditure by MPs of taxpayers' money; and the settlement of MPs' pay in the context of a complete reform of their remuneration. The future would be one of fine-tuning the scheme and listening to MPs to understand any concerns that they might have and how IPSA might respond. We had already started to bring together small groups of MPs to test possible innovations. This, I thought, should be a major means of maintaining contact and building trust. As I stepped down, these and many other ideas were being explored and taken forward.

A MEASURE OF SUCCESS

It is for others to decide what sort of fist I made of setting IPSA up and guiding it through its first six years. For my part, one of my principal ambitions, shared by my colleagues on the board, was to take the issue of MPs' expenses and remuneration out of the headlines. We wanted the media, the public and MPs to see that the challenges thrown up by the scandal of 2008–09 were behind us. A system had been put in place which, while always amenable to improvement, was working in the interests both of the taxpayer and MPs.

We wanted to arrive at the point where MPs' expenses and IPSA were no longer something for the front page – perhaps a piece on p. 23 in a slow news week. I think we made pretty good progress.

EPILOGUE

A LETTER TO MR SPEAKER

On 18 January 2018, I wrote a letter to the Speaker of the House of Commons, which I made public. It began:

Dear Mr Speaker,

May I first thank you and your Committee for accepting the unanimous recommendation of the independent appointment committee that I be appointed a member of the Electoral Commission. I was disappointed by the vote in the House this evening rejecting your committee's recommendation.

IN THE BEGINNING

In the autumn of 2017, I was asked whether I wished to apply to fill the recent vacancy on the Electoral Commission. There were (and still are) widespread concerns about interference through hacking and cybercrime in elections across Europe and the United States of America. There were (and still are) concerns about the funding of organisations involving themselves in elections and referendums. There were (and still are) concerns about the reliability of postal votes. These are important matters. I thought that my background might enable me to make a contribution towards addressing them. So, I said that, yes, I would apply.

The usual process associated with applying for a job in the public sector then began. It's a lengthy process.

The recruitment specialists recommended me to an independent appointment committee, established by the Speaker. I was called for interview. The appointment committee was chaired by Joanna Place, the chief operating officer of the Bank of England. She was joined by Sir John Holmes, the chair of the commission, and Bridget Phillipson MP, a member of the Speaker's Committee on the Electoral Commission.

After interviewing the shortlisted candidates, the appointment committee made a unanimous recommendation to the Speaker that I be appointed. He in turn put this recommendation to the Speaker's committee. They accepted it. The Speaker then, as required by the law establishing the commission, wrote to the leaders of the various political parties – including the Prime Minister – advising them of his recommendation and seeking their views. They all accepted his recommendation.

Just one further step remained to be taken. The relevant legislation gives the last word to MPs. This is done through a rather arcane procedure called a humble address. A member of the government, usually the Leader of the House, moves that the recommendation be referred to a committee of the House, where it can be approved without coming back to the floor of the House (I know, but pay attention!). This procedural device can be thwarted if an MP shouts 'object'. The recommendation has then to come back for another go. In my case, a couple of MPs shouted 'object' on the first occasion. So, back it came for a second time. This time there were several voices raised to shout 'object'.

What to do? The only way to get my appointment approved at that point was to bring it to the floor of the House. The procedure provides for a debate of up to ninety minutes, after which there is a vote. And so there was a debate (of sorts). There was then a vote. The recommendation that I be appointed, which had gone through so many stages, was defeated by seventy-seven votes to forty-six (there are 650 MPs, so less than 20 per cent of them thought it worth bothering with). So, that was it. I was not going to become a member of the Electoral Commission after all.

THE ROAD TO REJECTION

I had received the first warning that the path to my appointment would not be smooth when a colleague drew my attention to an article in the Huffington Post which appeared on 3 January 2018:

> MPs Block Ex-IPSA Chief Sir Ian Kennedy From New Watchdog Post As 'Revenge' For Expenses Crackdown.
> Labour and Tory backbenchers team up to halt new appointment.

As it happens, the team at the Electoral Commission had just made contact: the next meeting of the commission was scheduled for late January 2018. The suggestion was that I might be able to attend if Parliament acted swiftly in approving my appointment. Otherwise, if it took more time, I could attend as an observer. They also wanted to run past me the press statement that the commission was preparing to release, announcing my appointment. I suggested that they hold fire, suspecting that there could be trouble ahead.

According to Paul Waugh, the highly respected journalist who wrote the story in the Huffington Post, a number of grounds were cited by MPs to justify their action, the burden of which was that I had made their lives uncomfortable and I was to be punished. They included:

One senior MP told HuffPost UK that 'revenge' was one way of describing the move to block Kennedy's appointment.

'He threw bucketloads of shit over us after the expenses affair. Well, as they say in Australia: 'nobody comes off the rugby pitch with a clean Guernsey [jersey], mate'.

'What does he know about elections anyway? He has no knowledge or experience of elections. He's just a quangocrat.'

As their parting shot, Paul Waugh reported, 'Kennedy is also blamed by MPs for forcing a 10% pay rise on them, a highly unpopular move that put up salaries to £74,000, and which led several MPs to hand the extra cash to charity.'

Crocodiles and tears come to mind.

All of these grounds were spurious. Moreover, of course, they had nothing to do with membership of the Electoral Commission. This was just a display of power. The MPs were getting their own back because they could.

THE 'DEBATE'

After the second 'object', my proposed appointment was brought to the floor of the House. It was a surreal privilege to have up to ninety minutes of parliamentary time dedicated in some measure to trashing my reputation.

Things began courteously, but soon began to go downhill. An outside visitor may well have asked whether there were not other more important things to spend valuable parliamentary time on. But there are no limits to the lengths to which some MPs will go when it comes to what they see as assaults on their exceptionalism. Pettiness plumbed new depths. While the comments in the Huffington Post were unattributed, the protection of parliamentary privilege allowed the likes of James Duddridge MP and John Spellar MP to come out into the daylight.

The story of IPSA was one of righting a ship that had crashed on the rocks, a crash wholly caused by MPs themselves. But Spellar demonstrated through his intervention how some MPs do have a way with hyperbole and injured righteousness.

The MP who was a member of the appointment committee, Bridget Phillipson (Labour), defended the rigour of the process of recruitment and appointment and confirmed that I was the strongest candidate. This latter fact merely moved Mr Spellar to wonder about the process of making appointments such as these. He did not go further, so it was not entirely clear what he had in mind but it's even money that he was saying that any process which produced me as the answer was, by that very fact alone, a flawed process.

WHERE WAS THE ELECTORAL COMMISSION?

During all of this saga, where was the Electoral Commission and particularly its chairman? Well, apart from a couple of emails to me from the chairman, Sir John Holmes, describing what was going on, there was radio silence. It was a curiously passive performance. The integrity of the process of making appointments to an independent body was being undermined. I expected more to be done to protect this process if not me.

PETER OBORNE

Oborne had previously commented on IPSA in an article he wrote on 15 December 2011 on Open Democracy:

> I have relatively few political heroes, but one is Elizabeth Filkin, who briefly served as parliamentary commissioner for standards a decade ago. She was appointed to her post in the wake of a wave of

notorious financial scandals, mainly involving Conservative politicians. Her job was to clean up politics.

Filkin's mistake was to take her job description literally. She exposed an appalling pattern of bullying, arrogance and greed at the heart of Westminster. MPs were appalled.

However, instead of punishing the malefactors, they turned their fire on Filkin herself, using threats, malicious gossip and a campaign of media vilification in order to rub her out. It was an all-party effort – the Labour, Tory and Lib Dem whips offices were all gleeful participants – that soon made sure she was out of a job.

In retrospect, Elizabeth Filkin was the canary in the mine … Years were to pass before, thanks to the vigilance of the *Daily Telegraph*, voters learnt the hideous truth about the lies, thievery and moral corruption of so many MPs.

Today, history is repeating itself. Shamed by the expenses scandal, Parliament was forced to create an external body, the Independent Parliamentary Standards Authority (Ipsa), to regulate the payments. From the start, MPs bitterly resented having to submit their claims to it for authorisation, just as a decade ago they hated Filkin.

Their assault on Ipsa, which began within weeks of it starting operations in May last year, has taken place on a number of levels. First, in an echo of the vindictive campaign of character assassination aimed at Mrs Filkin, senior Ipsa personnel have been targeted. Both the chairman, Sir Ian Kennedy – a hard-working and decent man, committed to public service – and his admirable chief executive, Andrew McDonald, have been the subject of vicious attack.

In response to the story in the Huffington Post, he wrote a piece in the *Daily Mail* on 6 January 2018, clearly intended as a shot across the bows of those MPs aiming to 'take revenge':

MPs are set to mount a revenge attack on Sir Ian Kennedy, who used to regulate their expenses when he was head of the Independent Parliamentary Standards Authority. Vindictive back-benchers cannot forgive the way he stopped them feathering their own nests.

Now, they are plotting to stop him being appointed to the board of the Electoral Commission. I can think of no one more appropriate than Sir Ian — a man of genuine integrity — to run this independent body.

But how contemptible of these vindictive MPs to try to stop this worthy man fulfilling a vitally needed public role. Truly, it is impossible to exaggerate the low calibre of many MPs from all political parties.

On Saturday 27 January 2018, after the vote in the Commons, Oborne wrote in his column in the *Daily Mail*:

The horrific scale of the Commons expenses scandal exposed, in a deeply depressing way, the extent of decay of integrity in public life.

However, it seems that many still think they did nothing wrong — and, worse, harbour a bitter grudge against those who exposed them.

This became clear this week when the Commons voted to block the distinguished public servant Sir Ian Kennedy from being appointed to the board of the Electoral Commission, the body charged with ensuring fair elections.

The snub looks like a cynical and sordid act of revenge.

THE TWITTERSPHERE

My younger son, who acts as a lookout from time to time when the temperature around IPSA or other activities is high, told me that there was some traffic on Twitter. Besides MPs, it included the journalist Tim Shipman, whose considerable self-regard must have persuaded him that here was an opportunity to exact some revenge for his failing to bring me to heel in our first encounter in that meeting with the lobby all those years ago.

OF WRESTLING AND PIGS

On reflection, I confess that I'm with George Bernard Shaw:

> I learned long ago, never to wrestle with a pig. You get dirty, and besides, the pig likes it.

LAST WORD

Oh, a last word. Mr Speaker's clerk assured me that he would wish to reply to the letter that I sent him. Clearly second thoughts prevailed. I still await his response.

APPENDIX I

A TRIBUTE TO ONE AND ALL

I would be remiss if I did not record my gratitude to those I worked with at IPSA over the several years.

THE BOARD

My thanks must first go to my colleagues on the board. We were a small group, five in all. We got on. We worked hard. We felt that we were doing something important. We accepted that brickbats would be thrown at us. We were surprised sometimes by what came our way, but we kept at the centre of everything we did the fact that we were there to clean up a mess and put in place a system that would serve both taxpayer and MP.

The Parliamentary Standards Act stipulates that three of the four members of the board (other than the chair) must be respectively: ex-MP, someone qualified to be an auditor for the National Audit Office and a retired holder of high judicial office. In the category of ex-MP, Jackie Ballard gave us valuable insights into the life of an MP as we were finding our feet. She was followed by Tony Wright, a distinguished writer on politics, author of 'The Reform of the Select Committees of the House of Commons' and chair of the House of Commons' Public Administration Committee for eleven years. He was tenacious in argument but utterly committed to reaching decisions that everyone could live with. This generosity of spirit endeared him to all. In turn he was followed by John Thurso. John's appointment came at a time when IPSA was ready to reset itself. We had served one whole parliamentary term and managed a general election – a significant challenge. We were now ready to catch our breath, take stock and try to do a number of things better, not least replace our inadequate IT systems and improve the quality of the administration of the services that we supplied to MPs. John's appointment was opportune. Before becoming an MP, he had had a distinguished career in the hotel and service industry and in finance: just the man to help us to become more user-friendly. But fate intervened in the form of the death of an elected member of the House of Lords. John, as Viscount Thurso, was urged to stand for election to take up the vacated seat in the Lords. Unsurprisingly, he won. So, he was lost to IPSA.

In the category of auditor, Professor Isobel Sharp took a somewhat puritanical line as we began our work. She was succeeded by Anne Whitaker, who built on what had gone before and, in particular, put the management of our finances on a firmer basis. She also chaired the very important Audit and Risk Committee with great skill, not least in steering us through occasionally choppy waters. Most importantly, quite apart from her financial skills, she brought a breadth of vision and experience which we all greatly benefited from.

The third category was, in effect, a judge of the High Court or the Court of Appeal. It was invaluable to have as a colleague someone whose career had been dedicated to the evaluating of evidence and reaching conclusions based on that evidence. It was also an advantage in that the judge could act on behalf of the board as the 'qualified person' under the Freedom of Information Act 2000 in dealing with requests for the disclosure of information under the act and whether the exemption set out in section 36 applied.[125] In some ways, the appointment was challenging. IPSA worked in the messy, untidy world of politics in which most problems were wicked ones. Judges ordinarily tended not to have much experience of this type of world. So, it was important to appoint as the judicial member someone who had experience of the world beyond the law and the law courts. We were fortunate in being able to secure such members: first, Sir Scott Baker, who had presided over the inquest into the death of Diana, Princess of Wales; then Sir Neil Butterfield, who had served for a number of years on the parole board and was its deputy chairman; and then Sir Robert Owen, who joined the board directly after chairing the inquiry into the murder of Alexander Litvinenko.

All three of the judicial members were of enormous value. One particular quality born of their life on the bench shone through. They were professional listeners. They read their papers diligently and then listened to the presentations made by the executives and the views of their colleagues. And then they would speak, but only when they had something to say – a priceless gift! And, of course, their views were always worth hearing.

It is fair to say that the judicial members found MPs as a group rather a rum bunch. As with all colleagues on the board, they 'shadowed' MPs to get a flavour of what life at Westminster and the constituency was like. The impression gained was not always favourable. But, of course, judges work in a particular way. Walking through a supermarket saying hello to shoppers and listening to their gripes may not have appeared particularly onerous nor rigorous. But it's part of politics, connecting with the electorate, being seen and giving up your weekends when you'd much rather be doing a million other things.

---

125   That information need not be disclosed if doing so would prejudice 'the effective conduct of public affairs'.

The fourth member of the board was the one who did not have to be selected from a designated category. As the first occupant, Ken Olisa, was wont to remark that he was there to represent the interests of the rest of the UK's 60 million population who weren't ex-MPs, auditors or judges! Ken came to the board with a distinguished record in business in the technology sector and as an investment banker. He was tough-minded and personified IPSA's pursuit of evidence and reason to substantiate any position that we might take. He earned the disapproval of some MPs because of his preparedness to speak his mind and to remember those who were outside the Westminster bubble; that, after all, was why he was on the board. I found him a delight to work with. We were fortunate that Ken was succeeded by Liz Padmore, an experienced management consultant and non-executive who was also chairing an NHS Hospital Foundation Trust. She continued Ken's commitment to testing arguments and seeking evidence and reasons. She also chaired the internal Remuneration Committee with the necessary care given the context in which we worked. Overall, she contributed greatly to the mood of mutual support, energy and commitment which characterised the second board.

GETTING AWAY

As part of our way of operating, from time to time we scheduled what we called strategy meetings. Some were for half a day, others a whole day. Usually, for reasons of cost and convenience, they were held in our offices. In the early days, they were often tetchy as members of the first board differed considerably in the approach that we should take, some preferring a more prescriptive (some might say punitive) method. They took some persuading when it came to spending taxpayers' money, with the expenses scandal still fresh in everyone's memory. The strategy meetings were normally led by the senior executive in charge of policy, John Sills. He did a formidably able job in bringing positions together and proposing solutions.

It is a common practice for boards to get away from the office on occasions and spend half a day or more with executives talking about future plans and how to realise them. IPSA organised one such away day in April 2013 with the members of the second board. It was for a day and a half in a hotel outside Croydon. It was no lavish session in some luxurious watering hole. We were spending taxpayers' money. 'Spartan' was the order of the day. The board agreed, however, that when lunch consisted of soggy chips and bread rolls covered by mountains of rocket, we might have taken 'spartan' a bit too far. Indeed, the venue as a whole had a sense of faded gentility where nothing quite worked. But it was cheap!

The executive presented papers. This was particularly important for me as chairman. It meant that I could participate more actively in discussion. It meant also that members of the executive could take positions and argue their merits as one of the group rather than setting out options and standing back. Given the high quality of our senior executives, this was invaluable. They were not only on top of the details of the issue at hand, but also brought considerable experience of the ways of Whitehall and Westminster and of how to navigate our way through them.

The away day in Croydon was a resounding success. A large number of issues relating to pay and pensions were thrashed out in an informal setting. It was particularly useful in enabling us to get our heads around the complexities of different forms of pensions. By the time that we broke up after lunch on the second day we had answered all the key questions and decided on the way forward. The executive had worked hard. The board had worked hard. It paid off.

On another occasion, in April 2015, although we did not go away, we spent the day away from our desks. As part of the process of getting everyone ready for the general election of 2015, the director of policy and the director of operations had the idea of getting the board to play the role of the various categories of MPs – not standing for re-election, defeated, re-elected and elected for the first time – and their staff. We were suitably rehearsed in advance. Our staff then had to deal with the sort of questions that the various categories of MPs might raise. They also had to deal with the variations in mood which would be an inevitable part of the process. Sir Neil Butterfield, the ex-judge, who was cultivating a burgeoning career in amateur dramatics in deepest Devon once he had stepped down from the Bench, took to the exercise like a duck to water.[126] It was a great success, not only in identifying issues that still needed to be addressed, but also in bringing everyone together at a time when we all needed to be on top form. We finished with an open-ended question time, with staff firing questions at members of the board, not just about the election, but about all aspects of IPSA's work and strategy. This too was a success, not least in showing the range of opinion on the board and how we worked out solutions.

UPS AND DOWNS

As chairman, I was keen to foster some sense of collegiality in the board. To this end, I invited the first board to my house and laid on dinner early in the winter of 2011. It was a success. Ken Olisa remarked that it beat spending half a day with a 'relationship expert'. It was also very convivial. Ken and his wife then entertained us all in the summer at his lovely house in Ham. Some garden furniture collapsed, but otherwise it went very well. Isobel Sharp entertained us to dinner

---

126 He was able to draw on his experience as a struggling young barrister who during pupillage supplemented his income by performing as a conjurer at children's parties under the name of 'Uncle Neil, the cheeky trickster'!

at her offices at Deloitte. It was a somewhat subdued affair during which Jackie Ballard memorably took against a poached egg.

Unsurprisingly, all was not always sunshine and light, particularly in the early years. The challenges we'd been set were tough enough, but there was also an undercurrent of tension between some members of the board and the executive. From the very early days, it had become clear that a couple of members of the board held to the view that our senior executives, being ex-civil servants (or on secondment), could not really be relied on to give unvarnished advice. Their default position, it was argued, was to reflect the views and needs of government. In this way, IPSA's independence was at risk.

It was bad enough to have to manage the sniping of MPs and the media. Having to deal with internal rumblings was not something I could allow to gain traction. The criticisms and doubts were entirely without foundation. A passing acquaintance with the ways of civil servants, if they were to be regarded as such (which was itself inappropriate), would make it clear that they served whatever agenda was advanced by their current leaders. They might demur, or roll their eyes and describe some idea or proposal as 'ambitious', but they got on with what was asked for. IPSA's executives were no different. Indeed, the director of policy spent a year or so and a number of bruising encounters with MPs defending positions which he personally thought from the outset were misbegotten (such as the initial notion that IPSA would only reimburse 80 per cent of MPs' telephone bills and our initial approach to accommodation for MPs' and their families).

Given that relations were strained, the chief executive proposed a form of away day which, sadly, was not a success. I decided that the air needed to be cleared. It was agreed that we would convene on a Saturday morning at 10 a.m. at the house of one member of the board on the outskirts of London and spend the morning and lunchtime confronting the various strands of unhappiness and dealing with them. The meeting was to end at 2 p.m. It was to be chaired by a 'coach' at the suggestion of the chief executive. The consensus was that only he, of the senior executives, would be invited.

The meeting was, by any account, awful. The facilitator or coach in explaining what was in store made the cardinal error of validating all the prejudices of those on the board who were opposed to the idea in the first place and certainly didn't want to talk about themselves and others as if it were a meeting of Alcoholics Anonymous.

The board were, to varying degrees, sceptical of the exercise from the outset. Scepticism metamorphosed into disdain and even hostility as the morning went on. It was never going to be easy to persuade some colleagues to 'loosen up' and start talking about their feelings when they had spent the whole of their professional lives being super-rational. The facilitator sought to create a 'touchy-feely' atmosphere: more like an 'encounter group' than a board meeting. Some reeled back either in horror or in terror. Board members were not prepared to reveal, let alone tame, their 'inner chimp'.[127] There were embarrassing silences. There were increasingly forlorn exhortations to 'Say what's on your mind!' Homicide was undoubtedly on the minds of some…

Lunch, buffet style so that we could carry on bonding, didn't help. There was no alcohol! As the clock struck two, the facilitator was giving it a last go. But the meeting was scheduled to end by then. So, perhaps the most reluctant participant of all of us simply looked at her watch and said that her car was coming at 2 p.m. so should have arrived. She gathered up her bag and readied herself to leave. It was a fitting end. The meeting had exposed the dynamics of the group and where the fault lines were. It had made clear the varying degrees

---

127   See Steve Peters, *The Chimp Paradox: The Mind Management Programme* (Vermilion, 2012).

of empathy among the board. It had not brought anyone closer. But it had provided me as chairman with further insight as to how to manage our way forward. Beyond that, it was a car crash.

To his great credit, the chief executive did not give up. I agreed with him that the barely concealed antipathy of some members of the board towards senior executives needed to be dealt with as it was getting in the way. So, a further meeting was convened at IPSA's offices. The particular member of the board displaying the greatest antipathy was briefed and invited. I, the chief executive and other members of the executive teams were also there. Views were exchanged. The atmosphere was one in which colleagues were encouraged and felt able to say what was concerning them. After an hour, there was a somewhat chastened member of the board. I felt that the meeting had some effect.

THE EXECUTIVE AND STAFF

Although not formally members of the board, the senior executives were regarded as such in so far as they contributed to the formation of policy as well as being responsible for implementing it. The policy team assembled the data and arguments on this or that issue; the finance team managed the finances; the operations team dealt with the scheme of expenses and with issues raised by MPs and their staff; the communications team managed dealings with MPs, their staff, the media and the public; the HR team dealt with all matters relating to employment and offered advice to MPs and their staff when asked; and the compliance officer operated the system for responding to allegations of non-compliance with the scheme. Within the teams, there were specialists who, for example, handled telephone calls or requests under the Freedom of Information Act or the redaction of personal data from receipts.

The staff were outstanding. They were not particularly well-paid and endured the austerity wished upon those working in the public sector by the Conservative-led coalition government, receiving pay rises limited to 1 per cent while inflation hovered at 2–3 per cent for the whole of my time as chairman. They were united, however, in a sense of doing something important. They were making a difference in a small corner of the nation's constitutional arrangements and thereby helping to restore some confidence in Parliament and parliamentarians. This was enough for them to come to work, stay late when needed and help each other out. They were a pleasure to work with.

The executive was led for the first five years by Andrew McDonald. He was a career civil servant who was also a scholarly historian. He had a long and successful career in the Ministry of Justice, not least as regards his involvement in the Freedom of Information Act, and was an obvious choice to lead the setting up of IPSA. He gathered together a strong team of experienced colleagues and bright young 'fast-streamers' who prepared the ground for when I became chairman. Thereafter, he led the organisation with skill and humanity. I valued his thoughtful advice. I also was greatly impressed by his administrative skills. He astounded me, for example, by succeeding in closing down the offices in Victoria on a Friday evening and managing the move to Millbank so that we were open for business on the following Monday morning.

Andrew's time at IPSA was dogged by ill-health. He soldiered on uncomplainingly while often uncomfortable or in pain. Eventually, in January 2014 he decided that he should stand down. We gave him a wonderful send-off at a reception in the House of Commons, attended by many MPs who may have railed against IPSA, but who recognised in Andrew a dedicated public servant.

Marcial Boo joined us as chief executive in June 2014. In the interim, I had invited Paul Hayes, an experienced ex-chief executive, to come in for a few months and take an outsider's look at the organisation. He succeeded in ruffling more than a few feathers, but was enormously helpful to me and the board. At my request he met Marcial on a number of occasions and wrote a careful paper for the board advising on changes to how we operated. Marcial then came on board. He had very considerable experience in the higher echelons of the public sector, having worked in government departments and in the Audit Commission and the National Audit Office. He worked hard to earn the confidence and trust of MPs and was increasingly successful over time. The staff took to him. The role was a step up – he had not been a chief executive before – but he quickly grew into it. We spent long hours discussing the future of IPSA, particularly as the end of my term of office approached. I felt that I was leaving IPSA in very safe hands.

Andrew, Marcial and I shared a private secretary who looked after us and fixed things. We were blessed by having first Martyn Taylor, then Nick Lee, then Naomi Stauber. They all served IPSA with distinction.

Our first director of communications was Anne Power, who brought wide experience of Whitehall and a calm demeanour to the role. Mark Anderson took over and was brilliant in the tough days of dealing with committees of the House and then the two-year management of the debate over MPs' pay and pensions. He was unflappable and kept me in the loop, even if it was (and it often was) in the middle of Saturday lunchtime or Sunday evening. His curious affection for all things Stoke was regarded as a harmless eccentricity. Mark was followed by the equally experienced Matthew Lumby, who combined a supremely laid-back approach with a razor-sharp understanding of the value of silence unless we had something to say. His eccentricity consisted of following English (or UK) sports teams around the world with the ambition of visiting every country on the globe. But even when he was watching the cricket in Perth, he was only a text message away.

Our operations was initially led by Scott Woolveridge. His experience in commercial call centres and in the commercial world more generally was invaluable. Judith Toland joined us as director of operations to prepare IPSA for the general election of 2015. She had an outstanding record in both the public and private sectors. She spent over two years managing every detail and preparing the growing team. The result was a significant success. She then carried out a thorough review, identifying lessons to be learned and improvements that could be made. We were fortunate to have her energy, experience, dedication and skill.

The man whose stay at IPSA outlived even mine was the director of policy, John Sills. I cannot speak too highly of him. He gave his heart and soul to IPSA because he believed in what we were doing. He was particularly valuable to me as a colleague because his approach to strategy and tactics was often at variance with colleagues less willing to cut MPs some slack. It was important for me and the board to hear as full a range of arguments and options as possible. John guaranteed that this was the case. He was the epitome of a good public servant.

My heartfelt thanks and gratitude are due to all.

APPENDIX II

A NOTE FOR THE RECORD BY DIRECTOR OF POLICY JOHN SILLS AFTER A MEETING WITH LABOUR PARTY MPs, MAY 2010

THE WORST MEETING EVER

I joined IPSA at the beginning of February 2010, on secondment from the Ministry of Justice. I'd worked before with Andrew McDonald, when he was constitution director in the Department for Constitutional Affairs and I was the head of electoral policy. It was my favourite ever job in the senior civil service, and one that brought me into contact with a lot of politicians whom I really respected: Charlie Falconer, Harriet Harman and Chris Leslie. In late 2009 I had lunch with Andrew. He'd been appointed as the acting chief executive of IPSA. He needed a policy director. Would I like to do the job? I took about thirty seconds to decide. Yes, I'd love to. Like all people with an interest in politics, I'd found the expenses scandal shocking (and laughable), and the chance to work with Parliament to restore some faith in British democracy really appealed to me. How naive I was!

Fast forward to just after the general election of May 2010. We had the idea of meeting with groups of MPs to explain the new rules to them and take questions. The first one I was involved in – newly elected Conservatives – went quite well. It was very well chaired. There were some testy questions, but we got a round of applause at the end. It felt like we were doing the right thing.

The next day it was returning Labour MPs. I wanted to do this one; I wanted to help. About forty MPs turned up. The chair was Tony Lloyd, a nice guy. Just before the meeting, a new MP came in, needing some information about staffing contracts. I took time to help her and as a result had to rush up to the stage. I took my seat and had a slug of water. I was accompanied by an IPSA board member – our accountant, who didn't say a lot through the ensuing proceedings. Questions began immediately – they didn't want an opening statement. A very senior MP sat at the front and was beckoned to start things off. He stared at me with real hostility, pointed his finger at me and said, 'I will never use your system.' My mouth went dry. I respected this man. What should I say? I wanted to say, 'Well you won't get any money then, mate,' but of course I couldn't. It would have precipitated a riot. I asked a feeble question like 'Have you got a member of staff who could help you?' He replied, 'I do my own expenses.' OK, so where do we go from here? I can't remember what I said – probably something even more feeble like, 'We'll have to talk.' All I do remember is that by now I realised my hands were shaking so much that I couldn't pick up my glass of water.

And so it went on: two and a half hours. One MP from east London was asking me questions about travel costs, but every time I tried to answer he just started shouting. Another MP, from the north-east, kept on muttering, 'You think we're all crooks.' 'No, we don't,' I replied, but it didn't seem to register. The low point was about an hour and a half in. I'd kept my cool, but some MP started ranting about telephone bills. IPSA had had the bright idea of only paying 80 per cent of phone bills, on the basis that MPs were bound to make a few private calls, and this way, their claims would be much simpler. I did argue against this, but my view didn't prevail. I had to defend it. The ranting MP declaimed, 'Does IPSA only pay for 80 per cent of your phone bills?' I'd had enough. I said, 'I don't use my business phone for private calls.' Uproar! Braying, expletives. What had I done? One prominent MP shouted from the back, 'What you have said is a sackable offence!'

It more or less calmed down after that. Credit goes to Yvette Cooper, who strove to find some common ground. She was another MP whom I respected. I'd worked with her a bit as a civil servant in the Lord Chancellor's department. After the meeting ended she came up and apologised for the way things had gone: 'People are angry at the moment. We'll find a way to work together.' I really appreciated that. Then the MP who thought we thought they were all crooks came up to me. 'Well done,' he said, 'Don't take it personally.' I was new to this game. And it was just a game, But it didn't feel like that. As a senior civil servant I'd worked with some quite challenging groups: judges, lawyers, electoral administrators. They had their gripes, not least because we were so often having to cut funding. But they retained a basic courteousness. MPs, in private, clearly felt they didn't have to observe any of the normal standards of behaviour. IPSA was the enemy – we were fair game. I hasten to add that this never happened in any of the many one-to-one meetings I had later. It was a group thing. Put them all together and they egg each other on.

I went back to the office in time for a pizza lunch with staff, to acknowledge their achievements (paid for by the chief executive). And yes, I was wound up. I ranted, to anyone who would listen. My faith in politicians was severely shaken. That summer I thought long and hard about whether I really wanted to stay in the job. The idealism that I had when I joined had thoroughly dissipated. I could easily have gone back to the Ministry of Justice, from whom I was initially seconded. I came so close to saying, 'Fuck it.' But I never quite got there. I cared about our mission. I wanted to help MPs, despite everything. I wanted to help IPSA survive – it faced many existential threats in its early years. I helped create IPSA and eight and a half years later I was still there – proud of what we had achieved, loving the people I'd worked with. And hoping that, one day, MPs will twig that we have helped them get through their own existential crisis. That, actually, we are on their side.

APPENDIX III

REQUEST UNDER FREEDOM OF INFORMATION ACT AND RESPONSE

REQUEST, AUGUST 2010

I would like to request under the Freedom of Information Act:

Details of any instance where staff of the Independent Parliamentary Standards Authority (IPSA) have been abused, verbally or physically, or threatened by a Member of Parliament, officer of the House of Commons or Members' staff, since the establishment of the Authority;

Details of whether IPSA has referred any Member of Parliament to the Parliamentary Commissioner for Standards over their conduct or expenses claims;

And, whether IPSA has invoked any action or financial penalty against an individual Member of Parliament or House staff as a result of their conduct in person, or within written communications, with representatives of IPSA.

RESPONSE

I am responding to your request as the member of IPSA designated by the Lord Chancellor as the Qualified Person under s.36(5)(o) (iii) of the Freedom of Information Act. I can confirm that IPSA does hold information relevant to your request but that some of the information is exempt from disclosure.

As the Qualified Person I have conducted the public interest balancing exercise in relation to the engagement of the exemption at s.36(2)(c) (prejudice to the effective conduct of public affairs) of the Act, alongside consideration of the s.40(2) (personal information) exemption and our duties under the Data Protection Act, specifically paragraph 6 of Schedule 2. It is my opinion that certain forms of adverse effect would or would be likely to follow from a full disclosure of the information you request. However, I am also of the opinion that some of the information you request does not qualify for exemptions under the Act and should be disclosed.

In the process of my deliberations I have consulted the other IPSA Board members and senior IPSA staff.

Answering each of your requests in turn:

- *Details of any instance where staff of the Independent Parliamentary Standards Authority (IPSA) have been abused, verbally or physically, or threatened by a Member of Parliament, officer of the House of Commons or Members' staff, since the establishment of the Authority.*

Please find attached a digest of the recorded details of such instances.

- Incidents 1 to 8
- Incidents 9[128] and 10

---

128   For the sake of brevity, incident nine has been omitted.

You will note that individual names and place names have been redacted. It is my opinion that this information is exempt in respect of MPs under s.36(2)(c) and in respect of IPSA staff under s.40(2) of the Freedom of Information Act. In short, although the information is personal information, there is a legitimate interest in the public knowing the details of the conduct to which IPSA staff have been subjected. However, it is also very important and in the public interest that there is a satisfactory and effective working relationship between MPs and IPSA in implementing the new expenses regime. This would, in my view and in the view of those at IPSA whom I have consulted, be damaged by making public the names of the individual MPs concerned. I have therefore concluded that there is a greater public interest in withholding this information than there is in its release.

- *Details of whether IPSA has referred any Member of Parliament to the Parliamentary Commissioner for Standards over their conduct or expenses claims.*

IPSA has not referred any Member of Parliament to the Parliamentary Commissioner for Standards over their conduct or expenses claims.

- *Whether IPSA has invoked any action or financial penalty against an individual Member of Parliament or House staff as a result of their conduct in person, or within written communications with representatives of IPSA.*

IPSA has not invoked any action or financial penalty against any MPs or House staff. I should make clear that IPSA has a clear anti-bullying policy and that no member of staff who has experienced inappropriate conduct by MPs has wished any action to be taken against them.

INCIDENT ONE

Date: unrecorded

Member in lift – Asked how he was getting on with IPSA – the reply was 'awful', I offered help – he declined and said you're all fucking idiots.

INCIDENT TWO

Meeting with [deleted] MP

Date: Monday July 26 2010

[Deleted] greeted me very pleasantly. He had staff members in attendance at all times, which created an intimidating atmosphere at the points at which [deleted]'s behaviour was inappropriate.

After an initial discussion, I outlined the basic principles of the scheme. These were met with ridicule and derision by [deleted] and his staff.

I then endeavoured to take [deleted] through the basic processes of the system. At several times during the session, he exclaimed, 'This system is a fucking abortion!' which I found deeply inappropriate and offensive. His staff laughed and agreed with this and other comments which [deleted] made.

Other comments included, 'It [the system/scheme] will make the only people who want to be MPs rich people and losers'; 'That lawyer (Sir Ian Kennedy) is a stupid [unable to recall exact expletive as I was thrown off guard by the whole situation – but it was an offensive swear word], he has no idea what we do'; and 'I don't have a constituency office, but I might get one now to spend the budget because I am that pissed off.

At one point an external visitor entered the office. [Deleted] said to him, 'I'm doing my fucking IPSA expenses; it's fucking shit!'

INCIDENT THREE

[Deleted] MP

Date: Monday 10 May

Came to say that he would not be doing an induction session, throwing his personal details form across the desk at the facilitator [deleted]. When told that he would have to, became angry and patronising and would not accept the message. In addition to being angry and raising his voice, his body language and physical behaviour was unacceptable – he struck the laptop on the facilitator's desk and loomed over the facilitator in an intimidating manner. Incident witnessed by: [deleted].

INCIDENT FOUR

[Deleted] MP

Date: unrecorded

Stormed out of induction session and came to reception to ask questions about the scheme. Was rude when staff [deleted] and [deleted] were unable to answer his questions; was loud and disruptive (blocking the reception desk from other MPs who wished to register – and taking a while to move when asked to do so). Walked off on a staff member [deleted] in the middle of her explanation, branding all the trainers and staff 'monkeys'. Witnessed by [deleted].

INCIDENT FIVE

[Deleted] MP

Date: Tuesday 11 May

Very difficult and disruptive; angry, with anger directed to volunteer [deleted] to a degree. It appeared that the volunteer had difficulties going through the induction with him. At the 10 minute mark the volunteer burst into tears and a staff member [deleted] attempted to intervene. When the staff member offered to help, the MP dismissed him as 'condescending', at which point another staff member [deleted] pulled the volunteer (still in tears) out of the session. At this stage the MP immediately became contrite and apologised and the remainder of the session was conducted by a staff member [deleted]. The MP continued to be difficult, claiming that the system reduced him to a cipher, and that it 'made him not want to represent his country as an MP'. He later returned with a box of chocolates and a note addressed to the volunteer. Witnessed by [deleted], [deleted] and other trainers.

INCIDENT SIX

[Deleted] MP

Date: Wednesday 12 May

Complete unwillingness to engage with volunteer [deleted], system, or induction session – rude, abrupt, disparaging ('I don't do administration') used the word 'f*ck' and other violent language (e.g. 'I'm going to murder someone today'). Very angry until she realised she could give it all to her proxy; refused to sign declaration as her stated intention was to share her log-in details with her member of staff. Witnessed by [deleted] and [deleted] volunteer.

INCIDENT SEVEN

[Deleted] MP

Date: Wednesday 12 May

Didn't come for an induction session but came to one of the doors of the IPSA rooms (with [deleted] and [deleted] at the reception desk) purely to criticise IPSA in an aggressive fashion. His comments included: 'I'm going to attack you at every step'; 'I will be sending in FOI requests!'; 'Ian Kennedy is an idiot – his whole board are idiots'. (He didn't say who he was – we identified him from the photo book.) Witnessed by: [deleted].

INCIDENT EIGHT

[Deleted] MP

Date: Thursday 20 May 2010

Very aggressive with the trainer [deleted]. Asked her how much she was being paid to provide the induction. When the trainer explained that she was a volunteer, the MP asked what bonus she was getting. The trainer explained that she was not getting a bonus, nor any other payment for providing the training. The MP said that she was going to submit an FOI request to find out what bonuses the trainer and her colleagues were getting. She asked for the name of the trainer and grabbed the trainer's name badge in doing so. Witnessed: by [deleted].

INCIDENT TEN

Reporting inappropriate behaviour

A complaint regarding bullying behaviour from [deleted], [deleted]

MP for [deleted], towards myself, [deleted]. This behaviour took place late afternoon on 7 June in 1 Parliament Street.

Two witnesses [deleted] & [deleted] (who may have overheard some of the conversation).

SITUATION

[Deleted] came into 1 Parliament Street and demanded her card in an abrupt manner, 'I want my travel card! I was told last week that it would be here today, so I would like it now!'

I looked carefully for the card but had no luck in finding it. I politely informed [deleted] that her card was not yet with us, and that I would be happy to follow it up on her behalf.

She aggressively interrupted in a raised voice before I finished the above sentence, demanding 'Where is it? I was told last week it would be here today! You obviously lied to me. I want to know where it is now!'

I again politely explained we were only giving out the cards on behalf of another team, but I would be happy to take down her contact details and chase up the whereabouts of her card, when I next managed to contact [deleted].

To this she responded aggressively and snappily said 'I'm not giving *you* my contact details! *You* already have my contact details! *You* shouldn't need to ask for them!' (Throughout which she insinuated the incompetence of IPSA and myself.)

She then went on to demand where her card is. 'You are to tell me now! Where is my card? You are to tell me now!'

I politely explained that I was aware that there had been some problems with the courier and that only half of the batch of cards had arrived last week, but I would contact [deleted] and ask him if he could help with providing information as to when exactly her card would arrive.

Again she rudely interrupted, 'That's an outright lie! Couriers are given their products to deliver and they deliver them! This is obviously IPSA incompetence, so I want *you* to tell me where my card is now!'

She proceeded to order me to phone [deleted] straight away, and stood over me whilst I did this.

I tried to get through to [deleted] but unfortunately he was unavailable.

I explained that unfortunately [deleted] was unavailable, but I would chase up her card as soon as I could/as soon as I heard from him.

To this she replied 'How convenient!' in a sarcastic and menacing manner and insinuated again that I was lying.

[Deleted] proceeded to demand exactly where [deleted] was.

To which I told her what I thought to be the truth; that I was unsure, but he was probably in a meeting (I later found out he was at a funeral).

To this she responded that was insufficient and grumbled about how incompetent we all are and stormed out of the room.

Please note that throughout this whole incident [deleted] had an aggressive tone/manner, and she was very intimidating and belittling towards myself, with body language reflecting this. I was very close to tears by the time she left and I think if it had continued much longer I would have been visibly upset.

Signed:

[Deleted]

APPENDIX IV

LETTERS BETWEEN KEN OLISA AND MR SPEAKER

Rt Hon. John Bercow MP
The Speaker
Speaker's House
House of Commons
Westminster
London SW1A OAA

Ken Olisa OBE
Board Member
IPSA, 7th Floor
Portland House
Bressenden Place
London SW1E 5BH

T 020 7811 6473
E ken.olisa@parliamentarystandards.org.uk
www.parliamentarystandards.org.uk

13th September 2012   Our ref: BO-717

I write to you, following our meeting last week, to reiterate the concern I expressed about the way in which remarks made by me in the press have been interpreted and also – separately – to explain my decision not to stand for reappointment to the Board of IPSA.

As I believe was evident at the time, I was surprised by your comment that my position, recently reported in the *Evening Standard*, demonstrated an ignorance of Parliament's workings.

In my business career I have come to the reluctant conclusion that, all too often, perception trumps reality and I am sorry that my correctly reported comments should somehow have conveyed such a radically incorrect impression to you.

I can only assume that the misunderstanding arose from where I was quoted as saying that I believe MPs should be worried about having their pay and pensions debated in public.

This remains my belief evidenced by the tone of the public's comments received on our website, the opinions expressed to me on the various programmes in which I have taken part and the diligent opinion research carried out by IPSA. My view was reinforced by the so-called 'shareholder Spring' in which – in the period immediately preceding the interview – three FTSE CEOs lost their jobs following very public debates about their pay.

You once described the expenses scandal as having inflicted greater damage on Parliament than that wrought by enemy action in the Second World War. The fundamental changes introduced by IPSA were always going to engender opposition and scrutiny. But the scale of the reaction from within Westminster has been astonishing – especially given that our job was to clean up a mess not of our making.

The time, money and effort exerted by Parliament and Parliamentary bodies poring over an organisation with an operational budget equal to the taxpayers' subsidy for the Commons bars and restaurants has been entirely disproportionate.

In the less than three years since we began our work we have been subjected to investigations by:

- The National Audit Office;
- The Public Accounts Committee;

- The Speaker's Committee on IPSA; and
- The freshly constituted Committee on Members' Expenses.

While that volume of scrutiny could generally be considered an implicit attempt to erode confidence in our independence, the CME was explicit in theirs, proposing to introduce primary legislation to compel us to adopt the Committee's recommendations if we failed to do so voluntarily.

That barrage of formal investigations has been supplemented by a stream of regular parliamentary questions and debates about IPSA not, unfortunately, confined to ordinary MPs. Members of your committee on IPSA also displayed an animus towards us, as well as a surprising lack of knowledge of the workings of the body for which they carry some responsibility. For example, last May, Sir Bob Russell asked the Leader of the House, Sir George Young, for a debate on IPSA citing his 'discovery' that we claimed our full daily allowance even when our participation at meetings was only by telephone. Sir Bob and Sir George both served on the Speaker's Committee for IPSA, and it would have been my reasonable hope that they knew how we were paid – namely for the actual time spent on IPSA business and, moreover, that we do not receive allowances of any description.

The Leader's reply was of rather more concern when he said 'there might be an opportunity to address the issue of membership when the terms of office of some existing members run out and the question of reappointment, or the appointment of new members arises.' The response, while wholly unconnected to the question, does provide a powerful indication of the likely nature of discussions about IPSA inside your committee.

An indication which appears to resonate with your unsubstantiated criticism of me at our meeting in early October.

In my previous letter to you I said that both the perception and reality of impartiality were fundamental to the appointment process for the next Board of IPSA.

Given the sustained animus towards IPSA from within Westminster I therefore consider it wrong to add a former MP and a member of your committee to the formerly independent appointments panel. More akin to adding two former heads of bailed-out banks to the selection panel for the next Governor of the Bank of England than a declaration of process impartiality.

It would, in my opinion, have far better served the restoration of confidence in Parliamentary procedures had you:

- Appointed to the panel, two ordinary citizens with no connection to Parliament other than the payment of their taxes and the casting of their votes and
- Followed the guidance from the Officer of the Commissioner for Public Appointments and accepted the present Board's offer to be reappointed for staggered terms so as to produce a smooth transition to a new configuration in two or three years time.

In your letter to Sir Ian of April 18th you said that it was your intention that the appointment process should be independent of you and SCIPSA.

Sadly, that turned out not to be the case and none of the current Board members has chosen to apply for their jobs. So, just as MPs' expenses are again making headlines, the country is faced with the wholesale replacement of the IPSA Board members.

This is obviously bad for IPSA's independence. But it is also potentially very bad for MPs. We are in the middle of the project to determine Parliamentarians' remuneration. I am delighted to learn from Sir Ian that the proposed appointees to the Board are of the highest calibre. Let's hope that they have the time and freedom from Parliamentary interference to enable them to pick up the complex issues of pay and pensions in time to ensure that prospective candidates for the 2015 election know enough about their compensation to decide to begin the arduous process of selection.

We should be proud of what IPSA has achieved in less than three years. We achieved what the Office of Government Commerce described as 'the impossible' by getting a scandal busting system in place in less than six months and, while other legislatures remain wedded to the model of opaque, unreceipted allowances, the British public can gain confidence by visiting our website to analyse how much and on what their MP has spent – down to the smallest receipt.

No more moat cleaning, no more duck houses, no more mortgage flipping. The expenses scandal is truly behind us. It is a shame that so many of those who should have most welcomed a system that is fair, workable and transparent should have invested so much energy in undermining our work.

And it is a shame that, whether by accident or design, IPSA will again be scrambling to tackle a vital element of the public's confidence in Parliament and its processes – MPs' pay and pensions.

IPSA and its new Board, supported by our hard working staff, have important work ahead of them and are well positioned to rise to the challenges they face. It is to be hoped that our successors will be left alone to get on with it.

I wish them well.

Yours sincerely

Ken Olisa OBE
Board member

Ken Olisa OBE
Board Member
IPSA, 7th Floor
Portland House
Bressenden Place
London SW1E 5BH

Rt Hon. John Bercow MP
The Speaker
Speaker's House
House of Commons
Westminster
London SW1A 0AA

20 September 2012[129]

Dear Mr Olisa,

Thank you for your letter of 13 September.

I am happy again to express my gratitude for the diligence and commitment you and other members of the first IPSA board have shown, under Sir Ian Kennedy's leadership, in securing the establishment of the Independent Parliamentary Standards Authority. This was a challenging task, in challenging circumstances: it is entirely right and proper that this achievement should be recognised.

I regret that you have found yourself uncomfortable about the current process for the renewal of the IPSA board. The process is being conducted fully in accordance with the requirements of the Parliamentary Standards Act 2009 and with regard to the guidance provided on appointments to statutory office by the Office of the Commissioner for Public Appointments.

As you note I have engaged in lengthy correspondence on the procedure with Sir Ian Kennedy, and have considered very carefully the points which he has raised on the required competition. I do not believe that the inclusion in the independent panel of Peter Atkinson or Dame Janet Gaymer compromises the panel's ability to

---

129 Although this letter was sent on 20 September, it was not received by IPSA until 4 October.

consider candidates for IPSA's board with absolute impartiality: you may recall that, in addition to being an independent lay member of SCIPSA, Dame Janet is a former Commissioner of Public Appointments. I am pleased that Sir Ian himself was willing to serve on the panel under the chairmanship of Dame Denise Platt of the Committee on Standards in Public Life.

I have every confidence in the integrity and impartiality of the panel, to whom the task was handed over in July, and I look forward to receiving the panel's recommendations in due course.

Yours sincerely,

John Bercow
Rt Hon. John Bercow MP
Speaker

Rt Hon. John Bercow MP   Ken Olisa

The Speaker   Board Member

Speaker's House   IPSA, 7th Floor

House of Commons   Portland House

Westminster   Bressenden Place

London SW1A OAA   London SW1E 5BH

T 020 7811 6473

E ken.olisa@parliamentarystandards.org.uk

www.parliamentarystandards.org.uk

13 November 2012   Our ref: BO-717/1

Dear Mr Speaker

Thank you for your letter dated October 4th.

I appreciate your expression of gratitude for the diligence and commitment shown by IPSA's first Board. However, I regret that your letter served to amplify, rather than assuage, both of the concerns about which I wrote to you on September 13th. As our correspondence will become public I am writing to ensure that my position is unambiguously on the record.

My original letter made two points:

- My surprise at your assertion that I was somehow 'ignorant' of Parliament and its processes.
- That I had not reapplied for my position on the IPSA Board because I consider the appointment process to be fundamentally flawed.

Your reply was silent on the first point (and, therefore in the absence of any evidence, I consider it closed) and rebutted the second with arguments already debated in the earlier exchanges with our Chairman.

The two issues are linked, being symptomatic of the gratuitous hostility to which IPSA and I have been subjected since the creation of an independent regulator. I agree. At all times in the past 2.5 years the Board has seen our task as one in which we must work together with MPs to repair that damage and to restore confidence in the democratic process. Accepting always that our impact is limited to those areas where the determination and administration of expenses, pay and pensions can help to bridge the divide between Parliament and the public. It is self evident that gratuitously attacking MPs or Parliament would undermine successful completion of that mission.

Turning now to my decision not to stand for reappointment to IPSA I should say at the outset that I am grateful for your acknowledgement of my role (and that of my colleagues) in IPSA's achievements.

I regret therefore that the concerns relating to the (re)appointment of members of the IPSA board which were raised by our Chair in lengthy correspondence with you did not lead to any material change to the process.

I am particularly uncomfortable about the addition of a member of SCIPSA and a former MP to the erstwhile wholly independent panel. This may not impact the reality of the panel's independence but unfortunately it fuels the perception that appointments to the next IPSA board will lack the neutrality and absence of prejudices about the candidates exhibited by the original process.

I consider absolute impartiality – in both perception and reality – to be fundamentally important to IPSA's credibility as an independent regulator.

It is its absence that renders me unable to stand for (re)appointment.

In a motivating speech given in the thick of the expenses scandal, you said 'A scheme which fails in the court of public opinion will surely founder'. I am proud of my small contribution to ensuring that IPSA's solution avoided that destructive fate and I am saddened that I am unable to see our work on pay and pension through to an equally solid conclusion.

I do, however, intend to play a full part in preparing the ground for our successors in the hope that the change has no materially adverse affect on candidates' ability to plan for the next election. And, when the dust settles, I hope that the work of the first IPSA board will be judged on what we have actually done and said rather than on what others might attribute to us for their own reasons

Ken Olisa OBE
Board member

Ken Olisa OBE

Board Member

IPSA

7th Floor, Portland House

Bressenden Place

London SW1E 5BH

Rt Hon. John Bercow MP

The Speaker

Speaker's House

House of Commons

Westminster

London SW1A 0AA

14 November 2012

Dear Mr Olisa,

Thank you for your letter of 13 November in response to my letter to you of 4 October. I am grateful to you for taking the trouble to give me your views in such detail.

Only two substantive points need to be made in response to your observations. First, my unequivocal legal advice was that the IPSA Board appointments had to be made through a process of fair and open competition. That is precisely what happened.

Secondly, as I explained to the Chair of IPSA, I appointed an independent panel chaired by Dame Denise Platt DBE, a member of the Committee on Standards in Public Life. The Chair of IPSA, Professor Sir Ian Kennedy, also sat on the panel.

The interview process was entirely independent of Parliament. My colleagues and I took no part whatsoever in the process and, quite properly, I learned of the candidates recommended by the panel when, and only when, the Chair, Dame Denise Platt DBE, wrote to me on Monday 29 October.

You suggest, in the final paragraph of your letter, that the new Board, supported by IPSA staff are 'well positioned to rise to the challenges they face'. I wholeheartedly agree.

I wish you every success in the future.
Yours sincerely

John Bercow
Rt Hon. John Bercow MP
Speaker

APPENDIX V

LETTERS BETWEEN THE CHAIRMAN AND MR SPEAKER

Professor Sir Ian Kennedy

Chair

IPSA, 7th Floor

Portland House

Bressenden Place

London SWIE 5BH

Rt Hon. John Bercow MP

The Speaker

Speaker's House

House of Commons

Westminster

London SW1A 0AA

2 April 2012

Dear Sir Ian

RESTRICTED ACCESS: APPOINTMENTS TO THE INDEPENDENT PARLIAMENTARY STANDARDS AUTHORITY

As you know the terms of office of Sir Scott Baker, Jackie Ballard, Ken Olisa and Professor Isobel Sharp, ordinary members of the Independent Parliamentary Standards Authority, expire on 10 January 2013.

The Speaker of the House of Commons is required to select candidates for the Authority under Schedule 1 of the Parliamentary

Standards Act 2009, as amended. Paragraph 2 of Schedule 1 states that:

Appointment of chair and ordinary members

(1) The chair of the IPSA is to be appointed by Her Majesty on an address of the House of Commons.

(2) An ordinary member of the IPSA is to be appointed by Her Majesty on an address of the House of Commons.

(3) A motion for an address under sub-paragraph (1) or (2) may be made only with the agreement of the Speaker.

(4) The person the subject of the motion must have been selected by the Speaker on merit on the basis of fair and open competition.

(5) The Speaker must not select a candidate without the agreement of the Speaker's Committee for the Independent Parliamentary Standards Authority.

Andrew McDonald and the staff of IPSA have expressed the desirability of renewing the existing appointments, for varied terms, to enable future appointments to be staggered and to ensure continuity in IPSA's governance. The arguments for establishing a rolling programme of appointments are clearly strong. I have, however, been advised that the mandatory nature of the instruction in paragraph 2(4) above ('The person ... must have been selected by the Speaker on merit on the basis of fair and open competition') requires each board position to be subject to fair and open competition at the end of every fixed term. I have been advised further that were I, as Speaker, to direct that an appointment be carried out by any procedure other than on merit on the basis of full and open competition, that direction would be amenable to judicial review.

In view of the provisions of paragraph 2(5) of Schedule 1 of the Act (above) I have discussed this advice with the Speaker's

Committee, including its lay members. The Committee concurs with the advice I have received.

As a courtesy I wished to inform you first that I have therefore, in accordance with the statutory requirements, determined that a fair and open competition must be run for each post of ordinary member of IPSA.

I recognise that this determination creates significant uncertainty for yourself, your board and IPSA's staff, which I regret. It is my intention that the appointments which must be made towards the end of this year should be of varying lengths in order to provide IPSA with greater security in future. I hope you will be reassured that while, under the statute, I may not assuage the immediate difficulty I will do what I can to avoid a recurrence.

I also wish to take this opportunity to acknowledge the commitment demonstrated by the board, under your leadership, since 2010. The journey has not been, and is not, an easy one. Yet the repeated iterations of the Scheme, and the conclusions of the National Audit Office on IPSA's performance to date, are testament to IPSA's significant achievements, not least of which are its establishment by May 2010 and its contribution to the vital task of restoring public confidence in our democracy. I am grateful to the members of the Authority for leading and enabling IPSA's development to date.

The required competition must commence very shortly if appointments are to be perfected before the current members' terms of office expire. By reason of the mandatory requirement in paragraph 2(4) of Schedule 1 any board member wishing to be re-appointed for a second term, as permitted by paragraph 4(3) of the Schedule, would again have to apply and be successful in competition with other candidates. The existing members would be welcome to apply, and I hope that they will.

I have asked SCIPSA's secretariat to draw up an outline procedure for the appointment process, drawing both upon the precedent set in 2009 and OCPA best practice. I attach a copy for your consideration, and would welcome your comments or suggestions before I make my final decision on the format of the competition required. Since IPSA's board is part of the legal entity of IPSA I trust there will be no difficulty in IPSA funding and providing administrative support to the competition: the Speaker's Committee will be willing to consider any reasonable requests for additional resource which may prove necessary, in the context of IPSA's main Estimate 2012/13.

To this end, it would be helpful if IPSA officials should be able to bring an outline proposal for expenditure on the competition to the next meeting of SCIPSA on Wednesday 18 April. As there is some urgency to get the competition under way I would also be grateful to receive your proposed job description/person specification, and your comments on the attached draft process as soon as possible, and by no later than Friday 13 April.

It is my intention that this correspondence should be published when the competition is formally announced. I would be grateful if you would respect its confidentiality in the meantime.

Best wishes,

Yours ever,

John

Rt Hon. John Bercow MP

Speaker

Rt Hon. John Bercow MP

The Speaker

Speaker's House

House of Commons

Westminster

London SW1A 0AA

Professor Sir Ian Kennedy

Chair

IPSA, 7th Floor

Portland House

Bressenden Place

London SW1E 5BH

T 020 7811 64/3

E ian.kennedy@parliamentarystandards.org.uk

www.parliamentarystandards.org.uk

16 April 2012

Our ref: BO-626

Dear Speaker

APPOINTMENTS TO THE BOARD OF THE INDEPENDENT PARLIAMENTARY STANDARDS AUTHORITY

Thank you for your letter of 2 April in which you set out your proposed approach to appointments to the Board of IPSA in January 2013. I am replying in my capacity as Chair of the Board which, given that my own appointment runs until 2015 and is not currently at issue, allows me a degree of impartiality.

In view of your candour, which I welcome, I will express myself in as plain and direct terms as possible.

We both recognise, I know, the importance of maintaining public confidence. May I begin, therefore, by expressing my concern that it may be perceived, whatever the intention, that the approach proposed might be likely to result in the wholesale turnover of the current members of the Board? There is no doubt that IPSA has taken a number of decisions which have not proved popular with some MPs. But in our view, reinforced by the views of others, the decisions have been both necessary and appropriate (and where not, they have been changed). I am sure that you would not wish the temporary unpopularity of decisions to be perceived as providing grounds for challenging the continuing membership of those making the decisions.

Now that the Scheme of Business Costs and Expenses is stable and working well, the daily outpouring of stories about expenses has ceased. It is in nobody's interest for expenses once again to become a live issue in the shape of a debate about the future composition of the Board and what this might say about IPSA's role as an independent regulator. I make no apologies for pointing to the fact that there is much at stake here, not least the reputation and future standing of IPSA and, indeed, the reputation of Parliament itself.

There is, of course, in your letter much that is common ground between us. First, I agree that initial appointments to the Board must be based on merit through fair and open competition. This, after all, is required by the governing statute and was the basis on which the current Board was selected.

Secondly, IPSA's contribution has been significant and I value your acknowledgement of it. IPSA was set up to address the scandal surrounding MPs' expenses. We have succeeded in doing so. We have contributed to some restoration of the public's confidence, which is fragile and still easily shaken, as recent events have shown.

Thirdly, we agree on the importance of rolling appointments, so as to achieve a proper balance between continuity and change, recognising the value of the knowledge and experience gained by the Board over the past two years, and allowing the Board to meet both its immediate challenges and, in the longer term, to have in place appropriate and suitable succession planning.

But, although there is common ground, there are also clear differences between us. First, it is important to recognise that as regards existing members of a Board in the public sector, the norm is one of renewal. In the case of public appointments, it is established practice that serving Board members are only required to take part in a full competition if their performance to date has been assessed – usually by the Chair – to be unsatisfactory. This is not the case as regards members of my Board.

Secondly, as regards what I will call initial appointments to fill vacancies, a precedent was set as regards the process to be followed in 2009 when the current members were appointed. You are proposing to depart from that precedent, but I can see no good grounds for doing so. The original process of appointment was developed in line with best practice in public appointments. The governing statute, of course, makes no reference to the detailed process to be followed. My strong preference would be, therefore, to follow precedent as regards any future appointments to fill vacancies. Indeed, I would suggest that the departures you propose carry with them some risk, which I will detail later in this letter.

Thirdly, I am keen to stress that if your proposed approach were to be adopted, as set out in your letter (and putting aside views on what the governing statute may require, which I will refer to later) for appointments in January 2013, it would:

- put at risk the reputation of existing Board members (whose performance might unjustly be called into question because of the requirement that they apply afresh for their role);

- put at risk the reputation of incoming Board members (who may be perceived to be placemen/women of Parliament);
- put at risk IPSA's ability to deliver – in a timely fashion – its critically important work on MPs' pay and pensions. We have started our work, involving a fundamental review, to secure, for the first time, a long-term and stable settlement which commands public confidence. This is a challenging brief, with IPSA's initial view due by the spring of 2013. It will require the Board to take decisions on important and complex issues according to a demanding timescale. Continuity for the Board is, in my view, crucial, if we are to agree a new settlement in a timely manner. If we fail to form a view by spring 2013 the risk is high that pay and pensions will become a political football with a 'race for the bottom' and the opportunity for a considered settlement retreating in the face of an impending general election; and
- commit SCIPSA to a potentially expensive process comprising a full competition for four separate posts requiring national advertising and executive search which I am not persuaded, in these times of austerity, represents a good use of public funds or value for money.

For all of these reasons I would urge you to adopt the following course of action. First, as regards the current members of the Board, I urge you to adopt the standard practice of renewal. By doing so, you will allow existing members of the Board the opportunity to decide, for themselves, what they wish to do, including whether they wish to stay on for a further fixed term. I know that any member of the Board wishing to have his/her term renewed would be happy to accept a further term of just one or two years, recognising the need to balance continuity with change.

Secondly, as they relate to new initial appointments to fill vacancies, I would make two specific points on your proposed approach:

- you propose the possible addition of a former Member of the House of Commons to the independent selection panel. This did not form part of the process in 2009. Putting to one side for the moment the size of the panel (already potentially five members), the inclusion of a former MP – whoever it might be would, to my mind, inevitably introduce a perception of party politics into selection of the Board for the first time, given that a former MP will, with very few exceptions, belong or have belonged to a political party. This would be wholly undesirable given the need for IPSA to be and to be seen to be independent of political influence; and

- you propose the possibility of selected candidates being invited to meet either yourself or SCIPSA before appointment by Her Majesty on an address of the House of Commons. Candidates selected for appointment to some prominent public bodies are now invited to meet the relevant committee. I believe that the circumstances proposed here are not comparable: those proposed appointments have been of Chairs-designate and not of 'ordinary' members, and such meetings have no influence over the outcome of the selection process. SCIPSA, by contrast, has a responsibility to agree the selection of the candidate put forward by the Speaker. It, thus, has a power of veto. A meeting with SCIPSA would, therefore, be, and be seen to be, an additional and, necessarily, a formal part of the selection process with all that follows in terms of possible reputational risk.

As I said earlier, we have a shared interest in developing a process that will achieve a successful outcome and maintain public confidence.

I understand that your approach is based on legal advice that you have received. Views may, however, quite properly differ on the interpretation of, and intention behind, the governing statute. May I propose, therefore, that we find a way forward by jointly commissioning an opinion on what approach is called for as regards the existing members of the Board should they wish to continue, based on shared and mutually agreed instructions? This will allow us all to stand behind a process that we can then support both for the forthcoming and any future appointments to the Board. I look forward to your response to this proposal.

In the meantime, I have asked the Chief Executive and his team to contact your office separately over the potentially very high costs which would arise from your proposed approach. I suggest that we turn to them and to the agreement of role and person specifications for future members of IPSA's Board once the way forward has been settled.

Yours ever,

Ian
Professor Sir Ian Kennedy
Chair

Professor Sir Ian Kennedy Chair
Chair
IPSA, 7th Floor
Portland House
Bressenden Place
London SW1E 5BH

Rt Hon. John Bercow MP
The Speaker
Speaker's House
House of Commons
Westminster
London SW1A 0AA

18 April 2012

Dear Sir Ian

RESTRICTED ACCESS: APPOINTMENTS TO THE BOARD OF THE INDEPENDENT PARLIAMENTARY STANDARDS AUTHORITY

Thank you for your letter of 16 April, recording your concerns about the requirement for a full, fair and open recruitment competition to address the expiry of ordinary Board members' fixed term appointments in January 2013.

Appointments to IPSA's board are governed by paragraph 2 of Schedule 1 to the Parliamentary Standards Act 2009, as amended. They are made for a fixed term by appointment of Her Majesty on an address of the House of Commons, As I set out in my letter of 2 April, the mandatory nature of the instruction in paragraph 2(4) of that Schedule[130] requires each board position to be subject to fair and open competition at the end of every fixed term, all proceedings relating to the previous fixed term appointment then being spent. I have been advised by Speaker's Counsel that were I, as Speaker, to direct that an appointment be carried out by any procedure other

---

130   'The person the subject of the motion [for an address] must have been selected by the Speaker on merit on the basis of fair and open competition.'

than selection on merit on the basis of fair and open competition, that direction would be amenable to a successful application for judicial review.

I therefore have no discretion and must require a fair and open competition for the forthcoming and any future appointments to IPSA's board: this legal advice is supported by SCIPSA which, in its lay membership, has a considerable weight of expertise both in the practice of law and in relation to public appointments.

As I have indicated I recognise, of course, that the statutory requirement creates real difficulty for IPSA, especially in circumstances in which four appointments will expire simultaneously. I recognise the need to seek to avoid a recurrence of these circumstances in future. I cannot, however, accept your argument that existing Board members who have performed satisfactorily, and who wish to continue in office, should be exempted from fair and open competition because renewal may be presumed in other parts of the public service.

IPSA's board members are statutory office-holders within the governance framework created for IPSA by the Parliamentary Standards Act 2009. I have set out the implications of that framework in my second paragraph above. Such statutory provisions override conventions or norms of practice: this is recognised at paragraph 3.2 of the Code of Practice for Ministerial Appointments to Public Bodies (April 2012) which confirms that legislation relating to the particular public body or statutory office must be complied with. It is also the case that the Act's requirement for selection on merit on the basis of fair and open competition in respect of all appointments to IPSA upholds IPSA's values of openness, fairness, accountability and transparency, which we are agreed are essential to the maintenance of public confidence.

You raise concerns about two aspects of the draft process for the competition on which I consulted you on 2 April. As you have noted, the governing statute makes no reference to the detailed process to be followed. I therefore have a degree of discretion in respect of the detail and can assure you that I fully accept the value of the precedent set in 2009. It is my intention that, in keeping with precedent and best practice, the competition leading to the identification of candidates for appointment should be managed at all stages by a panel which is independent of me and of the Speaker's Committee for the IPSA. I shall give further serious consideration to the points of detail you have raised as I finalise the process.

At the close of your letter, you suggest that I should jointly commission with IPSA a new legal opinion specifically to enable existing members of the Board to continue in office should they wish to do so. The statutory requirement for a fair and open competition does not bar them from doing so, provided they are found to be the most meritorious candidates available in the competition. I have previously expressed my hope that the existing board members, who have made a significant contribution to IPSA's establishment, would be willing to engage with the required process. I am happy to repeat that expression here. I am also happy to make clear that the performance of the existing board members should not unjustly be called into question because the statute requires them to apply afresh, should they wish to be considered for a second term of office.

Your officials have been aware of the statutory requirement for an open competition since February. IPSA has not in that time advanced any formal legal opinion of its own, either to agree or disagree with the advice which it knew had been provided to me.

The necessary competition must now be initiated, if new appointments are to be made before the existing appointments expire in January 2013. To commission a further opinion at this late stage would incur additional delay and expense: in view of the urgency (and being mindful of the costs, which you have quite rightly pointed out are already potentially substantial) I decline this proposal.

I am grateful to IPSA officials who have provided me with an outline of the likely costs of the open competition. I have discussed this with the Speaker's Committee, both in view of its statutory role in relation to appointments, and its role in consideration of IPSA's estimate. I shall write to you separately to report on that discussion. I hope that we can now resolve the details of the process and initiate the competition as soon as possible. It is in IPSA's interest that the succession is settled properly and efficiently. To this end, please send me your proposed job/person specification by no later than Thursday 26 April.

Best wishes,

Yours ever,

John

Rt Hon. John Bercow MP

Speaker

Professor Sir Ian Kennedy   Rt Hon. John Bercow MP

Chair   The Speaker

IPSA, 7th Floor   Speaker's House

Portland House   House of Commons

Bressenden Place   Westminster

London SWIE 5BH   London SW1A 0AA

25 April 2012

Dear Sir Ian,

RESTRICTED ACCESS: APPOINTMENTS TO THE BOARD OF IPSA — INDICATIVE COSTS

Thank you for the note setting out IPSA's estimate of the cost of a full appointment process for the four posts of ordinary board member of the IPSA, each requiring full executive search. As explained in my letters to you of 2 and 18 April a full appointment process is required for each post upon the expiry of the current fixed-term appointments, by the mandatory instruction in paragraph 2(4) of Schedule 1 to the Parliamentary Standards Act 2009, as amended.

The estimate was discussed by the Speaker's Committee for the IPSA at its meeting on 18 April. The Committee noted that the estimated costs for the process as a whole were in the range £95–140,000 and that IPSA is formally seeking agreement for a total budget in the region of £100,000, to be included as a separate line within IPSA's main Estimate for 2012/13. This budget would be ring-fenced to ensure that unspent resource would be returned to HM Treasury.

The Committee is content for a new line to be placed on the

main Estimate 2012/13 for no more than £100,000 on the under-standing that the budget is ring-fenced as you have proposed.

Notwithstanding this agreement, the Committee recognises that the market for executive search services is very competitive, and believes that the formal tendering process should result in a com-bined price for those services which is substantially lower than the upper end of the indicative costs range provided in the note. The Committee would therefore encourage your officials to be mindful of the need for restraint and to make every effort to negotiate a competitive price. I should be grateful if you would advise me of the outcome of the tendering process and, in due course, of the costs of the recruitment process as a whole.

Yours wholly,

John Bercow
Rt Hon. John Bercow MP
Speaker

Copies to:
Andrew McDonald, Chief Executive, IPSA
David Stevenson, HM Treasury

Rt Hon. John Bercow MP

The Speaker

Speaker's House

House of Commons

Westminster

London SW1A 0AA

Professor Sir Ian Kennedy

Chair

IPSA, 7th Floor

Portland House

Bressenden Place

London SW1E 5BH

T 020 7811 6473

E ian.kennedy@parliamentarystandards.org.uk

www.parliamentarystandards.org.uk

26 April 2012

Our ref: BO-626b

Dear Mr Speaker,

APPOINTMENTS TO THE BOARD OF THE INDEPENDENT PARLIAMENTARY STANDARDS AUTHORITY

Thank you for your letter of 18 April in which you set out your response to the concerns that I raised in relation to the proposed process for the renewal of the Board of IPSA.

The point that you make concerning the principle of appointment on merit on the basis of fair and open competition need not detain us. I am as fully committed to it as you are. As I made clear in my earlier letter of 16 April, this was the basis on which the current Board was selected. My position was simply that the approach to renewal, rather than initial appointment, which is commonly accepted across the public sector should be followed. To do otherwise would, at the very least, raise questions about why the accepted norm is not being followed. This letter is not the place for legal argument but I am bound to say that the Code of Practice for Ministerial Appointments to which you refer, should it apply, merely requires that legislation be complied with. The issue here is what the legislation actually requires. Moreover, I am surprised that it is suggested that you, as Speaker, would be amenable (successfully or otherwise) to judicial review. This would be unprecedented. I regret, therefore, that you did not feel able to accept my suggestion that we jointly seek further advice.

I remain concerned that the process as currently defined may yet undermine the ability of IPSA's Board to respond in a timely fashion to a number of key challenges, not least the question of pay and pensions.

In relation to my two specific concerns about the draft process – the possible addition of a former Member of the House of Commons to the independent selection panel and the introduction of a pre-selection meeting with the Speaker's Committee for the IPSA – I am glad to see that you intend to give serious consideration to both points.

I will, therefore, await your response, following discussions with the Speaker's Committee, both on the final process that you are proposing and the budget to support that process. In parallel with that, we will send you a draft role and person specification.

Yours sincerely,

Ian

Professor Sir Ian Kennedy

Chair

Professor Sir Ian Kennedy   Rt Hon. John Bercow MP
Chair   The Speaker
IPSA, 7th Floor   Speaker's House
Portland House   House of Commons
Bressenden Place   Westminster
London SWIE 5BH   London SW1A 0AA

30 April 2012

Dear Sir Ian,

APPOINTMENTS TO THE BOARD OF THE IPSA

Thank you for your letter of 26 April, in reply to my letter of 18 April. I have noted the points you make and I will write again following discussions with the Speaker's Committee.

Yours sincerely,

John Bercow
Rt Hon. John Bercow MP
Speaker

THE FIRST BOARD LOOK BACK IN (SOME) ANGER: 'REVIEWING MPs' PAY AND PENSIONS – A FIRST REPORT'[131]

FOREWORD BY THE BOARD OF IPSA

This framework for the determination of MPs' remuneration is the last substantive publication from the first term of IPSA prior to the departure of the four ordinary board members. The circumstances which have prompted this have been amply recorded elsewhere but we – the chair and fellow board members – would like to take this opportunity to summarise the last three years and to offer some advice to IPSA's principal stakeholders.

When IPSA was established by the Parliamentary Standards Act in 2009, British democracy was reeling from the shock of the MPs' expenses scandal. The Speaker himself described the damage to Parliament as the greatest in recent history, 'with the possible exception of when Nazi bombs fell on the chamber in 1941.' The public, uncertain whether to be more angry about 'flipping' or duck houses, wide-screen TVs or moat cleaning, turned away in anger.

---

131 January 2013.

Restoring confidence in Parliament was a national priority – one endorsed by the leaders of the three main political parties and the majority of MPs.

We were appointed by a wholly independent panel, endorsed by both Houses of Parliament, received our Royal Warrant and, in January 2010, set about creating a regulator with responsibility to oversee the business costs and expenses and the administration of the payroll of 650 MPs and some 2,500 staff – a sum amounting to just under £130 million of taxpayers' money in the first financial year. To minimise the potential disruption to the workings of Parliament, we intended to have everything in place by the next election, but that date was not known with certainty until early April when the Prime Minister announced 6 May as election day.

One year after the *Daily Telegraph* had first published details of MPs' expenses and four months after our appointment IPSA – having consulted widely with the public – introduced a completely new expenses regime with the promise that it would be fair, workable and transparent.

In pursuing that promise, we were careful to base our decisions on the strength of the evidence and the power of the argument rather than on the volume of its delivery. This led us to take what were, in some quarters, unpopular decisions. For example, we resisted calls to ban the employment by MPs of family members on the grounds that there was little documented evidence of abuse, the employees in question provided trusted support and often good value for money, and it was a common practice amongst British businesses (many of which are family owned).

We also went to great pains to ensure that our system was fair to both the public and MPs. On one hand, the system now in place will be familiar to anyone whose employment requires them to claim for the reimbursement of expenses but on the other, our scheme is also designed to support MPs with special health, security or family needs, so that they can conduct their parliamentary duties effectively.

Behind the scenes our dedicated executive team led by Andrew McDonald had created a new organisation, secured accommodation and commissioned an online claims system. The Office of Government Commerce – the part of government charged with helping public-sector organisations ensure greater value for money – declared: 'The impossible has been delivered.'

Research told us that the public reacted positively to the changes but, rather than embracing the new system as a way of putting the scandal behind them, many Members of Parliament were either silent or hostile. So great was the reaction of some that we were compelled to erect signs in Portcullis House warning those attending our induction workshops that aggression towards our staff would not be tolerated.

Some of the Westminster opposition was overt and specific – an unwillingness to claim expenses online, resistance to registering their accommodation, a view that untested budget limits were too small, the rules too restrictive, the publication of claims unfair.

Some MPs, apparently determined to put the clock back to the days when expenses were administered by servants of the House, used their privileged powers to attack IPSA generally and some of us personally. In our first year and a half of existence, we were subjected to reviews by the Speaker's Committee on IPSA; by the National Audit Office and the Public Accounts Committee; and by a newly revived Committee on Members' Expenses.

We welcome accountability – transparency is an important value to us – but this was unusual, to say the least, for a new regulator which now employs less than fifty people and costs not much more than the House of Commons food and drink subsidy.

Of course we faced challenges, especially in the early months. The volume of transactions, telephone calls and emails, was surprisingly high – and they have not really fallen. We acknowledged that some of the rules on business costs and expenses were restrictive, and amended them when we had the opportunity in April 2011. We brought in measures to help MPs with cash flow – loans, direct payment facilities with landlords, extensions to MPs' payment cards. We made the online claims system simpler, responding to comments from its users. Slowly but surely the attacks from within Westminster became more muted.

Outside Westminster we received encouraging survey data that showed we were making progress in restoring the public's confidence in the expenses system. Unfortunately the various prosecutions and convictions of MPs who had abused the pre-IPSA rules served to remind the electorate of the scale of the scandal and so impeded the increase in confidence.

It is to be hoped that the passage of time will convince the public that a problem caused by a few should not be allowed to influence the appreciation of the many.

In 2011, in a sign that the government and Parliament recognised that we had successfully charted our way through the turbulent waters of business costs and expenses, we were given the powers to set MPs' pay and determine their pensions.

This challenge has been described as 'the Big Exam Question' – what should a legislator in a 21st-century democracy be paid? – and it is the first time in our nation's history that it will be answered by an independent body in consultation with the electorate.

Last summer, we commissioned detailed research into public attitudes on MPs' pay and pensions prior to launching a formal consultation in October 2012. We found the public sceptical of change that did not mirror their own experiences, but willing to listen when presented with evidence. But we discovered a weakness at the heart of our democracy – many members of the public have little knowledge about what MPs do, especially when they are at Westminster. Addressing that knowledge deficit is an important prerequisite to winning public support for changes to MPs' remuneration.

We see contributing to the restoration of public confidence in the MPs' pay, pensions, costs and expenses as a fundamental responsibility of IPSA.

Our democracy is a precious national asset and to appreciate its value we need only look to events outside the UK in the years since the expenses scandal rocked our collective confidence.

A barometer of the electors' confidence in the elected is provided by the way in which the latter manage taxpayers' money – especially when it benefits themselves. That is why the expenses scandal had such a profound effect on our country and why we should celebrate the progress that has been made over the last three years.

As four of us make way for our successors – the chair remains – we close with a message to our three principal stakeholders.

Parliamentarians: It is our experience that the vast majority of MPs are decent, honest, hard-working people committed to providing a service in which they believe. We hope our departure provides the stimulus for that hitherto silent majority to play an active and constructive role in realising the vision encapsulated in the Parliamentary Standards Act.

Press: Without the press and its persistence, the expenses scandal may never have come to light. It should take pride in having catalysed a current scheme which has consigned flipping, duck houses and moat cleaning to the archives. The IPSA website now publishes every MP's expenses down to the smallest item. Therefore ridiculing the reimbursement of legitimate business costs and expenses does no one any good. It is time to acknowledge the change and to move on.

Public: The UK now has one of the most transparent expenses systems in the world. Soon – and for the first time in our history – our MPs' pay and pensions will be determined by an independent body and not by MPs themselves. This is something of which we should all be proud and helps to restore our claim to be a leader amongst democratic nations.

As we prepare to hand over to our successors we pay tribute to IPSA's dedicated staff who, often in very difficult circumstances, have consistently met their key performance indicators and ensured that MPs and their staff have been paid and their business costs and expenses reimbursed in an accurate and timely manner.

We wish them, and the new board, well in their task.

Helping to restore the public's faith in Parliament and democracy is no small prize.

Sir Ian Kennedy, Sir Scott Baker, Jackie Ballard, Ken Olisa OBE, Professor Isobel Sharp CBE.

APPENDIX VII

TWO PAPERS WRITTEN BY THE CHAIR TO EXPLORE IPSA'S ROLE[132]

VALUE FOR MONEY – WHO SAYS?

INTRODUCTION

Recently, I appeared before the Public Accounts Committee. I was to be questioned on a report prepared by the National Audit Office on the value for money provided by IPSA (the Independent Parliamentary Standards Authority), which I chair. In opening the hearing, the chair, Margaret Hodge MP, asked me what I understood by value for money. This was not the first time: in my many years working in public services, I have frequently asked and been asked whether this or that public body, including those I have been responsible for, provides value for money (VFM). My response has always been: 'It all depends on what you mean.' This response has ordinarily been seen as unhelpful. So, I have also had to frame a second response which meets the demands of what has become the conventional approach.

In what follows, I want to explore that first response. It will necessarily involve a consideration of the second. I will be wholly concerned

---

132 Both were written in the summer of 2011 and were originally published on IPSA's website.

with the delivery of public services and, thus, the notion of VFM in the public sector as it relates to the use of taxpayers' money. VFM in the private sector requires a different analysis, not least to take account of the centrality of choice (not least to put their money elsewhere) which investors and consumers have, but which has not ordinarily been a feature of public services.

APPROACHES TO UNDERSTANDING VFM

There is a lot written about VFM. I am not going to take you down that path, though I may have to alert you to where it leads. At its simplest, VFM in the public sector means achieving stated aims in a way which makes best use of taxpayers' money. At this level, VFM is a very straightforward notion, not calling for much theorising. At another level, however, it is an extremely complex issue, but the standard theorising (and there is a lot of it) is, unfortunately, unhelpful. According to this standard approach, VFM as it is commonly used, has become a term of art. It is talked of in terms of objectives to be achieved. These objectives are represented as being so clearly articulated, so carefully adumbrated, that they have all the qualities of certainties. They are objective. Their presence or absence can be measured. As if to enhance this appearance of clarity and certainty, three words have entered the language as being the real keys to VFM: the '3 Es' or economy, efficiency, effectiveness. These words will tell you what is best as regards the use to which money should best be put. They have become the passwords to a world which is technical: a world which economists and accountants have claimed as their own. VFM is a technical term. They are the designated technocrats.

THE PROBLEM OF 'VALUE'

Of course, the problem which strikes anyone looking beyond the jargon is that the supposed certaintics are no such things. They are an illusion. There are no objective certainties which allow precise calculation and objectively verifiable measures. The reason is obvious. 'Value' is a term of judgement. It is, unsurprisingly, an evaluative term! It does not describe something which can be stated as an objective fact.

Of course, attempts are made to square the circle by saying that it is not the word 'value' that we should be concentrating on, but the careful articulation of the objectives which lie behind it. When we are assessing VFM, we are really assessing whether these clear, unambiguous and verifiable objectives are being met. And, it is said, these objectives can be stated with such precision that their presence or absence, whether they are being met or not, is merely a matter of factual determination. So, on this basis, VFM is about facts, objective evidence and certainties. There are at least two difficulties with this gambit. First, reference to 'objectives' is no less a matter of judgement than referring to value. Objectives speak to that which is sought after and desired rather than that which exists. And, secondly, setting the objectives down undoubtedly produces a list, but lists are always incomplete (irritatingly, they usually fail to include the very thing that crops up!). But, more significantly, such lists give only the illusion of objectivity, because the value decisions on which they are based, while central to the enterprise, are not revealed. The judgements are still being made. It is just that they are hidden and, to that extent, unaccountable.

THE KEY QUESTION

The pursuit of value for money, therefore, needs to be addressed differently. The question is not one of the definition of VFM and its central constituent element 'value'. Nor is it one of reciting a list of objectives, without identifying what lies behind them. This is because any consideration of VFM represents a judgement. The really key question is whose judgement is the relevant judgement. It is not what VFM means, or what the objectives are; it is who decides what it means, or what the objectives should be. What may be of high value to some may be valued less by others. Choices need to be made. Who makes them is the key. It is that simple.

THE '3 ES'

I have already mentioned the '3 Es' as being central to decisions about VFM. You only have to look at these '3 Es' to get the point that I am seeking to make. Consider whether a public service is meeting the test of the '3 Es'. 'Economy' is said to relate to the cost of the service. Is it economical? But whose view is to be listened to in determining whether the cost which has been settled on provides the proper level of service? How do you take account of the *quality* of the service from a number of perspectives, of which the perspective of the recipient of any service, especially public services, is the most relevant? The same problem arises in the case of the other '2 Es'. 'Efficiency' refers to what is got out for what is put in. Fine, but who decides what it is that should be got out, so as to judge whether you are efficient in getting it? 'Effectiveness' in turn is supposed to measure the impact, the effect achieved in any particular context. Again, fine, but, again, who determines which effect should be sought? A list of objectives may have been drawn up. But who decided on the objectives and whose hand wrote the list?

In short, to the proposition that the 'value' in VFM consists of achieving the '3 Es', you must ask: 'economical' at what cost as judged by whom; 'efficient' to what purpose as judged by whom; 'effective' to what end as judged by whom?

Those who dwell in the land of VFM are quick with a reply. As it happens, it takes the discourse into even more uncertain territory. It goes like this. VFM is really about 'achieving the right balance between the 3 Es'. Would it be cruel to repeat the question: the right balance in whose eyes, or, who sets the scale against which any balancing is to take place?

THE REAL WORLD OF VFM

The unavoidable conclusion is that, when we talk of VFM, we are firmly in the world of value judgements. In the realm of public services, the world which I inhabit, the importance of this obvious conclusion cannot be overstated. It is literally about democracy. Public services are paid for by the taxpayer. They exist to provide particular specified services to the public. The services must be provided in such a way that the public gets value for money. It must, therefore, be at the heart of the democratic covenant between people and government that it is for the public to decide what value consists of, what they count as valuable in the services provided.

ENTER THE PUBLIC

The moment that this proposition is advanced, and it is clearly correct, the notion of VFM can no longer be claimed by economists or accountants as their unique preserve. It is clearly the preserve of the public. It is for the public to determine the v in VFM. persu the technocratic approach has another line of defence. Yes, the argument goes, it is quite true: we are talking about judgements. But judgements about public services, including VFM, are vested quite properly in government and politicians. They are elected to decide on how taxpayers' money is to be disbursed. In deciding on how it is to be disbursed, they have the best information and serve as proxies for the public. So, when government or politicians pronounce on VFM, it *is* really the public after all who are deciding, albeit at second hand through their elected representatives. This is standard democratic territory. But, unfortunately, there is a catch.

RE-ENTER THE 'EXPERT'

You will remember that I said that the standard approach to VFM is to regard it as a term of art. Government and politicians have come to believe or have been persuaded to accept this approach. They have come to accept that VFM is a matter of expertise, best left to experts. As a consequence, they have largely passed responsibility to others, particularly the National Audit Office and until recently the Audit Commission. And these bodies, the 'experts' in VFM, see VFM technocratically, through the prism of the '3 Es'. 'Value' takes on a limited meaning, relating to cost, price and output. The underlying value choices which, as we saw, necessarily inform the decisions made, are not made explicit by the experts. All is science and calculation. These choices cannot, therefore, be subject to scrutiny to ensure that they, in fact, reflect what the recipient of public services would choose as being important, that they reflect what the public really values and wants from the services. They may just as well, and most likely do, reflect what the *providers* rather than the recipients of the services value. This is particularly true when the resources available to provide a service are, as is usual, under strain.

BACK TO REAL VFM

Seen in the way that I have set out, VFM poses wholly different questions from those conventionally asked. This is where things get complex. Seeking to reflect what the public values in the provision of any service is no easy task, even if it is the only right way to assess VFM. The public values different things at different times. And, of course, the public is not a homogenous entity. There will usually be several publics with several views.

Such untidiness, however, is the stuff of democratic discourse. It is an abiding feature of any public policy. Consequently, there are established mechanisms to address the challenge posed: the challenge being to elicit, in the light of available evidence, a considered and broadly representative view on a matter of public importance, having to do with the delivery of public services, as regards which there may be no obvious consensus.

DEMOCRATIC ENGAGEMENT: THE EXAMPLE OF NICE

One such mechanism exists in one of that most contentious of all areas of public policy – the NHS. Within the NHS, one of the most difficult challenges is to determine what medicines/drugs should be made available to patients through the NHS. Whether the words 'rationing' or 'resource allocation' are used, it is clear that, however much money is made available, choices will always have to be made as to what can be afforded and thus provided. And such choices often have to be made against a background of the special pleading of single interest groups, the effective lobbying of the pharmaceutical industry and professionals, and the significant interest of the media. What is involved is a major issue of value for money. It could not be more explicit. Does the purchase by the NHS of this drug for this group of patients amount to value for money for the NHS and thus for the taxpayer?

Since 1999 such decisions have fallen to be decided by the National

Institute for Health and Clinical Excellence (NICE). NICE was created by statute. You may think that by doing so, government has
conformed to the approach I referred to earlier whereby issues involving VFM in the NHS are seen as matters for experts and are
passed to experts. But NICE is different. Whatever government might
have had in mind, NICE has gone its own way. It has recognised
the central issue of the democratic covenant. It has earned the ad-
miration of countries around the world while routinely getting up
the nose of Big Pharma, patients' groups and government (thereby
proving it must be getting something right!). It operates a complex
system of assessing value, the basis of which is a calculation of QALYs
(Quality-Adjusted Life Years). The calculation is driven by a regard
for the values of the NHS and for the principle of the greatest good
for the greatest number of the population as a whole. In this way,
NICE explicitly recognises the evaluative nature of the exercise.
The Q in QALY reinforces the fact. And, in its analysis of QALYs,
NICE seeks to expose for scrutiny the underlying factors which bear
on quality and which it bears in mind. All of them are judgements.
All of them are available for debate and discussion (which routinely takes place). Admittedly, at one level, the calculation of QALYs
appears to be formulaic and driven by econometrics. But this calculation derives from a prior application of a series of judgements which
are explicit.

So, when NICE talks of VFM, it overtly sets out what it judges the
word value to signify; it takes two steps. The first is to be as clear as
possible as to the values and principles which underpin the objectives
sought; the values of the NHS. The second step is to decide whether,
as regards any particular decision, the decision best accords with those
values. This is where engaging with the public comes in. NICE takes

account of a range of factors from a range of interested parties. But, so that the judgement made should not simply be that of interested parties and its own experts, NICE also provides for the element of democratic engagement the importance of which I emphasised earlier. NICE seeks advice from its Citizens' Council. The Council was created by NICE. Its membership consists entirely of members of the public. They meet to discuss proposed decisions of NICE (whether, for example, to approve the provision by the NHS of a particular drug). They hear the relevant scientific and economic arguments. They weigh the opportunity costs inevitable when the resources available are finite. Cost, price and output are parts of the story, but they are not the whole story.

The injection of the Citizens' Council into the system of deliberation means that a central contribution to the judgement of what is to be valued, the VFM provided by the NHS, is vested in the public, through the proxy of the Council, a public which has been informed and then is free to make up its mind.

A device such as the Citizens' Council is central to any really genuine appraisal of VFM. It cannot, of course, be used for every detailed issue of the day. And, of course, other mechanisms of democratic engagement, local and national, co-exist and are of central importance. But, as regards the vexed issue of VFM, true democratic engagement is at the heart of things. VFM is not for technocrats.

This is not to say that there is no role for technocrats. Clearly, they do have a role, but it is a second-order role. What they can do, and it is of great importance, is to determine whether, once the choices have been made, the means of putting these choices into effect make the best possible use of the money available. Matters such as the ways in which contracts are let, staff are deployed, and money is accounted for are all part of this second order role. But in the case of public services, the first order issue, the values and objectives, and the last word on them must be with an informed public.

IPSA AND VFM

I mentioned IPSA at the outset. As an organisation funded from the public purse, it must, of course, provide value for money. You will have gathered by now that, for me, the crucial question is not what value means in this context, but whose view of value should be determinative. Unsurprisingly, there is significant disagreement. The perspective of MPs, by and large, is that IPSA exists to provide what they regard as important and only if it does so is it providing value for money. And, given that in the minds of many MPs, IPSA does not give them the support that they claim is their due, IPSA, by that token, fails to provide value for money. The taxpayer on that reasoning is getting a poor return.

What MPs are doing is defining VFM in a way in which it is assumed, without discussion, that they are the arbiters of what constitutes value. They could be said to be making this assumption because they see IPSA's scheme of expenses and costs as existing solely to do what they want. But if that is their view, it is clearly wrong-headed. IPSA is not the servant of MPs, created to serve their needs, though this is a prevalent view. IPSA is an independent regulatory body. It exists to serve the public interest. Its role, among other things, is to ask whether what MPs argue for is, indeed, in the public interest. That is what regulators do as regards those whom they regulate.

There may be another basis on which MPs assume themselves to be the arbiters of value. They may claim, as I set out earlier, that, as elected representatives of the public, they are the public's proxies in ensuring that the public gets value from the taxes levied. There are at least two problems with this approach. First, there is, of course, a clear conflict of interest. Second, and equally clearly, such a view also represents an attempt to return to self-regulation by the back door. But, putting aside these awkward truths, this role of proxies was, perhaps, what the Public Accounts Committee saw themselves as playing (though there were plenty of the other assumptions around, such as that IPSA is there to serve MPs and that MPs are IPSA's 'customers'). But if this was how the PAC saw itself, as the proxy for the public, its response was to do precisely what I referred to earlier. It commissioned the NAO, as experts, to determine whether IPSA provided VFM. It defined VFM in technocratic terms and brought in the technocrats.

As it happens, the NAO's response was fairly complimentary of IPSA, given the difficult circumstances in which it was established and has had to operate. But, that said, the NAO's approach was at best problematical. Two particular positions that it adopted warrant comment. The first reflected the view that IPSA exists to serve the perceived needs of MPs, to 'enable' them to carry out their parliamentary duties (avoiding, of course, what will be recognised as the crucial question – who decides the nature of the 'enabling'). The flaw in this approach, its under-appreciation that IPSA is an independent regulator established to serve the public interest, is something that I have already dwelt on extensively. The second position adopted by the NAO which is particularly problematic was its specific reflection on IPSA's preparedness to accept risk (IPSA's 'risk appetite'). IPSA could be more 'efficient' (save money), the NAO stated, if it were less risk-averse. In saying this, the NAO appeared to be defining value in technical terms, having to do with efficiency as it relates to the cost associated with risk. But in fact, of course, it was making *its* judgement about the proper balance of risk and where the public interest and the public's appetite for risk should lie. By doing so, the NAO was challenging IPSA's view as to where the public interest lies. But it is IPSA which is charged by Parliament to serve as the independent regulator. It is IPSA which, as a central part of that responsibility, must seek to determine and act upon what it, and it alone, judges to be in the public interest. Its judgement must be the product of some democratic engagement. It can be questioned if it is patently at odds with what an informed public is calling for. It should not be questioned, however, simply because others would wish for a different judgement.

I reach this view because it must be clear beyond peradventure by now that VFM is crucially something on which the public's view must be central. Compare the NAO's approach. It maintained that IPSA exists to serve the needs of MPs. This was what VFM meant: that what was done was what best met MPs' needs. And, to assess IPSA's success in achieving this, the NAO looked inwards and commissioned a survey of what MPs thought of IPSA. The response was the predictable 'turkeys voting for Christmas'. The NAO did not ask itself how the public might assess VFM. It did not look outwards to gauge the views of the public: what the public might regard as being of value in the disbursement of their taxes as regards the expenses and costs of MPs. The NAO did refer to a survey carried out by IPSA. But this was interpreted narrowly as showing an increase in the trustworthiness of MPs and Parliament. It was not viewed as central to the question of VFM. Of course, from the perspective of the public and of the Parliament which created IPSA to achieve that very result, it is a defining feature of VFM.

For IPSA, trust between the electorate and the elected is THE value most sought by the public and most in the public interest to seek to achieve. The extent of this trust currently is central to any assessment of the VFM provided by IPSA. IPSA was created as a response to a massive scandal which rocked the nation. Trust in MPs and our democratic institutions was at an appallingly low ebb. IPSA was created as an *independent* body whose task it was to replace failed self-regulation with real, effective regulation. Unsurprisingly, it was not welcomed in Westminster, once the dust had settled. Those who had enjoyed life for centuries without effective scrutiny and accountability, save of their own making, were suddenly being asked for receipts! The sunlight was too bright for some. Indeed, some even thought (and think) that IPSA is an assault on their very status as MPs, despite what Parliament may have thought in 2009.

This is the historical background (and it is a history which is barely a couple of years old). It should not be a surprise that, as an independent regulatory body, IPSA sees its principal aim as being to act in the public interest. The fundamental public interest was and remains, as surveys show, the restoration of trust in MPs. Nothing can be more important for democracy and, of course, for MPs.

So, the answer to the question whether IPSA is providing VFM does not lie in whether MPs or technocrats approve of what it does. The only answer is whether it is doing what a properly informed public wants it to do. This is so important that it is routinely ignored and why it is has been repeatedly emphasised here. Until it is accepted, IPSA will continue to lock horns with those who, for whatever reason, choose to ignore it.

From IPSA's perspective, it must, of course, regularly satisfy itself that its sense of what the public values is sufficiently acute; that, for example, it has got the balance of risk about right. This is where what I called democratic engagement comes in. IPSA must routinely check to ensure that it reflects what an informed public wants. To this end, IPSA is working to establish ways of going beyond surveys and taking the temperature of informed public opinion on a regular basis. Now that IPSA has the responsibility also of setting MPs' pay and pensions, this need to stay close to informed public opinion takes on even greater importance.

By gauging and giving effect to the views of an informed public about what value they seek to get from their taxes, IPSA will truly be able to monitor whether it provides value for money. It will also serve as the only valid basis on which those who would expose it to scrutiny regarding VFM may properly judge IPSA.

WHAT'S IPSA FOR?

IPSA was recently given what *The Guardian* called a 'clean bill of health' by the National Audit Office (NAO). We do provide value for money for the taxpayer. This verdict was just the latest. Our budget had just been approved after over three months of discussion and three formal hearings by the Speaker's committee (SCIPSA). The NAO had simultaneously approved our accounts. We then appeared before the Public Accounts Committee to be examined on the NAO's report on our value for money. And this is not the end of it. There is yet more scrutiny of our efficiency and cost-effectiveness in the offing: not just the PAC's report, but also the forthcoming review by the newly revived Members' Allowances (now Expenses) Committee. And we've only been in operation for fifteen months! As is well-known, there are some MPs who do not wish us well. Constant attritional scrutiny is one way of expressing this sentiment. Some might think it disproportionate. We have to get on with it, despite the very obvious consequence that it diverts us from providing the very service that MPs ask for.

What we want to get on with is to address the next important task that Parliament has set us. MPs' expenses and costs have been successfully dealt with through the expenses scheme, albeit there is still some way to go as we make the system increasingly simpler to operate. Success can be measured by the fact that 99.7 per cent of claims made by MPs are within the rules, claims are dealt with on time, and, critically, the public's confidence in the system has grown and continues to grow. Our next task is to tackle the questions of MPs' pay and pensions. This is what we are beginning to work on now. We want to engage the public and MPs in answering what I have called 'the big exam question' – what does a modern 21st-century Member of Parliament need from the public purse so as to do the job? This is an immensely important task. For Parliament to have given it to us constitutes a complete break with the past. For the first time, an independent body will determine what MPs should receive by way of remuneration, and recompense for their expenses and costs – the total package of funding, seen in the round.

As I've said, this is our next challenge. But, while we and most others believe that we have dealt with MPs' expenses and costs and are ready to move on, some would challenge that view. Some MPs do not want to move on. They do not accept that expenses and costs have been dealt with. They continue to assail IPSA, what it does and how it does it. Fundamentally, their criticisms and attacks are not just about the system that we have put in place (its rules and operation), though, as I have said, we recognise that they are not perfect and need regular attention. They go much deeper. Their concern is about IPSA's role; what exactly is IPSA for and what should we be doing in operating the expenses system? Till these questions are addressed and settled, they will continue to affect relations between MPs and IPSA, even as we move the discourse on to the broader issue of proper remuneration. These are the questions, therefore, that I intend to deal with in what follows.

Since we are dealing with MPs, it might be best to start with the law that Parliament passed in 2009 and then amended in 2010. The Parliamentary Standards Act lays on IPSA a number of duties. Of greatest importance in understanding what IPSA is for is the duty to 'have regard to the principle that Members of the House of Commons should be supported in efficiently, cost-effectively and transparently carrying out their parliamentary functions'. Notice that the duty could simply have been expressed that IPSA 'should support MPs in ... carrying out their parliamentary functions'. But it was not: instead the duty is to 'have regard to the principle that it should…' The difference is critical.

Why it is critical is because IPSA is a regulatory body. The 'regard' which the law requires us to give to the principle of supporting MPs is for IPSA, as the regulator, to decide upon. It is a matter of policy for IPSA. Obviously, we are keen to do all that we can to ensure that our regard for the principle satisfies MPs' needs. But, equally obviously, we must also take account of the public interest in carrying out our duty, as must any independent regulator. It follows that, since it is a matter of policy, the judgement of the way in which IPSA is to 'have regard to the principle that it should support MPs…' is a matter for IPSA alone to make.

The SCIPSA, made up of eight MPs and three lay members, is the body to which we must present our proposed budget for the following year. Its role is to satisfy itself, in deciding on our budget, that in complying with our statutory duties, we do so in an efficient and cost-effective manner. The logic is clear. IPSA decides its policy: the way in which it is to comply with its statutory duties, not least the duty to 'have regard…' (Obviously, the remedy of judicial review exists if we interpret our role wrongly.) SCIPSA then decides whether in carrying out our policy we do so in an efficient and cost-effective manner. If our statutory duty were simply 'to support' MPs in the performance of their parliamentary functions, SCIPSA would be entitled to ask a different set of questions about our efficiency and cost-effectiveness. But, to repeat, that's not our statutory duty. So, SCIPSA must not proceed from the premise that it is.

This conclusion as to the nature of our duty informs an issue of central importance to IPSA. It is quite clear that members of SCIPSA do not think that IPSA properly supports MPs in the performance of their parliamentary duties. This is also a view held by a number of MPs. The National Audit Office's recent survey of MPs' opinions tells the same story. This view of what IPSA should be doing (and, to some, is failing to do) by way of support, stems from a difference between IPSA's approach to its duty to 'have regard...' and what MPs (and, it appears, SCIPSA) believe our duty to be and what we should be doing as a consequence.

To illustrate this difference, a helpful starting point is the view put to us by SCIPSA that our role in administering the expenses scheme is that of 'client care' and that viewed from that perspective we are failing MPs to some degree. But, as we understand it, 'client care' is a concept used in the service sector (lawyers, accountants, private doctors) or in the retail sector to refer to being solicitous to the needs and concerns of clients (and regularly asking them for their views) for the obvious reason that it is the client who pays the bill and who could take his business elsewhere. In our context, of course, the analogy is seriously misleading. It assumes that our 'clients' are MPs. But if 'client care' means what has been suggested, it is the taxpayer who pays the bill for MPs' expenses. To that extent, it is the taxpayer who is our 'client'. It is the taxpayer whose interests we exist to serve. This is even more so because the taxpayer cannot go elsewhere: IPSA is the body charged by Parliament with dealing with MPs' expenses. Of course, IPSA must (and does) also weigh carefully the needs and concerns of MPs. But, to repeat, the analogy and the conclusions drawn from it are inapt.

Let's take the question of 'support' for MPs a step further. I have already explained that IPSA's duty is to 'have regard...' and that it is for IPSA to determine what that duty consists of, as it relates to the support of MPs. So, what 'support' means, and who decides become the big questions. As regards who decides, there can be no doubt that it is for IPSA to decide. That's our role. It is not for SCIPSA to decide. Their role is to comment on IPSA's cost-effectiveness, not to stipulate what we should be cost-effective about. Nor is it, secondly, for MPs to decide. The reason is so obvious that it needs to be stated repeatedly. If it were for MPs to decide what constitutes proper support, any semblance of independent regulation would collapse on itself. MPs would simply say that they want this or that from IPSA and IPSA's role would simply be just to hand it over. It would be as if a bank's executive responsible for regulatory affairs were to telephone the FSA and advise that his bank found this or that rule or operating practice a nuisance and demand that it be changed and the FSA would be expected to ask what changes would best suit the bank! This may have been how self-regulation worked for MPs. It isn't how independent regulation works.

To repeat, it is for IPSA, as the regulator, to determine what level of support is proper for MPs. In reaching its view, IPSA must, of course, act reasonably. It must listen to MPs. It must gather evidence, examine past practices and take the views of bodies such as those of the Senior Salaries Review Body (eg the SSRB's report in 2007 on what the proper levels of staffing should be for MPs). Ultimately, as an independent regulator, IPSA must then make its own determination on the basis of what, in the light of all the various factors and evidence, best serves the public interest. The public interest, as judged by IPSA, is the sole criterion. This is what IPSA has done and will continue to do, whether it is in relation to its decisions on staffing levels (which are currently being reviewed), the employment of connected parties, or the continuing and evolving modifications of its rules and operating procedures. It is not for others charged with scrutinising our cost-effectiveness to substitute their view of what is in the public interest for that of IPSA. Their role, their scrutiny must be confined to whether we do what we have decided to do in an efficient and cost-effective manner.

It follows that it is not for SCIPSA merely to hear that MPs wish for this or that and then to suggest that, if IPSA does not meet this wish, IPSA is therefore not cost-effective. To do so places SCIPSA in the role of establishing policy. That is not SCIPSA's role.

There is an even wider point which arises from what I have already set out. It may help if I touch on it here for the sake of completeness.

It has been suggested to us that there is an inherent tension, born of the structure of the legislation creating IPSA, between our role as a regulator and our role as a provider of services. In large part this suggestion grows out of what, in our view, is a misunderstanding of our role in relation to supporting MPs which I have already addressed at length: the notion that our role is to comply with whatever MPs may urge on us by way of their need for support. It also grows out of the notion that if, as a provider of services, we don't do what MPs and others expect, it's because we've got our regulatory mission wrong. The mission should, therefore, be revised (the scheme should be changed), so that it delivers the required services. On this view, the provision of services comes first and the services should be those urged by MPs. The regulatory framework should follow. The tension should be resolved by putting the cart where it belongs – before the horses! The supposed tension, on examination, therefore, becomes a device for urging change on IPSA, so that the scheme becomes a vehicle for meeting MPs' preferences and the services are provided accordingly.

We, however, do not recognise this supposed tension. IPSA, as a regulator, has established the scheme of expenses. In doing so it has made a variety of judgements, guided by its independent assessment of the public interest. IPSA has then put in place a series of operational mechanisms to give effect to this scheme, reflecting, necessarily, the judgements on policy underlying the scheme, together with particular judgements on particular aspects of operation, such as the level of assurance to be called for before paying out claims, or the level of risk to be tolerated.

The administration of the scheme, therefore, is informed by and follows the scheme and the policy lying behind it. There is no inherent tension between our duty to regulate and our duty to administer. Clearly and quite properly, IPSA must then be held to account as to how it delivers that administration. That is the role of SCIPSA: to determine whether, in its administration, IPSA is sufficiently efficient and cost-effective. There is a limit, therefore, to the extent to which SCIPSA may comment on IPSA's administration. It can say that our process for ensuring that claims are valid is inefficient or not cost-effective in x or y way. But it is not SCIPSA's role to state, for example, that IPSA's appetite for risk is inappropriate, or that a system based on allowances (as the term was used under the old system) would be better. Parliament left such decisions to IPSA alone to make.

APPENDIX VIII

MPs' PAY 1911–2010

**THE VALUE OF THE MEMBERS' SALARY FROM
1911–2011 IN CONSTANT 2011 PRICES
(HOUSE OF COMMONS LIBRARY)**

MPs' SALARIES AND GDP DEFLATOR 1911–2011

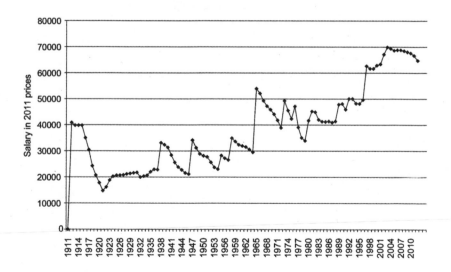

ACKNOWLEDGEMENTS

My thanks go to John Sills for his advice and counsel. He was a brilliant public servant and remains a good friend. His knowledge of IPSA is without rival.

My thanks go also to Jack, Tom and Andrea, who suffered through the long years of my chairmanship, often distressed for me at the latest tweet or blast on social media, and who have helped me as I wrote this account. My brother Alan took time off writing his latest novel[133] to give me invaluable advice.

Thanks are also due to James Stephens and Olivia Beattie at Biteback and to their brilliant editor Stephanie Carey.

---

133   Alan Kennedy, *The Things That are Lost* (Lasserrade Press, 2019).

INDEX

Afriyie, Adam MP 108–10, 112, 143, 157–8, 160–61, 163–6
Alexander, Danny MP 132–4
Alice's Adventures in Wonderland (Carroll) 65

Baker, Sir John 204–5
Baker, Sir Scott 261, 297, 322
Ballard, Jackie 259–60, 265, 297, 322
Barclay, Stephen MP 152–3
Batty, Ken 146
Beith, Sir Alan MP 156
Benn, Hilary MP 117–18
Bercow, Speaker John MP 1, 14, 19, 76, 80–81, 84, 122–28, 135, 168, 226, 228, 232–4, 251–2, 258, 285–96, 297–315
Blunkett, David MP 110
Boo, Marcial 116, 269
Brady, Graham MP 119–20
Brake, Tom MP 108
Brown, Gordon MP 10
Brown, Nick MP 137
Bryant, Chris MP 120
Butterfield, Sir Neil 261, 264

Cameron, David MP 34, 74, 107, 140, 220, 222
Campbell, Alastair 12, 15, 215
du Cann, Edward MP 208
Chartists 200

Chatterji, Professor Monojit 146
Clegg, Nick MP 105, 107, 220, 222
Clwyd, Ann MP 143
Coffey, Thérèse MP 116
Committee on Members' Expenses 108, 110–11, 155, 156–66, 337
Committee on Standards in Public Life 10, 40, 295
compliance office 86–94
Conservative 1922 Committee 84 (fn 46), 103, 118
Constitutional Reform and Governance Bill, later CRAG Act 6, 7, 46, 86–7, 93, 96, 185, 206
Conway, Derek MP 39
Cox, Geoffrey MP 209
Cox, Jo MP 101
Creasy, Dr Stella MP 154, 161
Cryer, John MP 120

Daily Mail 1, 11, 12, 13, 54, 106, 256–7
Daily Telegraph 1, 2 (fn 2), 11, 12, 15, 45 (fn 26), 126, 138 (fn 65), 143 (fn 68), 205, 224, 318
Davis, Peter 90–94
Duddridge, James MP 255
Duncan, Sir Alan MP 6–7

Eagle, Angela MP 118, 138
Electoral Commission 75, 83, 251–8

Evening Standard 123, 285
Expense@Work 44, 45 (fn 25)

Filkin, Elizabeth 126, 255–6
Freedom of Information Act (FOIA) 54,
   56, 61, 115, 142, 167–75, 236, 260, 268,
   275–83

Gaymer, Dame Janet 145 (fn 70), 146,
   290–91
Gillan, Cheryl (later Dame Cheryl) 137,
   138 (fn 66)
Gladstone, William MP 200
Grayling, Chris MP 107, 114–16

Hague, William MP 113–14
Harman, Harriet MP 14, 107–8
Harper, Mark MP 163
Heath, David MP 108
Hodge, Margaret MP 150–55, 323
Holland, Sir Anthony 145–6
Holmes, Sir John 252, 255
Huffington Post 253–4, 256
Hughes, Simon MP 173
Hutton, Lord 193

Jackson, Stewart MP 36–9
Johnson, Alan MP 30
Johnson, Boris MP 243 (fn 122)

Kaufman, Gerald MP 97
Kelly, Sir Christopher 10–11, 40

Lansley, Andrew MP 112–13
Lawrence, Sir Geoffrey QC 202–3, 211
Legg, Sir Thomas 138
Leigh, Edward MP 85
Leopard, The (Lampedusa) 49
Liaison Committee 155–6
liaison group 84–6
Lloyd George, David MP 201–2

McDonald, Andrew 23, 54, 68 (fn 38), 80,
   103, 116, 162, 214, 256, 265, 267, 268,
   298, 319
McMeikan, Elizabeth 145 (fn 70), 146, 233
McNally, Lord 171–3

Mann, John MP 110
Maude, Francis MP 132
Mill, John Stuart 200
Miliband, Ed MP 120, 220, 223
Morgan, Nicky MP 86 (fn 48)
Morse, Amyas 148–9, 152

National Audit Office (NAO) 68, 148–54,
   246, 259, 323, 333–4, 337
Newsnight 57
Norman, Archie 119

Oborne, Peter 126, 143, 255–7
Office of Government Commerce (OGC)
   67–8
Olisa, Ken (later Sir Ken) 122–4, 161, 262,
   264, 285–96, 297, 322
Onn, Melanie MP 121
Osborne, George MP 168
Owen, Sir Robert 261

Padmore, Liz 262
Parliamentary Commissioner for
   Standards 91, 92, 93, 277
Parliamentary Standards Act 3, 45, 96, 110,
   166, 29, 290, 307–8, 311, 317, 338
Pepys, Samuel 199
Phillipson, Bridget MP 252, 255
payment in lieu of notice (PILON) 238–9
Platt, Dame Denise 127, 233, 291, 295
Prince, Rosa 11
Public Accounts Committee (PAC)
   148–55, 163, 323, 333, 337

Raynsford, Nick MP 158, 162–3
Rose, Sir Christopher 15
Royal Institute of Chartered Surveyors
   (RICS) 30, 33, 37–8, 39 (fn 22)
Russell, Bob (later Sir Bob) MP 77,
   79–80, 105, 121–2, 137–9, 144–6, 147,
   163, 287

St John-Stevas, Norman MP 208
Sandys, Laura MP 137, 139
Senior Salaries Review Body (SSRB) 19,
   41, 46, 48, 178, 184, 189, 203–4, 211–12,
   341

Sharp, Isobel 260, 264, 297, 322
Shipman, Tim 10, 11, 12 (fn 6), 257
Sills, John 23, 55, 103, 106, 117 (fn 56), 159,
      162, 246, 263, 265, 270, 271–4, 347
Skinner, Dennis MP 69
Speaker's Committee on the IPSA
      (SCIPSA) 73, 75–81, 83, 87, 128,
      137–40, 170, 181, 299–300, 305, 337
Spellar, John MP 255
Spicer, Sir Michael MP 103–4
Stower, Tony 192
Straw, Jack MP 4, 5, 7, 49 (fn 29), 185,
      207, 210

Thurso, John (Viscount) 260
Times, The 214
Timms, Stephen MP 100
Toland, Judith 255, 270

Wakeham, Lord 49
Walker, Charles MP 84, 104, 118–20, 137,
      224 (fn 111)
Watts, Dave MP 120
Whitaker, Anne 260
Winterton, Rosie MP 137
Wintour, Patrick 14
Wishart, Pete MP 138
Wollaston, Sarah MP 86 (fn 48)
Woolas, Phil MP 77–8
Woolveridge, Scott 140, 270
Wright, Tony 229, 259
writ de expensis 199

Young, Sir George MP 26 (fn 14), 108,
      111–12, 116, 132, 157–8, 166, 287

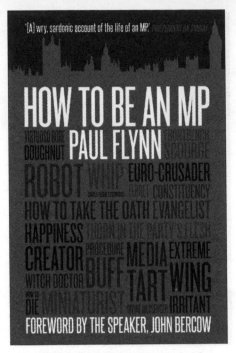

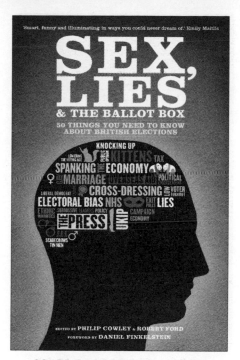